ROUTLEDGE LIBRARY EDITIONS: PURITANISM

Volume 9

THE PURITAN FAMILY

THE PURITAN FAMILY
A Social Study from the Literary Sources

LEVIN L. SCHÜCKING

LONDON AND NEW YORK

First published in English in 1969 by Routledge & Kegan Paul Ltd

This edition first published in 2021
by Routledge
2 Park Square, Milton Park, Abingdon, Oxon OX14 4RN

and by Routledge
52 Vanderbilt Avenue, New York, NY 10017

Routledge is an imprint of the Taylor & Francis Group, an informa business

© Translation 1969 Routledge & Kegan Paul Ltd

All rights reserved. No part of this book may be reprinted or reproduced or utilised in any form or by any electronic, mechanical, or other means, now known or hereafter invented, including photocopying and recording, or in any information storage or retrieval system, without permission in writing from the publishers.

Trademark notice: Product or corporate names may be trademarks or registered trademarks, and are used only for identification and explanation without intent to infringe.

British Library Cataloguing in Publication Data
A catalogue record for this book is available from the British Library

ISBN: 978-0-367-56981-5 (Set)
ISBN: 978-1-00-311164-1 (Set) (ebk)
ISBN: 978-0-367-62884-0 (Volume 9) (hbk)
ISBN: 978-1-00-311133-7 (Volume 9) (ebk)

Publisher's Note
The publisher has gone to great lengths to ensure the quality of this reprint but points out that some imperfections in the original copies may be apparent.

Disclaimer
The publisher has made every effort to trace copyright holders and would welcome correspondence from those they have been unable to trace.

THE PURITAN FAMILY

A Social Study
from the Literary Sources

LEVIN L. SCHÜCKING

*Translated from the German
by Brian Battershaw*

London
ROUTLEDGE & KEGAN PAUL

*First published in 1969
by Routledge & Kegan Paul Ltd
Broadway House, 68–74 Carter Lane
London, E.C.4*

*Printed in Great Britain by
The Garden City Press Limited
Letchworth, Hertfordshire*

© *Translation Routledge & Kegan Paul Ltd 1969*

*No part of this book may be reproduced
in any form without permission from
the publisher, except for the quotation
of brief passages in criticism*

SBN 7100 6381 4

*First German edition Die Puritanische Familie published by
B. G. Teubner Verlag, Leipzig 1929*

*Second German edition published by
A. Francke Verlag, Bern and Munich
1964*

Contents

Preface to the English edition ... ix

Preface to the second edition ... xi

Introduction: Puritanism and the Ideal of Sobriety ... 1

I MARRIAGE UNDER PURITANISM

1. Puritan literature dealing with marriage and family: the conduct books ... 18
2. The Bible as a model ... 19
3. Development of the Reformation's conception of marriage: exceptional position of Baxter ... 21
4. The most important conditions for successful marriage: the most dangerous errors ... 25
5. Basic relationship of the sexes in marriage: the position of women ... 28
6. The subordination of women: modification through the system of special duties ... 32
7. Limits to the subordination of women ... 35
8. Marriage as a sharing in erotic experience: sexual intercourse between husband and wife ... 37
9. Marriage as the sharing of a common religious life: spiritual self-revelation in prayer ... 40
10. The 'relaxed and pleasurable' process of sharing: spiritual understanding of the woman ... 41
11. Practical conclusions: consideration for femininity ... 45
12. The advanced nature of the concept of marital love ... 47
13. Theory and reality: Cromwell, Mrs Henry, Mrs Hutchinson, Mrs Baxter ... 50
14. Origin of the American feminist cult in the Puritanical mores of the English colonist. Ultimate grounds: the relation of female to male in love-making ... 53

II PARENTS AND CHILDREN UNDER PURITANISM

1. The family theocracy as the nucleus of the Puritan way of life — 56
2. Teelinck describes his stay in Banbury in 1604 — 57
3. Circumstances in Geneva. Luther's ideas — 59
4. Evidence for the beginnings of domestic religious discipline in Whitforde, in the Scottish catechism and in Thomas More — 61
5. Development of the characteristic features of the household congregation — 62
6. Origin of the family church — 65
7. The concept of the family: limitation of number of children, their first religious instruction — 67
8. Education outside the home — 70
9. The subordination of children — 72
10. Punishment in the family — 74
11. The work of revival — 76
12. The cultivation of industry and simplicity — 77
13. Parental concern in the choice of profession — 79
14. Parental role in marrying the children — 80
15. The unqualified necessity of parental consent — 81
16. Force and influence on the shaping of the will — 82
17. The examples of Hutchinson and Cromwell — 84
18. Reasons for the discomfort in family relationships: suppressed position of the mother — 85
19. The relations between the children in a family — 89
20. The ultimate religious purpose of the family: attitude to life — 91
21. Asceticism and hostility to youth — 92

III MASTERS AND SERVANTS

1. Servants as part of the family — 96
2. Duties of either party — 97
3. Change in views and circumstances — 101

CONTENTS

IV THE IMAGE OF THE PURITAN FAMILY IN LITERATURE

(a) *Milton's Conception of Marriage*

1. *Paradise Lost* as a conduct book 103
2. Intellectual and spiritual communion 104
3. The sharing of work. The duty of living together 105
4. Sharing of pleasures. Hospitality. Picnic with the angel 106
5. The reasons for the catastrophe. Eve as a representative of womanhood. Her weakness 109
6. Milton's Strindbergian conception of woman 111
7. Milton's Adam a prig 112
8. Puritanism and the unpuritanical in the relations between the sexes in Milton 113

(b) *The Family in Bunyan and Defoe*

1. Bunyan as husband and father 114
2. The basic idea behind the second part of *The Pilgrim's Progress* 115
3. The conjugal love of the Christian woman 117
4. Themes from family life in Bunyan 118
5. Defoe as a eulogist of marriage: its glorification in *Robinson Crusoe* 120
6. Defoe's books on marriage 123
7. The stories of conversion in *The Family Instructor* and *Religious Courtship* 123
8. The development of the feminine soul in Puritanism: Cromwell's daughter and Defoe's heroine 126

V THE CONVERGENCE OF ARISTOCRATIC AND BOURGEOIS CULTURE

(a) *The Role of the Family in Aristocratic Culture*

1. The cultural seclusion of the Puritan: the views of the fashionable world 129
2. Swift's attitude to the family. Chesterfield and Dr Johnson 132

3. Family propaganda in the moral periodicals   136
4. The family as a school of virtue. Description of the child. Cato's domesticity as a model   141
5. Family encouragement from other kinds of literature   143

(b) *The Family as a Literary Problem: Samuel Richardson*

1. Richardson's problems   145
2. The significance of *Clarissa*   146
3. The battle against the Cavalier ideal: Steele as pacemaker   148
4. Clarissa Harlowe and the Puritan family   151
5. Richardson the moralist   153
6. The Janus-head of Richardson's art. The receding of the religious element. Family problems old and new   154

VI THE FAMILY AS A LITERARY PUBLIC

1. Women's education and literature   159
2. The lady and literature   161
3. Richardson and the ladies   162
4. Fielding and the ladies   164
5. Fordyce's sermons   166
6. The humanizing of the family: relation between parents and children   169
7. Reading aloud in the family   172
8. Importance for literature: discovery of the family as a theme   176

VII CONCLUSION   181

Bibliography   185

Index of Names   193

Preface to the English Edition

In 1929 Professor Schücking wrote this book about the Puritan family as the arbiter of literary taste, an investigation of the relationship between literature and social values, and now, forty years later, this work is being presented for the first time to the English reader. Although in the meantime a number of relevant books have appeared which could not be taken account of in this work, it is still considered an essential study of this particular subject. The book frames in a vivacious literary style a scholarly treatment of the influence the Puritan family tradition had on the development of taste in English Literature, especially in the seventeenth and eighteenth centuries, and makes therefore both pleasant and informative reading.

The type-set of the second edition, which incorporated a number of significant alterations, was unfortunately destroyed in Leipzig in 1943 in an air-raid. This fact has added to the job of translating this book the arduous task of re-checking most of the references, which the author was unable to complete before he died. This was an exercise in detective-work which, however, had its own rewards for the sleuth. I wish to thank all people who have supported and contributed to this work, especially Mrs Elisabeth Schücking who was always eager to give the advice and assistance I needed, and has helped in this way to perpetuate the memory of her husband.

Munich,   H. J. HENTSCHEL
December 1968

Preface to the Second Edition

The first edition of this book appeared more than a generation ago—to be precise in the year 1929. At that time interest in English Puritanism was everywhere very slight. William Haller's book, *The Rise of Puritanism*, which, since then, has become well known, only appeared nine years afterwards and there was at the time a complete lack of monographs dealing with the origin and character of this highly influential movement with any degree of thoroughness. The Continental student observed with some surprise the exiguous nature of the part allotted to it among the forces that shaped English cultural development by such a work as G. M. Trevelyan's *English Social History* (which was published in 1944).

It is true that, in the meantime, there has been some change in our views, and I have considered a variety of aspects of the relation between English Puritanism and literature. Quite recently we have had a treatise by Laurence A. Sasek, *The Literary Temper of the English Puritans* (Louisianna, State University Press, 1961), a work which has reviewed this whole question with a new degree of exactitude.

Yet even now there may still be a place for my own account—I might add that towards the end of the Second World War a new edition of my work was on the point of coming out when a bomb hit the printing works and completely destroyed the type that had been set up in readiness for press. The justification for this work of mine is to be found in the circumstance that it seeks to perform a task too often neglected, namely that of establishing the basic facts and their sociological consequences. Indeed the significance of the very name of Puritan is by no means self-evident. The Puritans, historically regarded, represent a certain trend which, from the very start and for many years to come, lived on within the English Church. It appears in the 'sixties of the sixteenth century after the victory of the Reformation had been achieved with the accession of Queen Elizabeth in 1558.

The aims of this movement are usually described as a reform of the liturgy—by which was understood an excision of residual Catholic practice in worship—and the abolition—or transformation—of the existing Church constitutions. The origins of the movement are usually ascribed to the efforts made by such of the clergy as had been driven on to the continent of Europe during the reign of 'Bloody Mary' (1553-1558).

In exile these men had become acquainted with advanced protestantism, particularly of the kind that flourished in Switzerland, and now carried Calvin's doctrine back into their homes. Imperilled outwardly by the government's violent policy of suppression but strengthened internally by the same cause, the movement grew to ever greater size, and the more irresistibly it extended, the less uniform became its programme.

In the course of time, therefore, the term 'Puritan' came to designate a variety of groups. Recently the term has become increasingly suspect; indeed anyone seeking to get to the root of the problems that arise in the sphere of Church government, of liturgy, or even of theological doctrine, anyone who seeks to do justice to the character of the various groupings—groupings which attained such immense importance in the history of the seventeenth century—will find that he has little use for this word 'Puritan' at all and will be more interested in Presbyterians, Independents, Congregationalists, Baptists and, at a later time, Quakers.

Yet there is a side to the Puritan movement which differs from the one touched on so far and, as is shown by the history of the word 'puritanical' right down to its present and rather anaemic meaning of 'hostile to pleasure', ascetic, etc., it is perhaps the most important side of all. It has nothing whatever to do with dogma or ecclesiastical politics and is only concerned with that which lay nearest to the heart of the members of this movement, namely with the practical conduct of the pious man's life.

Here we are concerned with ways of life which, though in secondary respects they show deviations from the norm, nevertheless bear the same stamp in their main features or form circles, some wide, some narrower, around the same pietistic nucleus. If however our aim is to understand the highly individual character of this peculiarly English 'pietistic' piety, nothing will assist us more than the examination of the characteristic mechanics of that family theocracy which constituted the very heart of the religious life and which have by no means received the attention which they deserve. (An initial bibliographical survey has been provided by

PREFACE TO THE SECOND EDITION

Chilton L. Powell, *English Domestic Relations 1487–1653*, New York 1917.)

Certainly the use of the term 'puritanical' to describe this phenomenon is open to the objection that the latter was by no means confined—particularly in more recent times—to those circles that stood in opposition to the Anglican Church. But this need hardly disturb us, for the theoreticians of this family theocracy, people like Perkins, Gouge, Rogers and Baxter with whose doctrines we shall become acquainted in the pages that follow, all belong in the final analysis to the same camp, that is to say they must be grouped with those who, in their quarrels about the liturgy and Church government and in their political disputes, all swore allegiance to the same flag. True, their influence was so powerful that they were able to conquer large tracts of territory that lay, strictly speaking, outside their party boundaries so far as the pietistic form of life is concerned. For we cannot help observing—and we do so with a certain surprise—how, to quote but a single example, the ideals and forms of practical piety, as these take on a definite shape within the context of family theocracy, bear an almost confusing resemblance to the ideas of such a man as Richard Baxter (1615–1691) who was almost exclusively nourished and sustained by the old Puritan conceptions.

A typical instance of this can be seen in the case of the Anglican, Jeremy Taylor (1613–1667). However far apart such people were in their dogmatics and in their views on Church government, they were to an astonishing degree in agreement in their ideas concerning practical conduct, in such matters for instance as family duties. Yet a few generations later we find such a man as Daniel Defoe (1660–1731), the author of *Robinson Crusoe*, letting his exemplary family scenes be enacted in an environment which, as he himself explicitly declares, might equally well be that of dissent or Church of England.

Here then we are made to see quite plainly that the main trend of practical piety does not follow the line which divides Anglicans from Sectaries but rather one which separates the pious or 'saints' from the children of this world. The denominational label has no longer any significance so far as the characteristic pietistic self-reforming English piety is concerned. Indeed we can go so far as to say that—again to take but one example—the celebrated novelist

Samuel Richardson, though the product of an Anglican home, nevertheless came from a Puritan environment.

This circumstance should be kept in mind if we are not to take umbrage at the fact that though the pages which follow are supposed to be concerned with the world of Puritan ideas, yet ideas such as those of Taylor and Tillotson (1630–1694), which were alive in close proximity to that world have not been ignored, and indeed it would surely appear senseless to observe a boundary which, as has already been shown, did not really exist at all. By the same token we might usefully follow the ideas in question right into the eighteenth century and observe how they worked themselves out and were at least partly superseded in the age of Humanism.

Yet the study which follows seeks to do more than merely accomplish a single task. On the one hand, as has already been shown, it endeavours to lay bare the essential principle that shaped a way of life in the kind of religio-ethical community that has become more important than any other for the peculiar spiritual development of the Anglo-Saxon nations. For not only are the views held by the pious concerning such matters as love and marriage, parents and children and the like—the views on which I am endeavouring here to throw light—of such a kind that their nature must be grasped if we are to understand English thought in bygone centuries, but they are still operative at the present day and have helped to form the modern Englishman.

For this reason it seemed called for to perform a task which has hitherto been neglected, namely that of searching out the threads that lead back from the Puritan movement to pre-Reformation times—at least in so far as this movement helped to fashion family life and so produce a phenomenon that in this context is of immense importance. We thus would have to penetrate a borderland, but it is, I must add, a borderland across whose misty terrain we can only advance a step at a time. In all this an attempt, however modest, is being made to answer the question, whether and to what extent Calvinism must be regarded as the original source of the Puritan movement. It would also seem useful for our purpose to start off with a special enquiry dealing with the question of a national personality ideal, though this should not imply that it could furnish us with a formula of overall validity. No such formula could possibly be found; yet such an enquiry might well make it easier to find an explanation of many phenomena that

PREFACE TO THE SECOND EDITION

throughout the centuries have remained strikingly constant in the psychic physiognomy of Anglo-Saxons.

On the other hand if the approach is made by the literary historians, there will be a tendency to use the knowledge already won concerning this matter of family theocracy for a better understanding of some of the most important literary works of the time. In Milton's *Paradise Lost*, for instance, much is made plain concerning the history of morals and manners which could not have been rendered intelligible by any other means. A new light is also thrown on the works of Bunyan, Defoe and finally of Richardson. This may help us form a proper estimate of the ethical will informing the writings of these literary educators whose work has so far tended to be looked at from an exclusively aesthetic point of view.

In addition to this, moreover, I have scrutinized the fate of the family during the transitional period in which aristocratic has been superseded by bourgeois culture and we have thus been able to see the family in its full literary-sociological significance, while the importance for creative artists of its development in the eighteenth century as a comfortable community and reading public has been examined.

The territory we have set aside for examination is great indeed and the performance of the task which we have set ourselves has often been sketchy, fragmentary, and imperfect. Although the author has for many years concerned himself with the problems which are here examined, the studies that follow will in many cases go into greater detail and correct many faults. Nevertheless the author ventures to hope for a certain modest measure of approval from the growing numbers of those who believe that the study of literary history is unthinkable without the foundation provided by the history of morals and manners. For the art of peoples can never really be fully understood until we have understood the people themselves.

Farchant, Bavaria L. L. SCHÜCKING
Summer 1964

INTRODUCTION
Puritanism and the Ideal of Sobriety

Whoever seeks to determine the national character of a people is likely to find himself on treacherous ground. He is bound to be dependent on apparently fortuitous experiences. The sheer multiplicity of impressions is confusing and oppressive, not to mention the fact that, since they are determined by social, geographical and even biological factors, they are in a state of continual flux. His judgment therefore is in constant danger of losing that sureness which alone can endow the result of his enquiries with scientific value.

Yet it would be rash to abandon all further effort on the ground that—as in so much else—our conclusions can hardly ever evoke the *consensus omnium*. The agreement of a number of critical enquirers must be regarded as providing at least an adequate working hypothesis, which, if logically developed, can illuminate the most significant spiritual and intellectual processes that have shaped a nation's history.

Our present task is to examine the peculiar characteristics of the English and the special circumstances from which these derive. Through social intercourse or through the work of such storytellers as have remained true to life and nature, many of us have gained the impression of a certain very special character, a character sharply distinguished from its counterpart on the European mainland. I will not at this stage attempt a thorough-going description of the traits that make up such a psychological physiognomy. It will perhaps suffice if, as a foretaste of all that is to follow, I select one important phenomenon which more than any other strikes the modern observer.

I speak of the way the English regard emotion, an attitude that is evident in a certain economy of words. The vocabulary used for the ordinary purposes of daily life is indeed astonishingly small, a fact that is in keeping with the cult of a marked reserve. This reserve is accounted as good form and extends even to such things as facial expression and bodily gesture; it is a reserve that does not even disappear where we should least expect to find it, namely in the relations of lovers. A marked lack of tenderness is in essence nothing but the result of the contempt experienced for all persons —including oneself—that betray a dependence on mere emotion. It often seems as though this people has become so successful in building a dam against the natural flow of sentiment that the ability to give it free expression when there is an actual desire to do so has been almost entirely lost.

Palpably, then, to have oneself in hand is thought to be the one supremely important thing. The suppression of weaknesses, such as that of vanity, for instance—which other countries judge much less harshly—is as complete as the ability to meet the blows of fortune by coming to terms with reality. The recognition that something is inevitable—'it can't be helped'—has a much more decisive influence on them than on other human types. Hand in hand with all this goes the wonderful contempt for self-pity, though a poor opinion is also had of mere sympathy that is not accompanied by an immediate resolve to give practical aid, wherever this is possible. This kind of sympathy is regarded as mere sentimentality.

Such an attitude admittedly implies an exceptional sense of duty, it implies constant self-examination, sincerity and, at the very least, a quite unusual measure of self-awareness. In personal intercourse this makes itself felt as tact.

This same quality of self-knowledge and self-awareness has yet a further part to play. Allied as it is with an active self-criticism, a habit by no means incompatible with that sense of one's own worth which in the present instance has become part of the basic structure of feeling—this same self-knowledge is in the final analysis the foundation of that sense of personal dignity which is the most powerful regulator of conduct. In education this last often plays a decisive part. 'Is that the way a gentleman behaves?' is the question put to an ill-mannered child. Let me not be misunderstood. The sceptical observer may find that in the real world the qualities I have just described are all too rarely discovered. This does not affect the argument. What matters is that they are part of a kind of wish-image of personality on which these people strive to model themselves, and this fact is sufficiently important for us to try to trace its origin and history.

INTRODUCTION

Since this is its most obvious feature, we might well describe the ideal in question as that of self-control. Self-control has from the earliest times admittedly formed part of the principal aim of any kind of education.

As Thomas Lupset (1498–1530) says:

> The best is not to be angrie; the nexte is not to shewe in wordes or countenance your angre
> (*An Exhortation to yonge Men*, 1534, folio 29b)

But this idea of self-control is, as we shall see later, something much more complex and comprehensive than a mere injunction not to let oneself be carried away by such passions as hatred, anger and rage and so impelled to senseless acts which one is bound ultimately to regret. Yet that is really all that we normally understand by this expression.

Anyone who traces the past history of the complex of qualities here under review, undergoes an experience very similar to that which awaits him when he looks at Holbein's portraits which date back to the sixteenth century. These pictures, which are wonderfully true to life, show, to a degree that is often quite astonishing, a pronounced English physiognomy; they show us faces that could come from no other country in the world. This is true even of Shakespeare's characters—at any rate where he deliberately departs from his usual manner of portraying people and shows us the grandiose picture of a model English King—to wit, Henry V.

Now in this character, which is very palpably built up on a basic structure of *sobriety, godliness, righteousness* and *humility*, we witness again and again the submission of the instincts to the rule of rational thought, such thought receiving its direction from postulates that are essentially moral and religious. We also observe here —and in a very marked degree—that element of strong self-awareness to which I have already drawn attention.

How significant in this respect is Henry's reaction, while heir apparent, to his father's illness (*Henry IV*, Part 2, II, 2). He will not allow himself openly to display the sorrow which he actually feels because this in an heir to the throne would be regarded as hypocrisy. He prefers by means of an artificial gaiety to court the reproach of indifference, for he is quite convinced that his loose way of life would make people suspicious if he were to show any deeper feeling.

Yet what inner knowledge is hereby revealed! What purposive and conscious control over his outward expression! What watchfulness over his relations with those around him! And how prudent, withal, how practical, how coolly rational is his manner of accepting life and of coming to terms with it! Even evil has its place and he makes the best of it and lets it serve his purposes:

> There is some soul of goodness in things evil,
> Would men observingly distil it out;
> . . .
> Thus may we gather honey from the weed,
> And make a moral of the devil himself.
>
> (*Henry V*, IV, 1)

The more moral and religious considerations can be made to serve practical ends, the greater the stress that thus tends to be laid on them. His humanity moreover only reaches to the point where it can still serve his interests. His conduct appears to be dictated by the utilitarian principle, 'honesty is the best policy'. His conversion at the moment when he ascends the throne strikes one as having about it something of the transformation of the 'unregenerate' into the 'regenerate' man which we shall so often encounter at a later date, for it utterly wipes out his personal weaknesses. He is so completely master of himself that he can declare—and not without good reason

> . . . our passion is as subject
> As are our wretches fetter'd in our prisons.
>
> (*Henry V*, I, 2)

His coldly objective view of the duties of kingship might well have been inspired by the Calvinist conception of professional ethics. He has put aside all vanity; pomp is for him no more than worthless ceremony; pride is unknown to him and in his self-examination he repudiates every thought that is out of keeping with that humility which he recognizes as an actual duty.

From where does this type derive with its curiously bourgeois air, this type whose character is based upon a rationalism bent on self-reform and one deeply bound up with religion? One might well be tempted to assume a connection with Puritanism. Anyone who wished to trace what I am calling the ideal of sobriety back to a

INTRODUCTION

Calvinist origin might well adduce the argument that elsewhere—to wit in Geneva—the same cause had produced similar effects. Here too the prevailing concern with religion was anything but a *dévotion aisée*, here too, men were familiar with the unceasing task of self-mastery, here too that ideal of self-mastery exerted a heavy pressure on all vital functions of the spirit.

Again—and in England we can observe something very similar—the Calvinism of Geneva earned the reproach that its insistence on self-control led to an excessive reserve, to a tendency on the part of men to keep their true selves concealed. The result of this, it is alleged, was a withdrawal of the individual even from his own family circle and this in turn brought a torturing dualism in its train and—as with the English—hindered a man from opening his heart to others. Finally there is the clash between the demands of business efficiency and those of morals—a clash to which I shall frequently have to draw attention and which the co-existence of fidelity to religious precept on the one hand and an active rationalism on the other, was ultimately bound to produce. And this clash was yet another phenomenon not infrequently encountered in a Geneva setting.

Yet noteworthy as such a parallelism may be, we should not exaggerate its importance, nor should too much confidence be placed on a certain popular version of history, according to which a Calvinist outlook utterly alien to the spirit of the country was introduced from the Continent and settled on 'Merry Old England' more or less spontaneously, like so much mildew. Such an account of the matter is a hopeless over-simplification. It implies an unconscious confusion of Shakespeare's London with sixteenth-century England, it means that a geographically and sociologically limited part has been mistaken for the whole. Even so, we cannot deny—and the thing becomes particularly clear from the sixteenth century onwards—that great stretches of luxuriant cultural vegetation run irretrievably to seed for centuries before our eyes under the influence of a spreading religious pietism.

But the ultimate origin of the trend is quite a separate question. There is food for thought in the fact that Shakespeare, who most certainly was no Puritan, when drawing his picture of Henry V, the ideal English king, so clearly fashioned it—as we have seen—according to the ideal of sobriety. Unquestionably we are dealing here with an old popular image that has a long history behind it; yet we cannot really trace it back to the Humanists, for if the Stoic ideas of antiquity found such speedy favour among the English humanists, it was only because these undeniably pious people felt the presence of something that was akin to their own traditional ideal of personality. Thus R. W. Chambers has shown us—and his conclusions are highly instructive—how profoundly such a man as Sir Thomas More was rooted in the best tradition of mediaeval thought and strove to cling to all that was good therein. Yet anyone who had actually spoken with More would have been able to see in the man's whole spiritual make-up something that reminded him of the best type of Puritan to be encountered at a later date.

There was for instance the humility which, even after he had become Lord Chancellor, led him to kneel before his aged father; there was the quiet but indestructible gaiety and affirmation of life which was the product of a perfect balance of spiritual powers, a gaiety with which a certain ascetical quality could nevertheless be mingled—it was a favourite saying of More's that one did not get to heaven upon a feather bed. There was further the contempt for all luxury and ceremony; above all there was that incredible self-mastery which—so his son-in-law tells us—never deserted him. In sixteen years of continuous intercourse Roper never once saw him 'in a fume' and even when tearing the mask from the face of a slanderous accuser, he prefaces his remarks with the words 'I am sorry that I am forced to say this . . .,' thus displaying that strange over-sensitive and almost unnatural conscientiousness with which we have become familiar in Anglo-Saxons of a later generation. For these traits in his character he is assuredly indebted less to his interest either in ancient or more recent philosophy than to the religious influences of his early years.

Here surely we are concerned with a very ancient heritage, with a manner of life which has adapted the more ascetic ideals of ecclesiastical Christianity to the demands of practical life. What really shapes this manner of life is that scholastic-patristic teaching which prevailed throughout the Middle Ages and which at a quite early stage had, of course, absorbed ancient Stoic ideas.

Now this body of teaching, using the appropriate Latin terminology, had developed the ancient Greek concept of *sophrosyne* into the precepts of *continentia* or *sobrietas*, of *discretio* or *mensura*. How important a part was played by the idea of the 'middle way',

INTRODUCTION

into which the last-named concept was ultimately expanded, is something to which I need scarcely draw attention. What is really of moment is that, as we can see from Anglo-Saxon literature, the compromise between worldly and ecclesiastical demands—and a very effective compromise it was—was achieved at an extremely early stage and it was the ecclesiastical ideal that yielded more ground than the other. Thomas Becon's writings throw light on the beginnings of the Puritan movement in the English church. He expressly puts *sophrosyne*—which means discretion, the careful ruling of desires and passions—with sobriety under the control of the conscience:

> to live soberly, should seem to be so purely, discretely, modestly, temperately, and sagely to institute our life, that our conscience should never accuse us of any evil but testify with us, that we live and do all things godly.
>
> (*Catechism*, 1560)

The word that more than any other called to mind the ideal manner of life had from the earliest days been the adjective 'sober'. The Anglo-Saxon demand for full emotional control is echoed by the best-loved moral handbook of the fifteenth century, *Dives et Pauper*, where the author recommends one 'to be always sad and always glad'. Shakespeare uses it occasionally with the sense of moral superiority such as in *Julius Caesar*, IV, 2: 'Brutus, this sober form of yours hides wrongs'. However, it is only in the era of Puritanism that the word develops its full complexity of meaning and begins to be used in an even more exalted sense; it is only then that for the pious it begins to call up an image of the kind of person they themselves are striving to be.

'What is it that you want?' says the grown-up daughter in Defoe's very widely-read *Family Instructor* (1715) in obstinacy and despair when her mother has taken away her beautiful books, her plays, her French novels, her Boileau and Dacier, and when her converted brother gives as a reason that her father wished her to be 'sober', she exclaims:

> Prethee what do you mean by sober?... Can't I be *sober* as well with all my Books my mother has taken away, *as without them*? What can you tax me with that *is not sober*, that here is such a rout about it?
>
> (page 100)

We can see the same quality in certain Puritan memoirs, such for instance as the recollections of her husband which the admirable Mrs Hutchinson (1619–1676) has set down:

> The heate of his youth, a little enclined him to the passion of anger, and the goodnesse of his nature to those of love and griefe, but reason was never dethron'd by them, but continued governesse and moderator in his soul.
>
> (page 17)

What in his wife's opinion prevented him from achieving the ultimate standards at which a man can aim was thus his incomplete mastery over his feelings. The yardstick by which Oliver Cromwell is measured by his intimate Maidstone is much the same. Maidstone says of him that the heat of his excessively fiery temperament was always damped down and held in check by his moral powers. Great stress is also laid upon this quality where women are concerned and Puritan authors do not think it too trivial to record of a housewife, as Baxter does of his Margaret, that she never grew angry when servants happened to break the crockery.

Here then we touch the heart of the problem of Puritan man, and Milton's thought leads us in a similar direction when in *Paradise Lost* he attributes Adam's failure in his task to his 'uxoriousness', to his dependence on his wife, a dependence which results from an insufficient 'sobriety', an insufficient control of his instincts by his reason. In so far as Adam falls through a lack of 'sobriety', this clearly implies that all the evil in the world results from a lack of self-control. Incidentally, Milton has the same idea in mind when in *Samson Agonistes* he enunciates the very questionable theory that 'all wickedness is weakness'.

Those who regard such sentiments as being no more than a product of the Renaissance can point to the fact that Milton was often influenced by the thought of antiquity and that the relation between *ratio* and *passio* was a favourite theme of seventeenth-century philosophy. But to lay undue stress upon this is to ignore the degree to which Milton's ideas tended to be nourished by the religious views of his time, which placed the concept of self-control at the very heart of self-reform. This was particularly true of the Puritans, though the teaching of the Established Church often followed similar lines.

INTRODUCTION

Now it is undeniable that the peculiar character of Puritanism, and in particular the searching and tireless pre-occupation with the self, must have had the most far-reaching effects on the character as a whole. For these people did not merely search their consciences for actual sins, for failures in such matters as moderation, chastity, humility and vigilance; they scrutinized their whole range of capabilities and talents, their weaknesses, shortcomings and their whole temperamental make-up; they studied the reactions of their souls to certain impressions, the strength of their powers of resistance. They used every means to form a just estimate of themselves.

Even at an early age this probing of one's self plumbed the most surprising depths and the methods employed were astonishingly subtle. A good example of this is provided by the widely-read William Gouge in his *The Whole Armour of God* (1619) where he deals with the examination of motives and with the avoidance of self-deception. What, he asks, lies at the bottom of our actions? What causes us to behave in a particular way? Are we moved by a desire for popularity or for the esteem of others? Or by hope for some advantage? Do we desire the respect of some particular person? Or are we moved by a longing for quiet and by the wish to avoid excitement? Or do we want to do someone an injury? Do we in all matters strive for truth? Are we only strict in small matters, but not in weighty ones? (1627 edition, page 64). Such questioning was of course not invented by the Puritans but goes back in essence to the very earliest times. In the present instance however, it has a peculiar characteristic in so far as the religious person daily illuminates the whole of his inner self as though with subcutaneous rays.

We are familiar with such examinations of conscience from our knowledge of the life of the Catholic layman, but such men are only concerned to search out their sins so that they may ultimately confess them. In the case of the Puritan however, where a man's whole life was looked at from a religious point of view and where every evening prayer became a confession, a guiding principle began to assert itself that extended to the most ordinary incidents of life. One redressed the balance so to speak not merely at Easter or even monthly, but entered up even the smallest item of moral expenditure, and ruled off the account daily. I might add that this imagery is itself taken from Puritan literature, from the passages, to be exact, which deal with the duty of watchfulness over one's self (John Downame, *A Guide to Godlynesse*, 1622, page 611). Actually my references to spiritual bookkeeping are a little more than a mere simile, for the believer is summoned in so many words to follow his ordinary business practices and keep a proper ledger in this, the spiritual sphere, and even to draw up a written catalogue of his sins and shortcomings.

It seems reasonable to assume that the effect of all this was in many respects disastrous. Physicians frequently warn their patients against an excessive and over-intense preoccupation with their physical state since this can easily lead to much suffering from diseases that only exist in the sufferer's imagination. People can develop a moral hypochondria in much the same way. Certainly this must occur where the feeling of spiritual health is not very pronounced and especially where the power to distinguish between good and evil, between innocence and sin, is imperfectly developed, as in the case of the child. Indeed we can scarcely conceive of the tortures which thus became the portion of thousands upon thousands of pliable, morally over-sensitive, children's souls. But among adults, too, many of the more introspective natures must have run the risk of being well-nigh crushed under the pressure of self-doubt. Indeed it is significant in this connection that religious writing (that of Downame, for instance, page 803 ff.) is to a quite surprising degree concerned with religious melancholia, a very common affliction in those days apparently and one which was often explained as a particularly skilful temptation by the devil, though this diagnosis can hardly have been helpful in bringing about a cure. In the eighteenth century, when the devil had already begun to withdraw before the advance of the Enlightenment, other explanations were favoured such as 'natural weakness and timidity of temper' and a tendency to self-torture (Samuel Clark, *Self-Examination explained and recommended*, 1761), to all of which due regard had now to be paid.

Yet even among the healthy-minded, such self-examination could lead to the wildest exaggeration of religious scruple. Thus at the end of the sixteenth century, we find Puritans who would not permit themselves even to stroke their dogs. In the end, such men could only attain peace of mind by refraining from all activities that could in any sense be considered pleasurable. Actually, even men whose education should have shielded them against such unfruitful denial of life, tended to be vaguely hag-ridden by this idea and claimed, explicitly or implicitly, to regard the attainment of this aim as the supreme moral objective. Samuel Johnson for instance, in 1759 utters a warning against apparently innocent pleasures:

> Pleasure, in itself harmless may become mischievous, by endearing to us a state which we know to be transient and probatory, and withdrawing our thoughts from that of which every hour brings us nearer to the beginning and of which no length of time will bring us to the end.
>
> (*Rasselas*, chapter XLVII)

Taken literally, this doctrine represents nothing less than the unalloyed spiritual heritage of the Middle Ages, for even the most sinister asceticism justified itself by such arguments as these. For men like Johnson such ideas did not constitute the guiding principle of their lives. But the persistence among them of strong anti-Epicurean principles which they regarded as self-evidently valid, remains undeniable. Their very language gives adequate expression to what was in effect their attitude towards life; they spoke of pleasure as 'self-indulgence', thus implying a culpable and excessive consideration for the self.

The effect of the meticulous examination of conscience involved in all this must have been particularly unfortunate where those concerned tended by nature to be self-satisfied. In the final analysis, the standards by which we judge ourselves are purely personal. The same total of aptitudes and achievements which may delight one man will cause another to despair. It all depends on what we expect of ourselves on the moral level which each man seeks to attain. For this reason, not only do expressions of self-praise constitute unreliable testimony, as everybody will agree, but, a fact which is frequently overlooked, those of excessive self-criticism are, if anything more worthless still.

The practice of continually regarding themselves in a kind of spiritual looking-glass, causes those who are already over-pleased at what they behold to be confirmed in their fault. Indeed it is this habit of perpetual self-examination that helps to create the type for which the English language has coined the word 'prig', a word that denotes a person who is perpetually conscious of his own imagined superiority, and is continually and intolerably concerned to impress us with the excellence of his own example. With all his faults, however, such a man is but a relatively agreeable variant of the Pharisee—who is a product of a rather similar process.

On the other hand an attitude towards life which threatens to make every man his own inquisitor is fraught with the danger that it will deprive him of every pleasure in life and thus cause his best qualities to wither away. That is why we find these continuous warnings against moroseness along with corresponding injunctions to merriment:

> What is more frequent, than to see Religion make Men cynical, and sour in their Tempers, morose and surly in their conversation(?)
> (Defoe, *The Religious Courtship*, 1722, I, 3)

The answer which this question receives, namely that such people do not have a sufficiency of religion, implies a very considerable admission. I need hardly stress the fact that most people find it very difficult to unite harshness towards themselves with mildness towards their fellow creatures, especially when harshness and intolerance can claim to have divine authority.

The circumstance that a man's gaze is excessively concentrated upon himself produces yet another result; a certain obtuseness that is almost deliberate, a spiritual lethargy, a lack of that ability to enter into the feelings of others with which a more naïve person and one less preoccupied with himself is often better endowed. People so inclined often end up as the polar opposites of the artistic temperament. The latter concept implies a man inwardly unfettered and largely obedient to unconscious impulse. It is this that Eduard von Hartmann has in mind when he speaks of the 'self-forgetfulness and world-forgetfulness of the productive mood in the artist'. For the Puritan, however, self-forgetfulness and world-forgetfulness are grave sins.

As against all this, the introspective tendency which the religious life tends to produce must of necessity show some worthwhile fruits. We may indeed be sure that the old saw which says that self-examination is a condition of self-mastery is more often right than wrong. Admittedly, as I have just pointed out, this whole process can often involve a loss of simplicity and spontaneity. For the soul that through doubt has become uncertain of itself is offered a means of reassurance from without and also a pattern on which to model itself. For all of us, once the scales with which we

INTRODUCTION

weigh ourselves move against us, direct our gaze to the achievements and aptitudes of our neighbours and so restore the balance. Thus a vigorous dissection of ourselves can easily cause us to conform to an ideal type and indeed a certain spiritual uniformity is something that is actually aimed at in a pietistic community. The unhewn stones which must be worked upon if they are to find a place in the temple of God—a metaphor that occurs again and again—become very like each other once they have been made subject to the chisel. Daniel Dyke remarks in this context that whereas it is a pleasant sight to see two rows of men wearing the same livery, a single one differently attired spoils the whole picture. The peculiar kind of religious uniformity that tended to prevail at this time could scarcely be more tellingly illustrated. Yet it must be remembered that all this served to fortify the individual inwardly and so enhance his self-assurance. As a result he began to be armed against sudden assaults of emotion, and against external influence in general, in a manner which recalls the Stoic. It is of course true that Puritan writers such as Gouge frequently attacked the Stoic for his alleged deadening of sensibility and wrongly accused him of seeking to destroy all capacity to feel. This they declared to be sinful, claiming that to make oneself insensible to suffering was to seek escape from the chastisement of God. Yet when it came to the control of rage and anger and similar emotions they were no more able than were the Middle Ages to dispense with the wisdom of Seneca, Plutarch and similar writers and so showed that their own ideal of personality was in many respects similar to that of antiquity.

'Self-knowledge' then came to be regarded as a kind of inward independence and also as a form of prudence, involving, as it does, a fair perception of a person's relations to those around him. This is how God uses the word to Adam in *Paradise Lost* when the latter has fallen through a lack of self-control and God reproaches him by saying that it would not have happened 'had'st thou known thyself aright' (X, 156). Richardson, too, using a catchword current at the time, speaks of the darkest and most contemptible ignorance as being a lack of knowledge of one's self. Eliza Haywood in *The Tea-Table* (1725) expresses it thus:

> It has ever been allowed that to know one's self is the most valuable part of knowledge.

Nowadays we would express this lack of knowledge as a lack of knowledge of our true intentions.

The emphasis placed on this idea must have been all the greater in so far as it also represented the key to external success, such success being, as it were, the key-stone of the religious life. For however impressive the warnings of preachers may have been not to make external success and in particular not to make riches the sole aim of their life, however earnest their counsel to practice unswerving honesty and righteousness in business affairs and to prove dependable therein, the men of that day were nevertheless filled with the desire to come to terms with life as they found it and to do so with some measure of tangible success.

It was this form of realism in the outlook of the Puritan which caused Max Weber to speak of the Puritan outlook as one of 'asceticism within the world' (*innerweltliche Askese*). This description which seeks to unite the two opposites in question makes plain the weaknesses that must have been inherent in each. After all an 'asceticism within the world' is something like a contradiction in terms. In this imperfect world moral and external objectives simply cannot coincide. Yet it is the essence of the Puritan's character that he sought simultaneously to attain both. For in the final analysis this is what his striving amounted to and in one respect at any rate, such striving was a source of strength. For although this continual self-examination was fundamentally nothing than a more intensive form of mediaeval Catholic practice, it nevertheless differed most strikingly from the full loss of self in the religious life and from true contemplation. Religion for the Puritan was not really surrender at all; meditation and recollection were ultimately only valued in so far as they contributed to practical achievements; his mind was wholly fixed on action.

> .... to know
> That which before us lies in daily life
> Is the prime Wisdom.
>
> (*Paradise Lost*, VIII, 192 ff.)

He was always anxious to see results and regarded his life as a ladder on which he ascended and every situation as a platform from which he could survey the extent of his success and thus measure his progress.

INTRODUCTION

This would show him, amongst other things, how far he had advanced in the virtues of patience and perseverance which bring so many other excellent qualities in their train, for, as Marie von Ebner-Eschenbach has said, 'to speak of patience is to speak of courage, determination and strength'. All this could lead to such amusing consequences as—to quote but one example—the placing on New Year's Eve of moral new year resolutions into the family Bible by the individual members of that family, this being followed a year later by an enquiry, under the supervision of the head of the family as to the extent to which a higher level of morality had actually been attained.

In such relatively trivial things we can already discern a certain spirit of activism, a spirit that is continually seeking to achieve certain specific ends and manifests itself in the posing of a whole host of questions. But it is in the very nature of things that this drive of the spirit should be directed, not towards religious goals alone but also towards worldly ones, and here the outside observer is liable to suspect a certain divergence between a professedly moral principle and what are palpably the dictates of utility and selfishness, so gaining the impression of hypocrisy. This was as true of the sixteenth century as it is today and is well exemplified in the figure of Shakespeare's Henry V. Indeed our human nature is so constituted that where ideal aims and material ones compete with one another the former do not always gain the victory.

However, the practice of continued self-examination which the ideal of sobriety enjoined made any obvious compromise with moral standards impossible. An attempt at justification had, therefore, to be made by way of dialectic. The results of this approach have often produced astonishment in the non Anglo-Saxon world. The humanity which only goes to the point where self interest begins is a good example of the process. In other words, in this matter of 'asceticism within the world' either the world or asceticism is bound to be the loser. Again it was in the very nature of things that this ideal of self-control (compare G. B. Shaw, *Back to Methuselah*, 1921. Introduction, page 53) built up on 'self-knowledge', should produce yet a further result, namely, an enhanced self-respect which led to a typical and intense consciousness of personal dignity, a matter to which reference has already been made. We find much mention of this dignity in the literature of the seventeenth century, particularly in Milton, though where such dignity is to a marked degree in evidence externally, the word 'honour' and even 'majesty' is used.

The feeling which is at the bottom of it all, that a mean and contemptible action is 'beneath one', is described by Richardson as the only justifiable kind of pride. The attitude in question which serves to repress a purely utilitarian scale of values, was really a kind of substitute morality, making possible that 'generosity' which has played such an important part in the English wish-image of personality and has from a practical point of view been of such high importance. People felt that they had a duty to act in a particular way and that this was a duty not only towards society but also towards themselves, a duty, that is to say, to the moral ideal which each of them represented.

I have sketched certain characteristic effects of this ideal and if they are studied, their importance in the relationships which I am about to examine will be readily apparent. The resolve to have oneself completely in hand, a resolve that from a man's earliest years extended not only to such things as the control of gesture but affected the smallest particular that could give expression to his living personality, was bound to have far-reaching results. Not least of these—and indeed this was the chief object of all striving—was that it endowed him with a kind of emotional independence. But the price of that very independence was that men were kept at a certain distance from their fellows. Emotion involves and involvement makes men dependent, but a man must be able to stand on his own feet and not forfeit his independence to a desire for sympathy.

When in *Paradise Lost*, Adam before his Fall pours out his heart to the angel, a heart full of dreamy devotion to his young wife, the angel shows signs of misgiving and advises him not, as one might suppose, to adopt a more critical attitude towards Eve, but to cultivate a higher degree of self-awareness. The passage proves in characteristic fashion that in the opinion of that time all moral health was believed to derive from a man's thought about himself.

This acute awareness of self which is not distinguished by any sharp dividing line from self-control, produces ultimately a kind of isolating layer that encloses a man, a layer which is present even in those ages in which emotion is much in evidence. Certainly a man like Gellert was on more intimate terms with his manservant than his contemporary Richardson was with his wife. Yet this in no way

INTRODUCTION

invalidates anything I have written in the pages which follow concerning the astonishingly advanced character of the spiritual element in Puritan marriage, even as far back as the seventeenth century. These people too experienced profoundly, through each other, and in company with each other, but to a rather lesser degree *with* each other. The closeness of the relationship here finds expression through a wonderful tact, through a delicate but silent understanding, not through warmth or tenderness. Nor does the lover turn the loved one into a kind of *alter ego* by letting that loved one see into the last recesses of his or her heart, and by permitting him or her to share to the very utmost every hope, every care, every joy, every weakness and every strength.

There is nothing that makes us more keenly aware of the characteristic armour with which these people surrounded themselves than the use of the expression 'to give oneself away' to denote the full opening of one's heart. The rather excessive affection lavished on unreasoning creatures such as dogs and cats, creatures which as far back as the earliest Middle Ages have held a privileged position in the Englishman's emotional life, may well have served as a kind of substitute for that element in the relations between one human being and another, which at quite an early age he had accustomed himself to renounce.

The pages which follow may perhaps help to provide an answer to these different questions. For in them an attempt has been made to deduce from the material provided by the more important Puritan writings the nature of the relationship which in the Puritan world subsisted between one human being and another.

I

Marriage under Puritanism

1. *Puritan literature dealing with marriage and family: the conduct books*

Puritanism is almost wholly deficient in imaginative literature and indeed, given its attitude towards life in general, it was hardly likely to produce such a thing. The student therefore who seeks to rediscover the features of Puritan reality in the mirror of art is hardly to be envied. Now I am not the first to observe that Puritanism has produced systematic expositions of ideal conduct which in many respects provide us with a more exact and reliable picture of life as it actually was than could in any other context be obtained from the literature of the imagination. For all that, it is easy to be misled into treating noteworthy Puritan writers such as Richard Baxter as representative of the whole world of Puritan thought. Ernst Troeltsch is among those who have fallen into this error, for Baxter's writings are very far from embodying the most advanced ideas of the Puritan movement. Kluckhohn makes a similar mistake in his fine book on love in the eighteenth century, when he treats certain remarks of Defoe as typifying the Puritan outlook which are by no means characteristic of the main trend of Puritan thought.

Yet if we are anxious to determine the real nature of the Puritan mind we can find excellent material in the so-called conduct books, which are not altogether unlike the mediaeval *Summae* and set out to advise the believing Christian in every situation of ordinary life, and particularly in matters that concern the family. In these folios all situations from the cradle to the grave are considered with scholastic acumen, the specific group of duties which arise out of them being in each case defined. The ultimate sources of this literature (in which all the various works are heavily dependent upon each other) are the Bible, the ancient writers (particularly Plutarch and the Church Fathers, of whom diligent use is made) and, among more recent writers, Erasmus and Bullinger.

The origins of this *genre* are largely veiled in obscurity, though to quote but one example, Reginald Pecock in his famous *The Repressor of Overmuch Blaming of the Clergy* (1455) informs us that he was the author of an exhaustive examination of the duties and peculiarities of the married state (see C. Babington's edition, 1860, page 15). But this work has vanished without trace and so no answer can be given to the question as to whether use was made of it by those who later treated the same subject. If we would follow the direction taken by the further development of this form of literature, we should call to mind the names of Miles Coverdale, to whom we are indebted for the translation of the Swiss-German Bullinger's *Ehebuch* (*Christen State of Matrimonye*, 1541), of Thomas Becon (1512–67) to whose influential writings I shall now have frequent occasion to refer, of William Perkins, the author of *Oeconomia Christiana* which was printed in 1590 and enjoyed a considerable reputation, and of William Gouge, whose great work *Of Domesticall Duties, Eight Treatises* (1622) which went into several editions, offers, along with Matthew Griffith's *Bethel: or, a forme for families* (1633), the most comprehensive treatment of all the related problems.

All these works were, of course, accompanied by a host of smaller compilations; moreover with the spread of Puritanism in the seventeenth century the number of such treatises was further substantially increased. We shall see that among these the essay *Matrimoniall Honour* (1642) by Daniel Rogers (1573–1652)—like so many of the others, a clergyman with a Puritan outlook—should be accorded a rather special position. The works of Baxter, with all their extensive casuistry, fall into the second half of the seventeenth century and his famous *Christian Directory* (1673) stands at the head of them all. The close relation subsisting between Baxter's views and those of the Anglican, Jeremy Taylor is evident in Taylor's *Holy Living and Dying* (1650) and we shall on occasion be struck by a parallelism with that master of the pulpit, the famous Archbishop John Tillotson.

2. *The Bible as a model*
It is clear that the student who seeks to form a picture of the ideals that animated the Puritan Englishman has a larger body of material to draw on than is available to him in regard to any other set of men in any other period. What strikes us more forcibly than anything

else in this matter is the fact that the English Puritan sought to shape his life by the example of the Bible and particularly by that of the Old Testament. Thanks to this, the great historical achievement of the Jewish people, the creation of its own form of the Patriarchal family, gains an importance for posterity which, till now, has been insufficiently appreciated (compare Goodsell, page 48 ff.). It was of course the practice in regard to any department of life to search the Bible story for incidents involving conduct that was in any way worthy of emulation. No texts however were sought out with such persistency and care as those which threw light on family life. Not that such reference to the Old Testament as a guide for living was in itself particularly new. The fifteenth-century *Dives et Pauper*, for instance, teems with examples taken from this part of Holy Scripture. When in the following century, but still in pre-Puritan times (1547-9), Archbishop Cranmer was putting together the material for his marriage service, he fell back on the marriage of Abraham and Sarah as an illustration of the ideal marital relationship. This kind of thing had of course, always had its place in a certain kind of literature, but under Puritanism it became steadily more marked. One could write a book about Abraham in England which would be more voluminous than one written, say, on Cicero or Homer in England.

What excellent instruction this Abraham provided both in word and deed, as did his son and grandson! Thus the story of Rebecca's roasting of a kid for Isaac could with profit be applied to life, and teach us that a good woman must be expert in the kitchen. When Rebecca, as a maiden, waters her father's camels, this showed how a daughter can be useful about the house, while Isaac's desire to bless his first-born before he died, could teach us that the pious man, before leaving this world, must make his final dispositions.

How reassuring, moreover, it must have been, after listening to those disturbing counsellors, for ever jabbering about evangelical poverty and quoting Christ's advice to the rich young man—how reassuring it must have been to read of the enormous possessions of men who had been particularly pleasing to God, such as Abraham, Isaac and Jacob! Of course there were occasions where it was not considered proper to follow their example. In the matter of polygamy, for instance, no attempt was made to imitate them, in England. Indeed, when the Anabaptists in Münster, whose teaching was not so very divergent from the main trend of Puritan thought, took a more logical stand in this matter, it was the English who seemed to be outraged rather more than anybody else, and the horror which this practice inspired continued to be evident in their literature for a considerable time.

All this throws light on a certain weakness in the Puritan position. In the final analysis, the Old Testament, when used as a guide, can prove to be a two-edged sword. The disquiet thus caused is obvious from the frequency with which Puritanical literature feels impelled to warn against 'errors' (compare for instance Gouge, 1626, Treatise 7, section 11 *et passim*). Indeed, in Bunyan's *The Pilgrim's Progress* (1678) we have a Mr Self-Will, a quite dreadful person who points out examples of crimes in the Old Testament committed by the most venerable individuals that range from adultery to theft.

3. *Development of the Reformation's conception of marriage: exceptional position of Baxter*

Lively as was the attachment to the Old Testament and powerful as was its effect in shaping the general trend of ideas—the proliferation of Old Testament names to be found in England at this time shows the extent of its influence—it is nevertheless obvious enough that in many matters the actual selection of the figures which were to serve as examples was determined by certain fixed views already in existence at the time. So far as marriage is concerned, the views expressed are simply those of the Reformation. In no particular do these new ideas contrast sharply with the old. To the Middle Ages marriage was, more or less, a necessary evil. Virginal men held a higher place than any in the married state and the difference in the position of the two could actually be expressed in numerical terms. Thus we are told in Dan Michel's Middle English *Ayenbite of Inwyt* (page 234)—and there are plenty of similar utterances—marriage counts as 30, widowhood 60 and virginity 100. An enormously popular work, William Langland's fourteenth-century *Vision of Piers Ploughman* is very definite on the point:

> ... that here owen wil for-saken,
> And chast leden her lyf
> ys lyf of contemplacion,
> And more lykyng to oure lorde
> than lyue as kynde asketh,

And folwe that the flessh wole
and frut forth brynge . . .*

(C. Passus XIX, 76–79)

Since this is so, it is particularly noteworthy that there is not a single word about the moral superiority of celibacy in a book that was as widely read as was *Dives et Pauper* in the century which followed Langland—the century, that is to say, before the Reformation. However, we should not infer too much from this, since this work, in many respects an advanced one, still continues basically to adhere to the grossly sensual conception of the purpose of marriage, which the Church had from time immemorial defined as the procreation of children, their education and the avoidance of unchastity.

It was the Reformation that took a decisive step towards a more exalted conception. William Tyndale, for instance, who in 1524 had studied under Luther in Wittenberg, expanded the old ecclesiastical conception of marriage in his *The Obedience of a Christen man* (1528), declaring that marriage 'was ordained for a remedy and to increase the world and for the man to help the woman and the woman the man, with all love and kindness'. Cranmer, when composing the marriage service in his *Prayer Book* (1549) characteristically took over the two Catholic reasons for marriage and added the Protestant reason which he formulated as 'Mutual society, help and comfort, that the one ought to have of the other, both in prosperity and adversity'.

However, the essentially ascetical spirit of Christianity had in this case been much too powerful. The teaching of St Augustine, which clearly implied that sexuality was really the original sin, had so profoundly poisoned men's minds that it was impossible for the cleansing effects of the Reformation immediately to assert themselves. It is characteristic of England that the abolition of clerical celibacy was carried through against the wishes of a powerful minority and that Queen Elizabeth still had a positive horror of the thing. That was how it came about that the Established Church

---

* Those who surrender their wills
And lead a chaste life of meditation
Are more according to the heart of the lord,
Than those who live according to nature's commands
And follow what the flesh desires,
And bring forth fruit.

for a long time still continued to flirt with the idea of clerical celibacy while the old Catholic ideas continued obstinately to prove themselves anything but moribund. Well into the seventeenth century we still encounter the pious proverb that 'marriage fills the earth but virginity fills the heavens', to which a witty preacher named William Secker (*A Wedding Ring Fit for the Finger*, 1658) rejoined by asking how the heavens could be full when the earth was empty, while a devotional work with a readership as widespread as that of *The Whole Duty of Man*, which was published in 1659, gives one the impression that the Reformers had never effected such a thing as the spiritualization of the relations between the sexes:

> Now this vertue of *chastity* consists in a perfect abstaining from all kinds of uncleanness, not only that of adultery, and fornication, but all other more unnatural sorts of it, committed either upon our selves, or with any other. In a word, all acts of that kind are utterly against Chastity, save only in *lawful marriage*. And even there men are not to think themselves let loose to please their brutish appetites, but are to keep themselves within such rules of moderation, as agree to the end of Marriage, which being these two, the begetting of children, and the avoiding of fornication, nothing must be done which may hinder the first of these ends; and the second aiming onely at the subduing of lust, the keeping men from any sinful effects of it, is very contrary to that end to make marriage an occasion of heightening, and enflaming it.
>
> (pages 168–9)

It is the great merit of the Puritan movement within the Church —in this department always by far the most progressive—that it unmistakably followed the path pointed out by Luther and did not hesitate, in assessing the role played by the physical side of marriage, to draw the conclusions implicit in its basic conviction. This point is of great importance if we wish to evaluate Puritanism correctly as a whole—which we are all too often disinclined to do. The historian G. G. Coulton, for instance, once contended that:

> The puritanism of the Reformation was simply the strictest and most logical attempt yet made to realize certain thoroughly mediaeval ideals; its theory had long been the theory of the religious, but none had yet dared to enforce it wholesale.
>
> (*Contemporary Review*, 88 (1905), page 230)

As we shall see later, there is a considerable element of truth in this remark; nevertheless, it badly overshoots the mark and nowhere does this become more evident than when we examine marriage and the family under Puritanism. For it is precisely here that we can discern the very essence of the movement—the union of worldly and religious duties to the point where the two virtually interpenetrate one another.

The correctness of this assertion is not impaired by the fact that many generations later Richard Baxter (1615–91) of all people, shows signs of reverting to the basic Catholic point of view. For him, one of the chief reasons for marriage is concupiscence; the sexual drive is for him a 'disease' which gradually dies away in marriage, and he speaks of it in the tone of a mediaeval penitential preacher. The married state is, in such circumstances, little more than a 'remedy against lust' and when Baxter speaks of family life as a most wretched increase of all the miseries of existence, when he refers to a wife and children as 'the devouring gulf that swallows all', when he declares that marriage hinders the clergy in their task and cries out against the extent to which a married man is actually drawn away from his relationship to God, then it seems as though some mediaeval ascetic such as the author of the Early Middle English *Hali Maidenhad*, had risen from the dead (pages 36–8).

This fundamental hostility towards marriage on Baxter's part represents a noteworthy deviation from the very tradition which surrounded him; nor did it fail to arouse the most violent opposition. Indeed, when he made nonsense of the whole thing by entering into marriage himself, he encountered the most lively personal enmities. (Nor is this the only point on which Baxter agrees with the Catholic Church. He describes the position of the father as intermediary between the family and God and considers that he therefore ought to be as holy as a priest, 'that he may be fit to stand between them and God'.)

It is worth noting that Baxter's famous Anglican contemporary, Jeremy Taylor, stands out as a kind of polar opposite to him in this matter. True, Taylor occasionally has something to say in praise of voluntary chastity which, in so far as it implies mastery over natural appetites, he regarded as demonstrably on a high moral plane. Nevertheless, when he compares marriage with celibacy, he uses his finest eloquence to laud the superior spiritual riches of the married state, through which we have a wholly different experience of the heights and depths of life and which is the true basis of any worthwhile achievement.

We see here how completely Taylor identified himself with that conception of marriage which we could well designate as the general Puritan conception and which fails to find any kind of expression in Baxter at all. Actually, this Puritan conception could hardly help being what it was, since the strength of Puritanism rested on a kind of rationalism which was much too clear and objective to do anything but come to terms with one of the most important things in a man's natural life—in this case with the relations between the sexes—in a manner which benefited the whole moral personality.

Now the attempt has frequently been made to show that Puritanism sought to suppress both the sentimental and the sensual element in sex relations and certain examples have been adduced —that of John Wesley for instance—to prove that it was actually considered meritorious to enter into marriage without any kind of affection whatever. In point of fact, however, these examples belong to a later period and are really no longer Puritanical at all.

This whole matter is worth examining more closely, nor should such examination be over-difficult. The Puritan was very practical in his outlook on life and so came early to realize the vast importance of marriage in the life of the individual. It was therefore, only to be expected that we should find the subject most thoroughly scrutinized in the conduct books. We thus have plenty of material.

4. *The most important conditions for successful marriage: the most dangerous errors*

It is unquestionably true that the Puritan had a profound distrust of any marriage whose only foundation was mutual affection. A thoroughly Christian pessimism in regard to human nature served to shape his judgment. There were also the lessons learned from life over many generations, lessons duly set down in the writings of Bullinger and Erasmus. Daniel Rogers, one of the most generous-minded writers that has ever treated the problems of marriage and one endowed with quite exceptional delicacy of feeling, utters the sharpest warning to those who plan to build their lives on so uncertain a foundation. 'Poor greenheads' he calls them, and prophesies that when a year or two has gone by and they have skimmed the cream of their marriage, they will begin to reflect and envy the good fortune of others.

The cool prudence that informs these words is typical for the whole movement. It is moreover a prudence which does not stop short when it comes up against religion. For however permeated they might be by their religious ideas, however deliberately their devotion to God might be transferred to the day-to-day business of their lives—though according to mediaeval man such devotion was possible in the cloister alone—not one of these people ever made the suggestion that they should follow the example of the *Herrnhuter*—Moravians—and let the will of God decide, leaving it either to the elders of the community or to lot to select their wives for them. Religion, Rogers declared, could do no more than it was able and however much stress was laid on a married couple's having the same religious views—Defoe was later to make this idea the essential theme of a whole book, *The Religious Courtship*—nobody thought it sufficient to guarantee success in marriage. The truth is that where marriage is concerned a whole host of considerations must be taken into account and only one of these is mutual affection. It is true moreover that comparatively little weight is attached to this last. Gouge for instance, whose book *Domesticall Duties* was to have so wide an influence on ideas in the years to come, has admittedly little to say on this subject, save only that mutual affection must be present (Treatise 1, section 84). But the man of sense has a clear duty to search out the grounds for this affection, and here it is curious to note the way the ages concur; Baxter, for instance, sticks to the old scholastic terminology and insists that there is a 'sensitive' love which does not depend on the worth of its object and can also be found in nature. With this he contrasts 'rational' love and it is this last that must be present if marriage is to be entered into. Such 'rational' love implies an attitude which searches out the grounds of love.

Rogers, however, though going along most of the way with Baxter so far as his practical demands are concerned, is not averse to a trace of romance and discerns therein a certain mystical element that exists in love, an element that cannot be fully grasped by the reason. He finds most eloquent words to describe the mysterious sympathy which can bind two souls to one another; for the sake of that sympathy many external and tangible advantages are often wholly disregarded. It is that final instinct that is also widespread in nature, an example being that of the vine which, in such inexplicable fashion seeks to embrace the elm.

But such Platonic conception no more prevents him than it prevents Baxter from recognizing, with the very maximum of coolness and clarity, the practical demands of the world as it is. Apart from insisting on the supremely important matter of parental consent and from some indulgence in trite warnings against setting too high a value on beauty and riches, we find both writers of one mind regarding 'the sacred condition of equality', that is to say equality of wealth and rank together with an identity of religious persuasion. In the matter of age, however, it is usually assumed on purely physiological grounds that the husband will be from five to ten years older than the wife.

In dealing with this matter of marriage, wise counsels of antiquity tend often to be reformulated and freshly applied. Moreover we keep coming across matter which is also to be found in dissertations on marriage and the choice of husbands. Frequently, however, the fullness of the writer's own experience and the shrewdness of his observation are quite astonishing. Thus Rogers declares it to be a misfortune for a man to marry, as so often happens, a woman older than himself. For in the end this leads to improper relations with female servants and even to the murder of children and all kinds of other crimes. Quite frequently it happens that after the death of a wife who is older than the husband, the aforesaid husband marries a woman who is much too young for him and who then proceeds to make his life a misery.

Again, the inequality may arise when a man marries a woman of inferior status, who, being thus raised up through marriage, becomes lazy and arrogant. Such a wife may also make her husband's life a burden by continually suspecting him of insufficient respect for her, or alternatively, driving him to expenditure that is beyond his means. Incidentally, the insistence on equality of fortune does not mean that there is any iron rule in the matter; if there is disparity of worldly goods, education and special gifts can frequently restore the balance. Further, although we are urged not to enter into marriage without seeking the advice of prudent and understanding friends, it is plain that the unhappiness of many married couples is due to the fact that the husband chose his wife only because she was pleasing to others. Again, many marriages fail because the husband has married a wife who forced herself on him; experience shows that this soon leads to that husband's indifference.

Many similar observations are to be found in this literature. There is for instance Rogers' attempt to answer the question of whether differences of temperament militate against the success of a marriage, or in what circumstance a marriage contracted with an inferior—in the case of widowers for instance—can still admit of certain possibilities of mutual adjustment. Such speculations as these are, of course, not governed by any religious or canonical consideration. What they express is that cool prudence of a middle class whose psychology in this year of 1642 strikes us as astonishingly modern.

For here there is an insight into human nature, a grasp of the laws governing certain reactions, an insight that only comes into evidence in art after the passage of many generations. Indeed the assumption of the Enlightenment that the activities of the human mind are governed by ascertainable laws and that a knowledge of these can be made to guide our lives has here already become a working reality. The views expressed concerning the psychological effects of the union of two people from different social environments are particularly noteworthy. We can see here how psychological importance is already attached to differences which are very subtle indeed.

5. Basic relationship of the sexes in marriage: the position of women
All this makes it more pertinent than ever to discover the basic conception of the relation between man and woman in marriage prevailing at this period. We should therefore examine the traditional circumstances in which Puritan doctrine had to operate. Naturally there was great variation in these from one social stratum to another, but it is quite clear—and the accuracy of our information here leaves little doubt—that the position of women, when compared with that of the rest of Europe, was quite strikingly favourable in just that stratum which was to set the tone for future developments. This is apparent both from the picture drawn by literature and from certain external evidence. Indeed in Shakespeare's day this feature of English life was particularly marked, and it is not surprising that it often failed to be viewed with a sympathetic eye and that its less pleasing aspects on occasion

aroused tendentious comment. Certainly we find foreign observers expressing disapproval of a number of allegedly reprehensible propensities that characterized the English housewife—her passion for pleasure and finery, for instance, and her habit of perpetually gadding about. Thus Emanuel van Meteren, the Dutch Resident in London in Shakespeare's day, has not a word to say about English family life. When he describes the married women of England, it is always to tell of their perpetual comings and goings, now to a card party, now to a baptism, now to visit a woman in child-bed, now to church or to a funeral. He insists that—often to the intense annoyance of their spouses—they care for nothing but diversions and, unlike their Dutch and German counterparts, leave the care of the house wholly to their servants. We also have the testimony of Frederick of Würtenberg who in 1592 found that women in England enjoyed great freedom and were 'almost the masters'.

There can be no doubt that something real has been observed here. Gouge mentions in *Domesticall Duties* how the women hide their 'silken gowns and beaver hats' in their friends' houses and when their husbands are away they 'paint their faces, lay out their hair, and in everything follow the fashion' (Treatise 1, section 125). Shakespeare surely had such examples of the sex in mind when in *Coriolanus* he showed us the chatterbox Valeria trying to entice the General's 'gracious silence', his virtuous domesticated wife, to leave her embroidery and abandon herself to idleness. She proffers the excuse with which van Meteren has already made us familiar—a dear friend to be visited in child-bed. Valeria, that cockney Roman, has a poor opinion of work: 'You would be another Penelope:' she says, 'yet, they say, all the yarn she spun in Ulysses' absence did but fill Ithaca full of moths' (I, 3).

This lady has close spiritual affinity to Mistress Ford and Mistress Page of the *Merry Wives of Windsor* (a play which, recent scholarship suggests, originally had its setting in London). In Act II, scene 2 of the play Mistress Quickly remarks of Mistress Page:

> Never a wife in Windsor leads a better life than she does: do what she will, say what she will, take all, pay all, go to bed when she list, rise when she list, all is as she will . . .

In Act III, scene 2 we find the same Mistress Page on her way to visit Mistress Ford, whose husband she meets:

FORD: Well met, Mistress Page. Whither go you?
MISTRESS PAGE: Truly, sir, to see your wife. Is she at home?
FORD: Ay; and as idle as she may hang together, for want of company. I think if your husbands were dead, you two would marry.

Puritan writings which upbraid contumacious women provide further evidence that these passages reflect something real. Naturally enough certain traditional exaggerations tend to mingle with the truth—Noah's cantankerous wife refusing to go into the ark, for instance, had long ago proved itself a fruitful theme in the mystery plays. Nevertheless, there can be little doubt that behind much of this there lies a residue of genuine experience and observation.

There must surely be some significance in Gouge's descriptions (1626) of argumentative wives always contradicting their menfolk, wives who 'give and scoff at the very hearing of subjection, saying thus wives shall be made no better than children or servants'. One thinks here of women like Shakespeare's Beatrice in *Much Ado About Nothing* of whom Claudio says:

> she will die ere she make her love known; and she will die if he woo her, rather than she will 'bate one breath of her accustomed crossness.
> (II, iii)

Descriptions occur of women who are lazy, who lie late abed, women who, when their husbands ask them to do this or that, impudently reply, 'Do it yourself, I'm not your servant', women whose homes seem to them a prison, if their word is not law therein and who, when their husbands wish to exchange the country for the town or town for country, insist on remaining where they are, saying that they cannot abide the London fog or that country air does not agree with them.

Such references are frequent and the exactness by which they are characterized show that they are more than the traditional repetitions of ancient cautions against gadabout women. Even Rogers, who in many respects is thoroughly progressive, declares that there is a 'world of women' which vehemently rejects the idea of being subject to the will of husbands 'we have meetings of women-drinkers, tobacconists, and swaggerers as well as men'. It is thus not difficult to understand the significance of the catchword that goes back to the sixteenth century (van Meteren) according to which England was 'a paradise for married women', an idea which was later to beget the remark (Defoe, 1725) that if a bridge were thrown across the Channel, the married women of the Continent would all emigrate to England.

Clearly, however, this state of affairs is but the result of a long development which was brought about by something other than the fact that women possess the peculiar qualities which are so sharply in evidence in the passages to which I have referred. Indeed, we occasionally hear quite contrary things about English women. It is particularly noteworthy—since it illustrates the exceedingly active part which, as we shall see, women played in Puritanism—that so early a movement as that of Wycliff was largely dependent on women for support. What we learn from Pecock's *Repressor* in the middle of the fifteenth century makes this credible enough, for his book, which was directed against the dying Lollard agitation, abounds in complaints that women are so well read in the Bible that they dare to argue with the clergy. He complains that they conduct themselves very haughtily, and this obviously wounds his self-esteem.

However, the vigorous and independent part played by women in religious life that is here so very much in evidence, may well be the sign of a change of attitude between the sexes, a change that was in many instances fundamental. Of course, at this early stage it was still customary to look down on women and to regard them as intellectually and morally inferior to men. Given the Church's teaching on original sin and the fall of man, this could hardly have been otherwise. Yet in England, strange as it may sound, this cast-iron foundation of the belief in the inferiority of women was far from being immune from attack.

Strangely overlooking the fact that the Carmelite *Dives et Pauper* dates from the fifteenth century, Agrippa von Nettesheim's *De nobilitate et praecellentia foeminei sexus* (published in Germany in 1532) has always been regarded as the first book written in justification of women. Now the author of *Dives et Pauper* certainly showed great boldness at that time in attacking the accepted doctrine that women were more wicked than men and that the misfortunes of mankind had been brought about by Eve. Moreover in making this attack, he went contrary to custom and did not employ the courtly claptrap that derived very largely from the Minnesingers and had very little relation to ordinary life. He relied instead on the sober facts of experience, declaring that many more women were made unhappy by men—or, as he said 'deceived by the malice of men'—than contrariwise; he insisted that men were much more prone to vice than women, and that women had a much greater horror of sin and a much stronger feeling of repugnance towards unchastity. He also asserted that their piety was much more genuine, a fact proved by the large numbers of truly saintly women anchorites whom he contrasted with the numerous dishonest male hermits who lacked the fidelity to continue to the end. The view of the learned men, the 'clerkes', who made Eve responsible for the Fall was attacked with remorseless logic.

A work such as this, which had nothing to do with the Wycliffite movement, shows us clearly that a more exalted conception of women was coming into being even in such spiritual and intellectual fields as had not come under the influence of the Reformers. In public life too, there are here and there remarkable instances of women's initiative. A typical case is that of Duke Humphrey of Gloucester who had deserted his wife, Jacqueline of Holland—a Wittelsbach—and forced her to acknowledge the validity of the divorce (this was in 1428), hoping thus to be able to marry her sometime lady-in-waiting, Eleanor Cobham. On this occasion a group of outraged women forced their way into Parliament and solemnly protested against his conduct.

The raising of the position of women in England which these incidents illustrate was a long process whose beginnings may well date back to Anglo-Saxon times.

6. *The subordination of women: modification through the system of special duties*

Puritan writers with their strict adherence to the words of the Bible had, as a matter of principle, to set their faces against self-glorification and insubordination on the part of women as something un-Christian which accorded neither with the practice of the Old Testament nor with the teaching of St Paul. Using the imagery which the Fathers had so constantly employed, and which had also been introduced into the Prayer Book, they insisted that the relation of man and woman in Christian marriage was the same as that between Christ and His Church. This, by implication, determined the position of each member of the pair. The man, as St Paul's epistle to the Ephesians clearly shows, was the head, the woman, a member of the family. The function of the man was an office and was to be regarded as any other office in the State. As early a writer as Tyndale, in his *The Obedience of a Christen man* (1528) had already equated the obedience of a wife to her husband with that of servants to their masters and of subjects to the holders of authority as 'Servants of God'.

The fact that the superior administers his office badly no more justifies disobedience and refusal of duty than it does in the case of a prince or a clergyman. How strongly developed from the very start had been this idea of the unqualified superiority of the male is shown in Gouge (1626) in another connection, namely when he is discussing the duty of a man to show courtesy and friendliness towards the woman, and points to the fact that even kings and queens stretch out their hand to be kissed by their kneeling subjects, a piece of courtesy which men should regard as an example to themselves.

Such enhanced authority on the part of the man must necessarily lead him to desire a respectful attitude on the part of his wife, and this will express itself in the cultivation of a certain reserve and tactful silence in his presence. Erasmus speaks of *verecundum silentium*. Gouge further declares that when his wife addresses him, she should not do so in familiar terms or use his Christian name, still less an abbreviation thereof, let alone such disrespectful words as 'Sweet', 'Sweeting', 'Ducks', 'Chicks', 'Pigsnie'; rather she should use his surname with the prefix 'Master' (Treatise 3, section 14). In much the same vein Downame in *A Guide to Godlynesse* insists that the wife should by her whole attitude recognize the husband as 'the better part of herself'.

The ideas, as expressed by Gouge and others, that are implicit in this general view of the relations between men and women, have a distinctly mediaeval flavour and it is difficult to see how they could have been reconciled with that drive towards independence, with which, as we have seen, the women of England were rather especially associated. Actually difficulties began to occur even among sincere believers. In the preface to the second edition of *Domesticall Duties* Gouge tells us that women had taken considerable exception to the remarks he had made in a number of sermons on the subject of their 'subjection' and that they had especially objected to what he had said about the limitation of women's rights in disposing over common property.

These objections, which bear eloquent testimony to the high opinion that women had about themselves, were not wholly without their effect on Gouge, and in this second edition he introduces a number of formal alterations. Above all, however, he draws the attention of these rebellious women to a principle which from now on fills the whole of Puritan literature and in point of fact constitutes one of the most characteristic and certainly one of the most important points of the Puritan Credo.

The principle involved is this: in the family, as in certain other situations, there is a system of mutual duties. In marriage, for instance—the pattern of thought is traditional—there are common duties and there are also special duties of the husband towards the wife and of the wife towards the husband, duties which vary according to the special position of each. Now in such a system, the failure on the part of one party to perform its duties does not affect the obligation of the other party to perform the duties which are peculiar to itself. The sets of duties incumbent upon one party are quite independent of those incumbent upon the other. Children whose parents do not fulfil their duties towards them are thus in no sense relieved of duties towards their parents.

It is the same in marriage; the duties which the wife owes the husband and which are exactly determined by that 'subjection' on which the apostle Paul lays such particular stress, are firmly fixed for her. On the other side there are duties on the part of the husband towards the wife which relate to the same object and may run in a contrary direction. This being so, then, since the duties do not run strictly side by side, but cut across one another over a wide area, there can never be any doubt about their nature nor any claims by one party that the duty towards it should be performed by the other. *For the duty of one party is by no means the right of the other.* Rogers illustrates this principle, which Richardson was still zealously defending in the eighteenth century, by the amusing example of the married couple engaged in selecting a dress for the wife. If the wife has set her heart on a green dress but the husband wants to buy a red one, the wife must give way. This is all part and parcel of her 'subjection'. However, it is not handsome on the part of the husband to insist on his own choice, for in matters concerning a woman's dress he should let his wife have her way. This is part of the special duties of the husband towards the wife. In such a case, though the competing duties are clearly not of the same rank, they are none the less duties. In this way the Biblical principle of the complete subjection of the wife to the will of her husband loses the greater part of its force. However inviolate it may still appear to be, its substance has largely disappeared and the door has thus been opened to further developments.

It is with such ideas as this in mind that Gouge informs his infuriated female readers that they have failed to understand him. All he had done was to show them the uttermost limits to which this God-willed 'subjection' could be forced to go, even if the husband were to insist 'upon the uttermost of his authority'. But this was not to be understood as implying that the husband's demands either 'might or ought' to go to that limit, as was clear from the duties of the husband as Gouge had himself defined them in the book. If the husband fulfilled those duties, his wife would certainly have no grounds for complaint. It is undeniable that the psychological effects of this system would, in certain respects, contribute not a little to the creation of good relations between a husband and wife; for in so far as something is asked of the wife as a duty which the duty of the husband forbids him to accept, this makes for contentment on both sides, all the more so since that quality of 'generosity', which fits so well into the English ideal of personality is at the bottom of the matter.

7. *Limits to the subordination of women*
Nothing in all this should be taken to imply that the husband should renounce his dominating position, though the actual manner in which Gouge wanted to see this superiority respected—even in matters of external form—soon fell into disuse. It is significant that Rogers (1650) was already expressly demanding that the formal 'Master' on which he had himself insisted should disappear as a form of address between married couples and that the more intimate 'husband' and 'wife' should be substituted. Nor is the duty of subjection understood in quite so comprehensive a sense as before. Gouge for instance, recognizes the principle that obedience on the part of the wife is not demanded of her where an action is contrary to the will of God—such unlawful actions, I might add, included visits to the theatre—but a wife's duty to accompany her husband wherever he goes, derives, as it did with Perkins before him, from the story of Abraham and Sarah, to which Gouge also adduces the example of the continual migrations

of the Patriarchs. The only exception that he would allow was where it was obvious that a husband moved from one country to another in obedience to a mere whim. Rogers, however, took a different view, holding that a wife need by no means follow her husband to 'a remote plantation'. True, Sarah followed Abraham in all his wanderings, but their case was rather different, for in those days God's living voice could be heard from heaven, assuring them of His protection. There was in these circumstances no room whatever left for doubt. So, thanks to a variety of causes, the strict form of subjection, which was once insisted upon, gradually began to grow more loose.

Most remarkable of all is the change in the position of women in regard to property rights. It was here, as we have seen, that Gouge encountered the heaviest opposition from his female public. This did not prevent him from continuing to stress the lack of any rights on the part of the woman and even to appeal to civil law in support of his argument. Rogers refrains from any advance beyond this point. Baxter, however, sees matters very differently, for he concedes a kind of 'joint-propriete' to the wife and justifies this, among other things, by pointing to the fact that, in the event of death or divorce, she can claim a third of her husband's property.

Mrs Hutchinson described how these theories worked in practice in an ideal Puritan household, she declared that her husband's fortune was so much at her disposal that he never asked for any account of her expenses. There can be no doubt that a pleasanter and easier relationship between husband and wife was beginning to assert itself. Jeremy Taylor, for instance, who, though not a Puritan, lays down rules of conduct which are virtually indistinguishable from the Puritan ones.

> A husband's power over his wife is paternal and friendly, not magisterial and despotic. The wife is *in perpetua tutela*, 'under conduct and counsel'; for the power a man hath is founded in the understanding, not in the will or force; it is not a power of coercion ...
>
> ('The Marriage Ring', page 139)

In these words Taylor is merely expressing in a more developed form what many others had said before him. No better example of this can be found than the description given by Mrs Hutchinson of Colonel Hutchinson as a husband:

For conjugal affection to his wife, it was such in him, as whosoever would draw out a rule of honour, kindnesse, and religion, to be practiz'd in that estate, need no more, but exactly draw out his example; never man had a greater passion for a woman, nor a more honourable esteeme of a wife, yet he was not uxorious, nor remitted not that just rule which it was her honor to obey, but manag'd the reines of government with such prudence and affection that she who would not delight in such honourable and advantageable subjection, must have wanted a reasonable soule: he govern'd by perswasion, which he never employ'd but to things honorable and profitable for herselfe: he lov'd her soule and her honor more than her outside, and yet he had even for her person a constant indulgence, exceeding the common temporary passions of the most uxorious fooles:

(page 12)

8. *Marriage as a sharing in erotic experience: sexual intercourse between husband and wife*

The above example shows how far we are from exhausting the real character of Puritan marriage if we concentrate wholly on this principle of 'subjection', basic as this conception unquestionably was. Indeed, even so fanatical an advocate thereof as Gouge is very far from claiming that, in stressing this aspect of the matter, he has said the last word on the subject of matrimony. For him too, marriage primarily consists in a perfect sharing.

With this idea however, we touch on Puritanism's greatest and most admirable cultural achievement. Yet if we are to assess it at its true value, we must compare it with the attitude towards marriage taken up by the whole civilized world prior to the Puritan movement, at the time of that movement and thereafter, or rather, we must compare it with the world's view of the relation between the spiritual and the sensual. Neither the Renaissance nor the Reformation had succeeded in building a bridge between these things and even Shakespeare, whose instinct for the natural is his principal title to undying fame, speaks of the act of love as 'the expense of spirit in a waste of shame' (Sonnet 129). Even Luther and Calvin, though vast changes were initiated by them—and most particularly by Luther—could neither of them completely rid themselves of the conceptions of the mediaeval Church.

The courtly world all over Europe on the other hand, though it had largely put aside the Church's views, continued nevertheless till well into the eighteenth century to be governed by the assumption—the truth of which it regarded as self-evident—that spiritual and sensual love were two distinct and separate things. Since marriage had its sensual side, this clearly implied that it could no longer be equated with love in its highest form. In contrast to this, the cool realism of the Puritans recognized marriage as being essentially a sharing of spiritual-sensual experience—a mixture of religion and nature, as Rogers calls it.

This is made very plain by the whole manner in which the subject was treated, for it showed a complete lack of inhibition in its readiness to theorize on the erotic side of marriage. Although here, as elsewhere, Puritan writers to some extent remained within the patristic tradition, the Puritan product was distinguishable from the equally prolific but rather repulsive Jesuit output by the cleanness of mind with which these delicate matters were handled and above all, by the honesty and consistency with which nature was recognized for what it is and accepted as such.

As early a writer as Perkins (1558–1602) in his *Oeconomia Christiana* speaks of marital intercourse as being itself neither good nor evil, 'est congressus viri et uxoris natura sua res indifferens neque bona neque mala' and he insists that such intercourse should proceed with holy mutual joy as a comfort and as mutual testimony of love and goodwill—a conception which is repeated in a very similar form by Gouge in the words 'with good will and delight, willingly, readily, and cheerfully'.

It is true enough that in certain respects the Catholic traditions were respected in so far as marital intercourse was considered unfitting at certain times, especially in times of fasting or on such days as the Sacrament had been received; in this matter, moreover, as in others, it was held that pleasure should not be sought for its own sake. This principle still finds expression in Milton's *Paradise Lost* when the common sexual experience of Adam and Eve is made to appear wholly justified and is indeed exalted as the divinely willed expression of their 'inner unity', whereas the purely sensual satisfaction which Adam and Eve obtain for themselves after eating the apple is definitely made to appear sinful.

But writers were not necessarily narrow-minded; Jeremy Taylor, for instance, who in this field, as in others, is almost indistinguishable from the Puritan, enumerates the following as sufficient reason for marital intercourse:

a Desire of children, or to avoid fornication, or to lighten and ease the cares and sadnesses of household affairs, or to endear each other.
(*Holy Living*, chapter 2, section 3, 2)

But a great many things can be brought within the scope of these very elastic limits. It is also worth observing the manner in which the Puritan reacted to a theory which echoed the ancient patristic doctrine that intercourse with a woman was sinful if she showed any signs of pregnancy or was weaning her child. This was a theory which in England had been abandoned by the Catholic Church before the Reformation but which continued to guide certain Baptist sects, and—to quote but a single instance—was responsible, to a considerable degree, for the moral catastrophe that befell the Anabaptists in Münster.

Strangely enough this theory was to find a fanatical advocate in Defoe. Gouge, however, and numerous other writers, utterly rejected it and their grounds for doing so were characteristic of the exalted view which they took of marriage, for, unlike the mediaeval Church, they could not bring themselves to believe that the procreation of children was the sole purpose of the institution. The unprejudiced view of sex and the ready acceptance of the facts of life is also evident in the way that Puritan casuists treat the question of whether a man and his wife ought ever to be separated from one another for a lengthy period of time—say by reason of the husband's business—a question that might well have arisen in that day, for this was the time of the rise of the East India Company. The Puritans found a very simple answer to this problem. It was that the determining factor was the physical make-up of the individual concerned, something, that is to say, in which one person differs markedly from the next.

Thus the Puritan's method of treating the erotic element in marriage recognized that it had an important part to play. Nevertheless, he was very far removed from the mediaeval conception which saw the be-all and end-all of the institution in sexual relations. Indeed, this is a matter in which we can note a very considerable development, for whereas Gouge deals with these questions in the most searching and exhaustive manner, his successors tend to regard this erotic element as being essentially marginal, its place in their exposition being largely taken by reflections upon the spiritual relationship between husband and wife, reflections that often display a marvellous refinement of feeling and a remarkable skill in psychological analysis.

9. *Marriage as the sharing of a common religious life: spiritual self-revelation in prayer*

Since the Puritan movement was essentially pietistic in character, it is not surprising that in these spiritual involvements with one another on the part of husband and wife, a common care for religious interests should have a leading part to play. For the enormously increased importance of the part played by the woman in the lives of her husband and her family can only be explained by the effort that began to be made—an effort that was in part anticipated in the fourteenth century by the Wycliffites—to equip the wife in such a fashion that she could accompany her husband faithfully and with understanding on all his journeyings in the religious life.

If she were to carry out this task, it was essential that she should have made up her mind about all relevant problems and thus become autonomous in religious matters. As such, it was only natural that she should have been taken sufficiently seriously and have come to be regarded as a person of sufficient importance to form the subject of biographies. This is exactly what had happened by the end of the sixteenth century and it is significant that Baxter should have written accounts of the lives of his stepmother, his mother-in-law, his old housekeeper and his wife.

This respect for women as moral and religious personalities was bound, to some extent at least, to affect their positions in the family theocracy. Whereas for centuries a woman had at best been regarded as a spiritual and intellectual guide to her daughters, she now assumed the role of deputy, taking her place at her husband's side, when, as priest and king, he administered his kingdom, supervising the training of his family in such matters as catechism, religious knowledge, moral principle and the practice of prayer. Perkins, it must be admitted, is here a conspicuous exception and does not take this view of women. Perkins apart, however, the trend is unmistakable. Writer after writer insists that wherever a husband shows himself unfitted for this task, whether spiritually or physically, the wife should replace him.

But these observations by no means exhaust the part religion has to play in effecting a closer union between husband and wife. The possibility of complete mutual self-revelation which it provides contributes both to their eternal salvation and binds the partners of a marriage to one another utterly and completely (compare Thomas More, *Utopia*, 1516). A further effect is that husband and wife form a closer community within the wider community of the family. The forms in which this narrow community finds expression may, admittedly, sometimes seem strange to us, for there was more involved here than the common cultivation of religious interests or a joining together in spiritual reading and prayer. There was also the form of devotion called 'humiliation' in which prayers were offered which, besides being forms of confession, consisted chiefly in the enumeration of the sins, weaknesses and failures of the other partner in the marriage—accompanied, of course, by an appeal for forgiveness—sins and weaknesses of which that erring partner was thus, for the first time, made aware. Naturally enough there were also prayers of thanksgiving for any virtuous inclination that may have been observed. Thus the concept of confession underwent a curious change.

The religious exercise described above, which can be shown to date back to a very early age—a reciprocal confession by laymen was already known in the Middle Ages (compare Hautkappe)—seems to have survived in England for a very long time. For instance, we are told of something very similar in the life of Elizabeth Barrett-Browning, who was said to have been in the habit of learning the nature of her various sins from the lips of her father, as he knelt in prayer by her sick bed. Her biographers seem to have regarded this whole business as an almost unpardonable oddity, but Barrett senior may well have learned of the practice from Defoe's *Family Instructor*.

10. *The 'relaxed and pleasurable' process of sharing: spiritual understanding of the woman*

The sharing in religious and erotic experience forms only a small part of that vast variety of relationships between husband and wife of which the rules of practical conduct in force at that time made people explicitly aware. A feature of these rules which is both basic and noteworthy is the insistence on an agreeable understanding between husband and wife, and here again it is the Biblical injunction to regard women as the weaker vessel (*1 Peter*, III, 7) and to show her consideration as such, which is the essential starting point. Actually the things that are regarded as weaknesses in this connection may well surprise us. Snawsel, for instance, in his *A Looking Glasse for maried folkes* (1610) puts the following definition into the mouth of a model wife:

> The wives infirmitie toward her husband is,
> when she cannot put up wrong at his hands.

Where we are concerned with real weaknesses there is a temptation which is not always successfully resisted to fashion a pedestal for male superiority. But nowhere is any of this so strongly marked as in Baxter, who in this particular, as elsewhere, remains very closely bound to the Patristic view—save only that he knows how to employ the techniques of spiritual analysis that belong to a new age.

> And it is no small patience which the *natural imbecility* of the *female sex* requireth you to prepare. Except it be very few that are patient and manlike, women are commonly of *potent fantasies*, and tender *passionate* impatient spirits, easily cast into anger, or jealousie, or discontent: and of weak understandings, and therefore unable to reform themselves. They are betwixt a *man* and a *child*: Some few have *more* of the *man*, and many have more of the *child*; but most are but in a middle state. Weakness naturally inclineth persons to be *froward* and *hard* to *please*; as we see in children, old people, and sick persons: They are like a sore distempered body: You scarce touch them but you hurt them. With too many you can scarce tell how to *speak* or *look* but you displease them. If you should be very well verst in the art of *pleasing*, and set your selves to it with all your care, as if you made it your very business, and had little else to do, yet it would put you hard to it, to please some weak impatient persons, if not quite surpass your ability and skill. And the more you love them the more grievous it will be, to see them still in discontents, aweary of their condition, and to hear the clamorous expressions of their disquiet minds.
>
> (*Christian Directory*, page 480)

This reminds us of Juan Luis Vives' (1492–1540) contemptuous opinion of women; most women, he says, are querulous and difficult to satisfy—'Querulae sunt pleraeque feminae et difficiles'—but the judgment of many other observers was already becoming less sharp and less arrogant. True, even these still assumed that a woman tends to lack self-control, and that thanks to her inferior judgment, she readily gives way to temper was an idea which had long been affirmed and continued long to be repeated (compare Vives and Gouge, Treatise 2, sections 8, 9).

One begins nevertheless to sense the dawning of a wholly new age and one not uninfluenced by the natural sciences. Certainly we feel this when a writer like Rogers cautions us against the too ready acceptance of such generalizations and insists that we are here not so much concerned with traits of character as with the effects of depressions, with 'faintnesses of spirits' and over-work. We should, we are told, accept the fact that a woman is constitutionally a more delicate creature; to quote a much used image, she is like a piece of Venetian glass which must not be grasped too firmly. Indeed Rogers does not hesitate to refer to the menstrual pains in this connection.

The conclusion to be drawn from all this is that the man shows his manliness, that is to say, his superior understanding, by showing consideration for these things, by exercising self-control and, above all, by refraining from any rebuke for as long as his wife is in an over-emotional state (Gouge, Treatise 2, section 9). Very typical of this connection is Baxter's story (*Christian Directory*, page 540) of the good and pious woman who, for all that, got into such an excited state that she threw a burning candle into her husband's face. The man a clergyman (Baxter?) refrained from using any violence in return.

Further, although women have a tendency to give way to vanity, men should still show understanding for such a fault. It is in the nature of woman to adorn herself, it is in her nature to show certain playful tendencies which it is best for a man to overlook, letting her do as she pleases when she wishes to indulge them. Indeed no less a man than Thomas Aquinas said certain things which are still valid today about women's rights to adorn themselves and make themselves attractive to their menfolk (compare Ziegler, page 295).

It may happen that a wife claims certain things to be necessary for her children and particularly for her little girls, and here too the husband should not show himself too strict. Even a man of such rigid virtue as Calvin, so Rogers declares, had to make certain concessions in this matter after his marriage. Finally, to quote a charge which anti-feminist writers have always been in the habit of making and which Vives repeats, women all too often show themselves incapable of keeping a secret—but husbands should not because of this withhold all information about their affairs, rather should they make a prudent choice and keep silent on certain matters.

It is instructive to note how reflections of this kind on the weaknesses of women are by no means incompatible with a very real degree of respect for them, such respect having replaced the condescending tolerance of an earlier age. This change of attitude is particularly striking when such a man as Rogers turns his gaze from the weaknesses of women to their strengths and by putting achievements which in their case we tend to take for granted into perspective, contrives to change our whole standard of values. What burdens a woman carries during pregnancy, when her child is born and while it is being weaned, and how handicapped she is liable to be by this and by her greater depth of feeling! So strong are the effects of all this that the death of her child will inflict upon her more tortures in a single day than those endured over a month by the husband. How much work she does, despite her lack of strength! Indeed, what man would patiently attend to all the niggling trifles and endure the continual racket made by children? What man would endure all the petty worries that their care and upbringing entails? Yet all these things her inborn instinct for love causes her uncomplainingly to accept. Are not the achievements of women in these matters downright superhuman?

But Rogers goes beyond such observations as these, he attempts an analysis of ideal womanhood as such. What, he asks, are the specifically feminine graces? There is, he tells us, that modesty which causes a woman to behave as though she were quite ignorant of her merits. There is that forgetfulness of self which causes her to submit to the inevitable with patience and good will. There is the equable temper, the uprightness, honesty and practical piety in which women excel men. There is that ready sympathy which expresses itself in deeds of neighbourly love and there is the union of all these qualities in that wonderful 'amiableness' and 'cheerfulness' of soul which enables her to remain calm in misfortune, much as the bird that continues to sing upon a withered twig. Add to this her bodily charms and who faced with such an incomparable catalogue of merits would not be ready to forget her undeniable faults?

11. *Practical conclusions: consideration for femininity*

The practical conclusions that men were bound to draw from all this are obvious. A certain consideration for women had always been required from men, indeed the principle is quite old and goes back to Patristic times. Erasmus was among those who had warned men against turning a wife into a serving maid, and Bullinger takes over the attitude from him, though oddly enough his translator Coverdale considers this admonition to be superfluous. Perkins at least goes so far as to consider the question of whether it is lawful for a man to beat his wife and emphatically denies him any such right. Gouge discusses the same problem with an arresting thoroughness and reaches the conclusion—incidentally quoting St Chrysostom as his authority—that this is only permissible in self-defence ('se defendendo'). Generations later Baxter uses almost identical arguments with identical results, though with the characteristic reservation that the husband does not actually lack the necessary authority to inflict such chastisement. When we take into account the fact that over a long period English law acknowledged the husband's right to inflict 'moderate correction'—Richardson mentions the fact that Talbot when Solicitor General (1726–33) (*Correspondence*, 1806, VI, 186–7) quoted the authority of this law in court—we cannot help recognizing a markedly progressive element in the moral principle as enunciated by these writers.

But it is not in this that the principal achievement of these men is to be seen, nor can we discern it in the repeated injunction never to lose one's self-possession in the presence of one's wife, for that is a very ancient precept, and, for that matter, self-control has over the course of time become the very essence of the Puritanical attitude of life. It is all too true, of course, that self-control can be combined with a very low estimate of womanhood, an estimate of which we occasionally become conscious even in Baxter's work— as when he quotes the conduct of a nurse towards a screaming child as an example of that admirable patience which a man should display when confronted with feminine irritability.

Actually, the most remarkable feature in all this gradual change of opinion is that a new duty is now imposed in addition to all the existing ones, in addition, that is to say, to the duty of love, to the duty of remaining faithful—in which there is no difference made between the sexes—to the duty of giving thorough instruction, of providing materially for one's family, of respecting the good name and the dignity which a woman should enjoy both among her immediate and among her wider circle of acquaintances. To all these different duties there is now added the duty of consideration or, to use the phrase current at the time, of displaying the 'tender respectiveness' which a wife has the right to enjoy. Nowhere in this whole movement is the astonishing ability to apply to the circumstances of ordinary life the findings of a most delicate psychological analysis more sharply in evidence. Thus Gouge as far back as 1622 insists that a husband should never forget that his wife is an extremely sensitive person, that he should not adopt an arrogant tone towards her, and should not scold her too violently—it is pointed out that wives become accustomed to excessive scolding by their husbands much as jackdaws become accustomed to the noise of church bells. A husband, moreover, should often speak of a wife's deserts and should never reprove her in front of others; he should never threaten her nor speak to her with a dissatisfied expression. He should never be backward in small outward signs of tenderness or in the giving of those little presents which women love. It is by these means that he will keep her love.

There is also a detailed enquiry into questions of practical care, particularly in regard to pregnancy and birth—and here there is some sharp criticism of those who refuse to engage some kind of domestic help or allot a room without a fireplace for a wife's confinement, and ignore the necessity of a special diet for the mother-to-be. Particularly harsh things are also said of the husband who shows himself mean towards his wife in money matters, who, when she is ill, is ready enough to produce tears but refuses to buy medicine, or for the man who throughout his life shows his wife a friendly face but never lets the thought enter his head about what is to happen to her after his death, although this is a magnificent proof of the genuineness of his love.

But Rogers has a list of duties far more extensive than this and not only does he describe these duties in the minutest detail but he displays the most penetrating understanding of the essential character of women. Moreover, everything that Rogers has to say in this connection seems to be dictated by a respect for womanhood which in this particular form is wholly without precedent. Indeed not the most humane and advanced moralist could aim higher than much that is to be found in Rogers' code of conduct. Thus he declares that the husband must be to the wife as the eyelid is to the eye, he must care both for her spiritual and for her bodily health. He is enjoined not to let her go to bed too late or get up too early—the good housewife, like Shakespeare's Imogen, would get up at four o'clock—he is bidden to relieve her even against her will of such work as he can and, if the state of her health makes this desirable, to let her have a change of air. In a word, he must never in any circumstances be remiss in protecting her interests. Indeed his solicitude must be apparent on his face, 'let thy hollow cheeks, pale face, sad heart, be as a calender', so runs Rogers' admonition 'in which others may read thy wives infirmities, their number, their measure and how long they have continued'.

The fact that the wife's duties towards the husband are enumerated with the same meticulous care, cannot erase the impression that we here have before us the very earliest literary evidence of the change in attitude towards women which was so markedly to differentiate Anglo-Saxon culture from that of the Continent.

12. *The advanced nature of the concept of marital love*
All the various demands made in this connection derive in the final analysis from an astonishingly advanced conception of love. For to a man like Rogers love was not what it was to his contemporaries in other spheres of life, something connected with the conventional 'gallantry', a gallantry which could go hand in hand at times with the grossest brutality. It was, in a word, not just a romantic feeling which from its very nature can lead an individual into a kind of intoxication of delight, only in due course to let him return to the trivialities of everyday life. It denotes for him a rather more exalted form of existence, a transfiguration of the commonplace, resulting from the fact that each partner is conscious of having the support of the other in sustaining his dignity and self-respect.

A particularly enchanting expression of Rogers' ideas is to be found in the imagery which he employs on one occasion to describe the common effort of a married couple to master the problems of life. He likens them to two people cutting a tree trunk with a large saw, each of whom is at every moment completely dependent upon the performance of the other of the self-same duties on which he— or she—is engaged. The relation between the two remains the same even after advancing age has caused the physical side of love to disappear. Jeremy Taylor writes:

The marital love is a thing pure as light, sacred as a temple, lasting as the world; *amicitia quae desinere potuit numquam vera fuit*, said one; 'that love that can cease was never true'.

(*The Mysteriousness of Marriage*, pages 38–9)

He thus displays a faith in the eternal duration of love which was still quite alien to Luther (compare Kluckhohn, page 11). Nor could it be expected that Luther should feel differently about this, for such ideas as those expressed by Rogers necessarily postulate a receptivity for spiritual values that could in a previous century only rarely have been found. We can say this with complete confidence while fully recognizing that the power to give expression to feeling is by no means identical with the ability to experience it. In a word, to conceive of married love as Rogers did argues a most delicate craving for sympathy, a desire to live in an atmosphere that is both comfortable and warm with a sensitive ear for the dissonances in a life of shared feelings and experience and a corresponding delight in its harmonies—all this to a degree hardly perceptible in Shakespeare though he lived but a bare generation earlier. When there is such spiritual accord the whole idea of 'subjection' loses much of its practical significance.

But there were those who had the wisdom to see—and see very clearly—that such happiness in marriage would not come easily but would have to be continually won afresh, that it had to be protected in those struggles with natural instinct which continually threatened to destroy it. That explains why people were preoccupied with the problem of preserving love in marriage to such a degree that there would be no difficulty in constructing a little vade-mecum for married folk from the prudent counsels that abounded on the subject. In such a compilation we would find severe and plentiful warnings not to let one's marriage suffer shipwreck through trifles, through such petty grounds of offence as would be nullified by that mere modicum of mutual consideration and self-control which outside the house would be taken as a matter of course. Much urgent advice is given never to let ill-humour gain the upper hand but to uproot it completely immediately it becomes apparent. Above all the idea of the value of individual personality is developed in a very positive and precise fashion. Each partner in a marriage is urged to study the individual characteristics of the other, for only thus can each be accorded the justice that is due to them.

MARRIAGE UNDER PURITANISM

The origins of such views are to be found in the most ancient observations on the subject—such, for instance, as the naïve moralizing of Plutarch. Such moralizing frequently recurs in Puritan writing. One should not confront elephants when wearing a white dress or bulls when wearing a red one. We must add the interesting fact that the beating of a drum so excites the tiger that he tears himself to pieces. Snawsel (1610) further expands Plutarch's zoology by citing the example of the horse which can be tamed by terms of endearment, whistling and pats—from all of which we may learn that a husband too has his likes and dislikes and that a good wife will be diligent in finding out what they are and be guided by that knowledge.

But these counsels are now also applied to the husband and in their new and expanded form, not only require that he should show understanding but also that he should display an attitude of respect for the whole character and personality of his partner. This is regarded as providing the most solid ground for mutual liking. As early as 1622 we find Gouge forcefully affirming that a man should love his wife for being the kind of person that she is. Rogers develops this thought still further by recommending the husband always to keep his gaze fixed on the special nature of his wife's merits and always to remain aware of those features of her character which first aroused his love; never in any circumstances must he indulge himself by dwelling on his wife's faults, nor must he ever compare her with other women. He must always say, 'There may be many excellent wives but you excel them all'. It is the essence of love that you should feel that no one even comes near to her in any particular. Thus marriage is by far the most personal relation that can be imagined. It is a relation that is so close that the rational judgment which is valid in all the other circumstances of life must in the matter of marriage yield to the counsels of 'tenderness and a respective heart'. Even adultery, though in the judgment thereof there is no such thing as a dual standard of morals, can be forgiven where there is real love.

It is, one might add, highly instructive to observe this conscious fostering of love and hostility towards certain pleasures which is so characteristic of Puritan thought. The most rigorous school of thought, as we have seen, condemned all pleasure whatsoever out of hand. Other writers however, took the view that popular holidays, theatres, love stories, masquerades and so on were not only sinful in themselves, and for that reason alone to be avoided, but also represented certain specific temptations to which our natural weakness would readily fall a victim. Despite this, however, pleasure was not in itself to be condemned, for just as the body needs rest, so, Downame declares (page 266), the spirit needs relaxation, stimulation and variety. This may be achieved through the contemplation of nature, a physical exercise, the chase and the more unexceptionable forms of art. Nor is this earth by any means a vale of tears; toil and vexation are not intended to be the whole of life and a cheerful spendthrift is always better than a morose miser. Indeed, all Puritan writers attach great weight to a certain unfailing lightness of heart—'sober cheerfulness', Lucy Hutchinson calls it —which must be maintained in all our daily doings.

13. *Theory and reality: Cromwell, Mrs Henry, Mrs Hutchinson, Mrs Baxter*

I have sketched out the general theory of marriage, as it is developed in the conduct books, and noted its loving and sympathetic examination of all those things, both great and small, that are liable to affect the inner lives of married people. Yet the picture that emerges is necessarily something quite different from the living reality, for, as in the case of Rogers to whom I have frequently referred, we are dealing—at least to some extent—with exceptional people whose spiritual refinement cannot be regarded as typical of the age. Sociologically speaking they represent only a relatively thin stratum. A spiritualization of the relations between the sexes such as we find in writings like these, postulates the possession of spiritual organs, the development of which could scarcely have been favoured by the coarseness of the age. We might just conceivably find something of this kind in a vicarage or in the upper ranks of society, for here, even where those concerned had remained untouched by Puritanism, we can on occasion discover evidence of surprisingly advanced views on the spiritual relationships of marriage, views that go back to a remarkably early date (compare E. L. Godfrey, page 189 ff.).

In what I have just written I may perhaps have tended unduly to separate the human relations between husband and wife from the religious ones, as though the former could have a sort of independent life of their own. I may thus have produced a somewhat distorted picture, for in actual fact these two sets of relations are so closely interwoven that they cannot be separated from each other at all. For we must not forget that, being essentially a pietistic movement, Puritanism saw the necessary completion of human relationships in something more than mere religious unanimity. Puritans looked upon the attitude towards God and towards Divine Grace as being the supreme determining principle to which all purely human bonds were subordinate. 'Dear Heart, press on,' writes Oliver Cromwell to his daughter Bridget after her marriage —his letters were full almost to bursting with those religious exhortations with which the head of a family was expected to edify those with the care of whose souls he was entrusted:

> Dear Heart, press on, let not husband, let not anything cool thy affections after Christ . . . That which is best worthy of love in thy husband is that of the image of Christ he bears. Look on that and love it best, and all the rest for that.

The violent suppression of normal human inclination that this kind of thing suggests, was often, no doubt, nothing more than an outward affair, to which, by providing it with impressive labels, the religious jargon of the time imparted a somewhat fictitious value, and it is all too probable that in many cases natural and human relationships were no more subject to suppression than in any other pious Protestant home. For instance, anyone reading Mrs Hutchinson's recollection of her husband, will sometimes gain the impression of a damper placed on ordinary natural feelings. But he will find no violence in the life of this man, who delighted in fine pictures and flute-playing. Yet where there are more restricted horizons, where the counter-pressure of cultural interests is weaker, where owing to the force of circumstance the whole view of life tends to be a narrower one, there indeed natural freedom of feeling tends all too easily to be put in fetters—and heavy fetters at that. It is noteworthy that even a man like Rogers, who is so profoundly conscious of the happiness obtainable within these limits and analyses it with such rare delicacy of touch, nevertheless remarks, 'Marriage happiness is but the liberty of a prison' (page 321). Here he is not referring to marriage alone. What he has in mind is life itself with all its self-imposed duties, of the nature and effects of which he is so deeply aware, life with its oppressive lack of freedom.

When we consider these self-denying restrictions, the 'cheerfulness' of which we hear so much, and which itself was so largely a matter of obligation, acquires a slightly displeasing and equivocal character. Where cheerfulness stands for the victory of optimism over the difficulties of life and the buffets of fortune, we must admit it to be admirable and worthy of emulation, but there is something positively gruesome about it if it grows, so to speak, from out the grave of natural human feeling. Indeed, there are times when one can speak of a positive perversion of such feeling. There is for instance, the case of the Reverend Philip Henry's mother, who was herself a typical seventeenth-century Puritan. This good lady was able to die happy since the fact that she left six half-grown children behind her was as nothing compared to the certitude that she herself would go to heaven. Here, surely, we have a perversion of human feeling that is still very much on a par with the monastic asceticism of the Middle Ages, and indeed this ideal of a cheerfulness of soul that must, whatever the circumstances, always remain unimpaired, represents, as I endeavoured to show in the Introduction, nothing less than a survival of a distinctive clerical-mediaeval attitude to life.

Nevertheless, it is just among those Puritan families whom political circumstance has pushed into the full glare of history that we so often find a marital set-up not so very different—particularly in this matter of the strength of purely human feelings—from the picture drawn by theorists which I have endeavoured to describe above. Several references have already been made to the wonderful harmony of Colonel Hutchinson's marriage, a harmony which lasted beyond the grave. Even a man with so enigmatic a character as Oliver Cromwell is seen at his very best in all that concerns his marriage. Even here, of course, the great difference in education and the traditional inequality in the position of the partners in a marriage was still bound to have its effects. She addresses him as 'You' while he, in addressing her, uses both 'Thou' and 'You'. (Even a generation later a clergyman's wife in Lancashire closes with the words 'and so I remain, dear husband, in dutiful obedience, your dutiful wife'.) Oliver Cromwell, however, not only asks his wife's advice in important family matters, but his relation to her is so warm and personal that after thirty-one years of marriage —though he has nothing else to tell her—he takes the opportunity of writing to her that he loves her and thinks of her ('Yet indeed I love to write to my dear who is very much in my heart'). To her he opens his heart and while to others he feels under the necessity of appearing as a man of energy and strength, he confides to her on another occasion—he was fifty-one years old at the time—that he already feels the weight of his years: 'I assure thee, I grow an old man and feel the infirmities of age marvellously growing upon me'. She however replies in the same tone of solicitous and tender love and declares that her life can be only half a life while he is away from her.

Baxter's wife plays an even more important part in the life of her husband, who describes her as 'The brightest as well as the bravest of his human helpers' (*sic*). One might add that in spite of all Baxter's theorizings about the subordination of women, his own wife—due no doubt to her background, intelligence and education—shows little sign of that 'subjection' about which her husband is so emphatic. That she felt she should have taken no account of her husband's weariness when he sat silent at table but should have sought to engage him in (spiritual) discourse does not suggest that she was inhibited by that pleasing timidity in the presence of her lord and master which Gouge still treats as the self-evidently necessary condition of a good marriage. Baxter, who felt compelled to set a high value on her spiritual aspirations, could hardly take exception to these and similar instances of feminine initiative. Actually Baxter's marriage was a singularly happy one.

> We lived in unviolated love and mutual complacency, sensible to the fellowship of mutual help. These near nineteen years I know not that ever we had any breach in point of love or in point of interest.

These examples show that the picture painted by a Daniel Rogers, idealized though it might seem, may well have taken its colours from the real world.

14. *Origin of the American feminist cult in the Puritanical mores of the English colonist. Ultimate grounds: the relation of female to male in love-making*

The impression of Puritan marriage which we have by now contrived to gain will be quite sufficient to enable us to set aside the current view of the causes of present-day American feminism. This cult is not, as is usually supposed, the natural consequence of the alleged scarcity value that women once enjoyed in the colonial territories. Actually, the colonists in question—the Pilgrim Fathers of 1620 illustrate this very well—brought with them into their new homes not only their religious traditions but also the English middle-class mores of the day, which I have here endeavoured to describe and which already display this characteristic to a very marked degree.

The ultimate cause of this phenomenon, which can be observed all over the Anglo-Saxon world, is a question in itself. Dibelius took it to be a late result of the knightly ideal of the High Middle Ages but this can hardly be correct. This knightly ideal was, of course, international and was just as pronounced in France and Germany (in England an unbroken tradition was maintained in some matters, which in other countries had yielded place to new forms). But that is not quite the point. The point to note is that this idolization of women consisted, very largely, in the externals of gallantry which have nowhere completely disappeared in social usage.

It will be difficult to reach general agreement as to the ultimate causes in this matter. Seen through idealist spectacles the advantageous position of women in England might well be regarded as due to an enhanced sense of justice on the part of the male; alternatively, some will be tempted to ascribe it to some supposedly unique excellence in Anglo-Saxon womanhood. The realist, however, will see it as something for which English women have contrived successfully to struggle and will attribute such success to that basic trait of the English character which we encounter again and again in both men and women, namely that markedly rational and practical habit of mind, that keen instinct which enables them to turn a given set of facts to their own advantages.

The facts in this case are the facts of sex, in other words, the key to the mystery is to be found in the relation between male and female lovemaking. The truth is that while women have need of men, the need of men for women is the greater of the two. The cool and objective recognition of this truth quickly made women alive to the advantage which nature had thus thrown into their laps.

At a level of culture where men are permitted to use their superior physical strength to exploit the weakness of women, women cannot turn the fact of their indispensability to their own advantage any more than a slave can do. As manners became more refined, however, and the level of culture began to rise, men became increasingly subject to certain moral constraints, and force being thus morally at a discount, women succeed in compelling their men-folk to face the facts of nature.

The concessions on the part of the men were for a considerable time very grudgingly made; indeed van Meteren speaks in quite unambiguous terms of male unwillingness to recognize the freedom of married women. Gradually, however, they learned to accept the situation and to make a virtue of necessity—a very typical process this, in which the Anglo-Saxons, thanks to their coolly rational habit of mind, have always achieved a rare virtuosity. In time the whole female sex was to benefit from the success of the struggle which their married sisters had waged. The Puritans, however, whose rational habit of thought so often astonishes us, sought in their turn to find a new formula to fit the facts. It was a formula which was ultimately to have immense influence.

II

Parents and Children under Puritanism

1. *The family theocracy as the nucleus of the Puritan way of life*
We have seen the Puritans' thorough treatment of the subject of marriage and have been able to assess the importance which they attached to this institution and the degree of psychological acumen with which their study of it was pursued. Indeed, this last was so considerable that many of the findings dating back to this period will retain their validity for as long as marriage exists.

It is thus easy to understand how the family became the very centre of life to a degree without parallel in previous ages. It may well be said that the whole Puritan movement has its roots in the family and that we cannot even begin to understand it if we leave the family out of account. Religion is for the Puritan family religion. Divine worship is, not incidentally but primarily, family worship.

What the movement aimed at was essentially the interpenetration of faith and conduct, the injection into practical activities of an ethico-religious content to a degree that was to affect every phase both of public and private life, so that the effects penetrated to the very core of personality and permeated the whole man. But none of this was possible unless pressure was brought to bear from all sides and brought to bear continuously. Only the family could supply the leverage by which the process of self-reform was to be set in motion. Baxter, in *Christian Directory* (1673) states:

> So that it is an evident truth, that most of the mischiefs that now infest or seize upon mankind throughout the earth, consist in, or are caused by the disorders and ill-governedness of families.
>
> (page 514)

And Bunyan in 1663 expresses a similar thought on the title page of his *Christian Behaviour* in affirmative form when he refers to this as:

the Fruits of true Christianity, shewing the Ground from whence they flow, in their Godlike order in the Duty of *Relations*, as *Husbands, Wives, Parents, Children, Masters, Servants*, etc.

Thus the attempt was made to create, cell by cell, the new political entity, the great religious 'bee-hive'.

The principal duty fell upon the head of the family. His thorough knowledge of the characters of its members made him better fitted for this task than the clergyman. Moreover, it was more fitting that he should undertake the task because he himself was responsible for bringing children into the world bearing the stain of original sin. Also the practical results of their being born again affected nobody so strongly as himself. Thus the home was deliberately and not illogically transformed into a church. It was no longer that the family went to the temple, rather the temple came into the family and fashioned it anew.

The law governing this process is an iron one and admits of no exceptions. For as we read again and again in St Augustine, God is a God of order both in the Church and in the home (compare Dyke, page 52 and Rogers, page 270). Resistance to that order is virtually impossible and it manifests itself in the religious exercises which take place at intervals throughout the day, so that life itself becomes a kind of divine worship.

2. Teelinck describes his stay in Banbury in 1604
Naturally enough a variety of forms began to develop early in which such disciplined living found expression, but although the differences between those who practised great strictness of observance and the less strict was considerable, the essential pattern of the lives of the elect, the 'saints' or 'Godly', was unmistakable. Its example had very wide effects. The father of Dutch pietism, Teelinck (born 1579) stayed for eight or nine months in 1604 in the home of a citizen of Banbury. He gives us a description in the preface of his *Huysboeck* (1639) of the arrangements with which he there became familiar and which ultimately became for him a kind of model. Here was a completely pietistic household. In it not only were religious duties performed in between the daily tasks, morning and evening prayers being regularly recited and grace being said before and after meals, but an ideal was attained, an ideal described in rather barren words by Teelinck, but nevertheless an

ideal which was always before the minds of these people. It consisted of achieving the same aims as the monk while at the same time remaining engaged in active life in the world. This meant that all intellectual life was caught up in the life of religion.

The day began with morning prayer and with the reading of a chapter of scripture. At midday there was more Bible reading, a prayer was said with the family on its knees and after that would come the blessing of food. Anything in the Bible passage which had been read that provided food for meditation or required exposition was then made the subject of table-talk.

After the meal a psalm would be sung, while in the evening each devoted himself to running over in his mind the events of the day, such recollection being followed by a prayer. Any sermons preached during the week were reverently attended. A special afternoon, namely that of Saturday, was set aside for the catechizing of children and servants. Sunday, however, provided the central point of all these religious exercises; on that day the streets would be quiet and free of all disturbance though in a number of houses you would hear the singing of spiritual songs.

The focal point in the two-fold church attendance on Sunday was the sermon and this served to stimulate further religious activities. The sermon was often noted down and invariably formed the subject of discussion first at meals and then quite possibly in the evening in the presence of the servants and children who would all be asked how much of it they remembered. The evening also provided an opportunity for the free discussion of any grudge members of the household might bear one another and for drawing one another's attention to small faults. If anyone were to go out, he would seek the company of someone who could—and would—expound a psalm to them or some chapter of the Bible. Aid for the poor, the visiting and comforting of the sick and oppressed, were part of recognized duties which were all conscientiously performed.

The picture drawn by Teelinck already illustrates the end of a certain phase. He can already tell us that unbelievers in Banbury were compelled to keep quiet out of consideration for the rest. Here, therefore, the battle which was beginning all over the country had already been won. The long-term consequences of that victory, discernible even today, are known to all of us. Knowledge of the pietistic household was disseminated by innumerable writings on the subject of religion in the home and this caused the institution to spread right across England. These writings comprise the true and ultimate source from which flows the stream of English piety.

Naturally different aspects of religious life assumed a variety of outward forms. In the household of a prominent lady such as Lady Hoby (1528–1609) where the chaplain played a considerable part, the lady of the house had already organized a sort of Sunday school. However, the ordinary citizen could usually only find time after his day's work and the evening meal to devote himself to his religious interests. Thus Philip Stubbes (*A perfect pathway to Felicitie*, 1592) recommends psalm singing after dinner—Falstaff, too, regarded psalm singing as the essence of Puritanism—though its place might be taken by thorough application to the word of God, 'conversing, reasoning, disputing and talking of the word of God in reading, expounding or interpreting of the same'. Then there was the confession within the family of individual sins, private meditation, thoughts of penance, prayers, etc. We learn from the recalcitrant wife in Snawsel (1610) that the constant kneeling which accompanied these exercises made her dead tired.

Though there seems to be so much variation of form, especially among the sectaries, though in some cases the claims made by the family on the individual may be greater, in some rather less, though the pietistic character may in some cases be stronger and in some weaker, yet a certain common denominator remains, the nature of which has been made so very clear to us in Defoe's *Family Instructor*. It is the manner of spending Sunday which among so large a proportion of English families has continued to this day—so much so that nothing is more typical of the social life of this country, nothing that is spiritually of greater importance.

3. *Circumstances in Geneva. Luther's ideas*
All this raises an inevitable question. Just from where does this pietistic family community derive? The most usual answer is that it derives from Calvinism and undeniably Calvinism shows certain similar features, though in other respects it is markedly different. Certainly we find a theocracy in Geneva, but it is not a family theocracy. We can learn for instance from the autobiographical writings of Andreas Ryf (1562) a very great deal about the kind of thing that happened in Geneva, where, as Ryf tells us:

alle quatember die bredikanten durch die gantz Stat gond, allemoll 6, 8, minder oder mehr Hüser in eins zemenberieffen, doselbsten jung und alte personen visitierren, examinieren, ires glaubens halben rechtfertigen, berichten, underwüsen und lehren, ehe daß sy zuom nachtmol gondt.*

Such examination by the eldest of the different groups completely made an end of the family community as we find it in England where the father represents the highest authority. The 'bredikanten', preachers of Geneva, are here very different from the English clergy who, as Teelinck tells us, were 'seer besoekich ende ghemeensaem mit dem volcke' (very free and easy with the people). Of course people had to prepare themselves for the examination by the preachers and very definite provision is made for this in the church (compare Choisy, page 233). Thus when the apprentice Ryf receives from his master, 'selbs underricht und im Glauben und der Religion geiebet' (individual instruction and exercise in faith and religion) then the work of the master, as the wording clearly shows, is simply supplementary. Such exercising in religion is certainly not part of a general religious instruction within the home as the Puritans practised it, and when Ryf uses such emphatic language in telling us of the 'herlichen Haußzucht und guotten Polecey' (patriarchal discipline in the home and good government) but only actually mentions the morning and evening prayers which were spoken while kneeling and in which first the lady of the house and then later the apprentice himself was the leader, the difference between this and the English practice is too obvious to dwell on. Above all the sanctification of Sunday with such a degree of strictness is completely unknown in the Geneva system. Calvin himself played skittles on Sunday afternoon and visited his friends.

As to Luther, the spirit of the community which he founded is an altogether different one. It is quite true that, as Tyndale's views about marriage very clearly show, he exerted a very important influence. Moreover, he thoroughly approved of the very high value placed on the family as a result of Puritanism. His own marriage in particular formed a model for Puritan usage. His conception of the family as the 'primal authority from which all other

* Every quarter day the preachers go through the whole town, call together about 6 or 8 houses, more or less, visit the young and old alike, examine them, correct their beliefs, instruct, lecture and teach them, before they go to dinner.

authority and rulership derive', is by no means uniquely his own and his saying that 'the head of the house should punish his child like a judge, instruct him like a doctor and preach to him like a parson or a bishop' merely echoes the words of St Augustine, 'Quilibet pater familias, quia super intendit domui, episcopus dici potest'—words that were also known in England.

It is certainly worth noting that Luther too demands a weekly catechizing of children by the father, but actually this appears to have been a practice that was common to all Christians and went back to the Middle Ages. For all that, his tone is utterly different from that of English pietism. This being so, it does not seem too unlikely that this English form of pietism, though it was certainly influenced by the Reformation and though under that influence it may to some extent have been forced to develop new trends, may nevertheless have its source in certain indigenous practices.

4. Evidence for the beginnings of domestic religious discipline in Whitforde, in the Scottish catechism and in Thomas More

There is much that supports the above conclusion. It is perfectly true that a book for the guidance of life such as the fifteenth-century *Dives et Pauper* states that collective prayer in church is better than individual prayer, which means in effect that it leaves family prayers and family worship completely out of account. This book, of which Cardinal Gasquet states in his *Eve of the Reformation* (pages 284 and 298) that it was the most popular of all religious books of instruction in that century, permits certain freedoms on a Sunday. Naturally enough it enjoins that the day should be devoted to 'praying and worshipping of God and ghostly songs', to the giving of alms, to establishing peace and unity of mind, but it has no objection to innocent merriment on a Sunday and actually itself gives licence for spiritual games and dances such as are customary at Christmas and Easter. Actually *Dives et Pauper* is in many respects strikingly liberal and a much stricter note is struck by the Catholic Richard Whitforde in his *A werke for householders* of 1533.

Whitforde very definitely insists that at every meal, both at midday and in the evening, someone should recite in a loud voice the different sentences of the Lord's Prayer with long paraphrases, as well as *Hail Mary* and the Creed. He also demands that the head of the house should take upon himself the burden of supervision and should, at least once a week, hear the whole household recite the Commandments, the seven deadly sins and so forth. Moreover, he should while in church, exercise supervision over those who have been entrusted to his care.

Above all, every opportunity was to be seized to listen to sermons, which were considered even more important than the Mass. On Sunday all worldly pleasures such as the baiting of animals, football, tennis, skittles, cards and so on were forbidden, as were also visits to inns. Instead of these the reading of the abovementioned book or of similar works was enjoined and this was to be done in the presence of as large a company as possible who were to be gathered together for this purpose.

That these are not isolated individual opinions is clearly shown by Archbishop John Hamilton's celebrated Catholic catechism for the Kirk of Scotland. It is interesting to note that John Hamilton was ultimately hanged on the gallows in his archi-episcopal robes by his compatriots when they considered the measure of his sins to be full; they were clearly people who favoured drastic measures. What is more immediately to the point, however, is that in Hamilton's catechism the father was enjoined on Sunday to instruct his children and, as head of the household, to do the same for his servants, the subjects of instruction being the articles of faith, the Lord's Prayer, the Commandments and the doctrine of the deadly sins. On Sundays pleasure of any kind was strictly forbidden. Instead, in addition to divine worship, there was to be reconciliation with neighbours and almsgiving.

We can learn what actually took place in a Catholic family at the time of the Reformation from the descriptions which have come down to us of the household of Thomas More who most certainly was no innovator in religious matters. He prayed in company with his children and arranged every evening for devotions in his chapel, devotions in which the whole of his household took part on their knees. He even dedicated a weekday, namely Friday, to special exercises. Further, he frequently gave his children religious instruction. There is here, surely, a clear tendency to cultivate an intensive religious life, both within and outside the family circle.

5. *Development of the characteristic features of the household congregation*

Of course, the Mass still had a very important part to play in all this and piety was much more formal than with Puritans. The prayers, for instance, were the Lord's Prayer and *Hail Mary*, which were recited in a fairly stereotyped fashion. Whether there was any discussion of the sermon during the Sunday meal and afterwards is doubtful, though we must not wholly rule out the possibility, for we know that when Europe was still Catholic sermons were given at irregular intervals and on the whole very rarely. Other groups however may have been in existence which directed their attention to the sermon rather more than to anything else.

The first definite mention in England of children's instruction is probably that which occurs in Coverdale's translation *Christen State of Matrimonye*, a translation of Bullinger's work made in 1541. A more detailed treatment of the theme was attempted in Becon's *Catechism* (1560, folio 520 f.). From now on the subject begins to appear continuously in Puritan writing. Moreover, the custom began to spread through all strata of society and through all denominations and persisted in so determined a fashion that, as we learn from Lytton Strachey, even Queen Victoria while still a six-year-old child was examined in the afternoon by her mother on the sermon to which she had had to listen in the morning.

This can hardly be adduced as evidence of pre-Reformation practice; the reading of a religious book at table, however, is quite another matter, for here we have an ancient Christian practice, some memory of which may perhaps linger in Becon's insistence that a child should read a chapter of the Old or New Testament at meals and that this then should form the subject of discussion. By Teelinck's day the thing had become quite usual. The honest baring of one's heart to one's companions on Sunday evening, the reconciliation and mutual encouragement to virtue, things which we can again read about in Teelinck, are also—as we saw—to be found in the Scottish Catholic Catechism. Finally the examination of conscience at the close of every day, which Becon was already recommending, is after all an essential part of Christian life. Indeed at a very early stage of Christian history, it would have been possible to study the excellent and detailed description of this identical moral exercise in the pages of Seneca. It was an exercise, moreover, in which, at the time of the Reformation, Catholics too were instructed, as a matter of duty, to engage under the form of a daily confessional prayer. How such things preserve their pristine character largely unchanged and yet take on the typical colouring of those whom they affect is shown by a comparison of the advice given to the Catholic in the event of his waking in the night with that given to the Puritan suffering from sleeplessness. The Catholic is enjoined to think of the sufferings to which the Saviour in 'His Passion' was subjected at that hour of the night, while the Puritan is counselled to meditate on God's love and grace and urged to enquire of his conscience whether he has been fully obedient to some particular Commandment and much else of a similar kind. In a word, the Puritan in such a matter is more influenced by considerations of practical ethics (Downame). We might well add that this particular example of the contrast is of rather special interest in so far as it is implicit in one of the most famous poems of English literature, namely Young's *Night Thoughts*.

Another characteristic of Puritanism, and one which decisively influenced its character, was the idea of keeping the Sabbath holy. Those who have attempted to trace the origin of such strict Sabbatarianism have often tended to attach excessive importance to the struggles that took place at the turn of the sixteenth century. In this discussion a very influential book, and one which was the source of much controversy, namely that of Dr Nicholas Bownd of 1595, invariably looms large, but people tend to forget that the beginnings of this movement, which, as we shall learn from Teelinck, was already very powerful in Banbury in 1604, date back to a point of time that was whole generations earlier. For instance, in Becon (1560), who was Cranmer's chaplain and whose writings certainly had great influence, we already find strict rules forbidding any kind of amusement on Sunday whether this consisted of games, dancing, animal baiting, skittles, shooting or the organization of any kind of fair. In place of these, one is expected to spend the time in training body and soul by means of pious, spiritual exercise. Only for servants was the rule slightly relaxed, for these were permitted 'to take some honest pastime for the recreation of their weary bodies' (folio 516b). Indeed Becon already shows in almost every particular the unmistakable Puritan-ascetic attitude towards life. For instance, he disapproves of people who spend their time studying the ancient writers, he is against painting, sculpture, and singing by trained singers in church (folio 546b), he will not even allow servants to sing worldly songs at their work and his warning always to bear one's self in gesture, word and deed as though God and his angels were visibly present, shows us how much the Puritan and the pious Catholic had in common.

PARENTS AND CHILDREN UNDER PURITANISM

6. *Origin of the family church*

For this reason alone I find it hard to follow Douglas Campbell when he traces the origin of Puritanism to the influence of Dutch Calvinist refugees (some 75,000 such families being said to have entered the country under Elizabeth). The beginnings of this form of pietism, which was one day to assume such mighty proportions, are admittedly veiled in obscurity. Yet the origins of those particular features which I have described make it plain that what we have before us here is a change of direction on the part of what was already an indigenous trend, a change brought about by influences coming from the Continent.

The trend itself is an old one. How thoroughly religion permeates life in Langland's *Piers Plowman*!—and that takes us back to the fourteenth century. There is, moreover, considerable significance in the fact that the only occasion when the poet mentions his family, his wife and daughter—to whom he refers by the somewhat odd name of Kytte and Kalote—is when he summons them to take part on their knees in the penitential procession on Good Friday (B XVIII, 427)—a circumstance which surely shows how closely even in those early days family and religion were bound up with one another. I might add that, as Cardinal Gasquet points out in *Parish Life in Medieval England* (page 153), Langland wants both Sunday morning and Sunday afternoon wholly reserved for religious exercises, though of course he is thinking of exercises performed in church. For in those days, the layman lacked that sufficiency of religious education which would have prevented him from being utterly dependent upon the clergy in every detail of his life. As time went on things changed; in the fifteenth century the clergy was complaining, as we can see from Pecock, in a very lively manner of the religious independence on the part of the laity which the Wycliffite movement had brought in its train. Indeed the Wycliffites were actually referred to as the 'Lay-Party'.

By the beginning of the sixteenth century, however, a lively religious interest had come into being in London mercantile circles, as is clearly shown by the prosecution of Hunne in whose house a thickly annotated Bible was found. Such reading of the Bible in family circles was very characteristic of the Wycliffite movement and Lechler has shown that around 1450 Pecock was violently criticizing this as a habit that was still very much in fashion at that time. That such 'Bible folk' had already developed a vigorous religious family life is something which we can safely assume, and indeed, where could those women of whose delight in Biblical discussion Pecock complains, have gained their religious knowledge unless it was from collective study within the home?

Some importance attaches to these facts because of the light they throw on the origins of Puritanism itself. Many have got into the habit of treating the religious permeation of ordinary life as something peculiarly Calvinist; but this is an error. We know that long before Calvin the various Baptist sects were already propagating this idea though they did so admittedly in conjunction with their advocacy of Christian Communism which Troeltsch (page 365 ff.) sees everywhere as the essential mark of the sectary type (as opposed to the ecclesiastical type). In England, however, at a very early stage—the beginning of the sixteenth century to be exact—we not only find quite simple folk with a religious life of their own, but also wealthy citizens like Hunne whose religious interests had undergone very considerable development. Men of the latter sort frequently financed the printing of religious books; they were often definitely anti-clerical, but, being typically hard-headed Englishmen, were unlikely to have had much sympathy for communism.

It is only natural that people like these differing, as they so markedly did, from the sectary type with its ideals of poverty, continence, brotherhood and equality—it is only natural, surely, that people like these should have been drawn towards the highly distinctive sort of family piety that I have described; for the two things go together and it is in the very nature of the family that it should have within itself a certain capitalistic bent. By and large then, we can, I think, form a picture in our minds of a religious family community which, in some respects, still has a slight sectarian air, and think of this as the foundation on which Puritanism was built.

Of course there is a special reason why this 'family church' became as important in England as it did. It is to be found in the general feeling that the scope of the Reformation had not been as wide as it should have been and also in that neglect of religion by the Government, which for decades almost attained the dignity of an official policy. We know that Elizabeth displayed a quite surprising indifference to her subjects' needs in this field, we know how scantily the country was supplied with preachers, we know how efforts at self-help and especially the conventicles organized on the Swiss model—'prophesyings' as they were called—were, from the 'sixties onward, forcibly suppressed by the State. Thus religion was forced back within the protecting walls of the home and left to the family.

7. *The concept of the family: limitation of the number of children, their first religious instruction*

In such a setting the religious life always takes much the same form, it turns the family into a theocracy in which the Bible is at one and the same time the code of law and the constitution which is continually consulted. Holding the Bible in his hands and supported by the mother, the father as *pars imperans* rules over the *pars subdita*, that is to say, over the children and the servants.

It is God's will that a man should have children. Only the wicked look upon many children as a misfortune—so we already learn from Lowth's translation (1581)—whereas the faithful regard it as the highest form of good fortune. In the Puritan family, therefore, large numbers of children were the rule. 'I hope she will be fruitful,' wrote Oliver Cromwell to his son concerning his daughter-in-law and it is noteworthy how in this department, religious faith utterly nullifies the rationalist attitude towards life which prevails in most other matters.

To employ means to prevent conception or to limit the family to a single child in order to enhance its worldly fortune, is regarded as a direct counsel of Satan (compare Rogers, page 139). A passage in Milton exemplifies this very well. When Adam and Eve are shut out of Paradise, Eve suggests that they should nullify the curse of God by having no children, but Adam declares the very thought of the thing to be sinful, for it amounts to a defiance of God and rejection of the yoke he has imposed on man (X, 1045).

The family indeed stands under God's special protection, for that reason a prayer precedes cohabitation, prayer welcomes the new-born child; I need hardly mention the importance attached to baptism. Further, parents are warned against handing over the new-born child to a wet nurse, as was largely the practice not of the fashionable world alone but also of the middling strata of society, as can be seen from the heresy trial of Hunne which took place at the beginning of the sixteenth century. Indeed, in the towns and in the villages around London, women had for centuries been making what was often a very questionable business out of wet nursing. In many cases this turned into something that was simply the manufacture of angels. Bishop Tillotson declares, no doubt with a certain amount of exaggeration, that very often scarcely one out of five children reached the age of one year. It is not unnatural that this abuse should from the earliest days have been vehemently resisted by the Church. To put an end to such gross neglect of maternal duty which Tillotson refers to as 'one of the great and crying Sins of this Age and Nation' (*Six Sermons* 1694, Sermon III, 'Concerning the Education of Children', I, page 103), all manner of physiological and hygienic arguments were adduced and reference was also made to the will of God as expressed in the Bible. It is true that here again the Anglican shows his true nature, for he leaves a little back door open by including among the cases where a mother is not obliged to suckle her infant, the 'authority of the father' (*The Whole Duty of Man* is even less insistent on this matter).

When the child made its first efforts to speak, care was taken—this too is a Catholic custom—that its first words should be words with a religious significance; it was especially encouraged to say such words as 'God', 'Jesus', 'faith', 'love'. As soon as it could form sentences it was taught to say 'God alone can save me'; 'Christ has redeemed me'; 'Abominate pride'; 'Learn to die'; 'Harm no one and serve all'; 'All men are brothers'. The religious instruction of the child had to begin at as early an age as possible, and in this particular the Puritan method of education did not greatly differ from that employed by the secular world.

Thus, to take but a single instance, Elyot's *The Governor* (1531) declares that, contrary to the rules of antiquity, there was no need to wait till a child reached the age of seven before beginning its instruction; antiquity had an easier task, in so far as it did not have to learn the ancient tongues. Naturally enough the Puritan justified the practice on religious grounds. As Defoe very forcibly put the matter, it was necessary to gain a start on the devil and this was achieved by introducing into the child's mind a number of things which it did not yet understand but of which it would become fully conscious at a later stage after they had lain hidden within its soul, as throughout the winter corn lies hidden within the earth. It is with the same hope that a child was given the Bible to read at an early stage.

A good indication of the kind of situation people took for granted is to be found in Becon's *Catechism*. This work presents the whole system of Christian doctrine in a dialogue between a father and his son, and the son is represented as being less than six years old. Nevertheless, it is assumed that, thanks to the father, the preacher and the school master, he has an adequate knowledge of his subjects. Actually a considerable number of instances of quite astonishing precocity are to be found recorded in the memoirs of this time. Mrs Hutchinson, for instance, tells us that she was taken along to listen to the sermon at the age of four and was then able to repeat it with a commendable degree of accuracy, a circumstance that may perhaps explain the introduction in Defoe's *Family Instructor* of a child aged five or six who enters into a dialogue with his father which would do honour to the most learned theologian. We should however not ignore the fact that in this case an exception has been quietly treated as a rule. The scene is only realistic in so far as— given the kind of education that prevailed at the time—it would have been natural enough for a child to babble about matters of religion though it did not understand them at all. But just as in strictly Catholic countries people have no misgivings about producing little toy versions of the altar and of the sacred vessels used in the Mass, so in the present instance the playing of a kind of children's game with sacred things was not felt in any way to be a desecration. On the contrary, Thomas White exclaims in *A Little Book for Little Children* (1702), 'Oh, how precious a thing it is to hear a child praying, as soon, nay sooner than it can speak plain!' A child who, like little John Ruskin preached sermons about 'Dod' from a kitchen chair, was not only a frequent and typical phenomenon in the Puritan nursery but for nearly three centuries an extremely popular one. Something of this has lasted to the present day, for even now when bad weather makes it unwise to take small children to church, we can see the eldest holding a kind of divine service for his little brothers and sisters. Also religious toys are far from having gone completely out of fashion as we can see from those Biblical and Catechismal texts which are written out by the mother and are then marked out with pins by children too young as yet to learn them by heart. Such wholesale permeation by religion of the whole of a child's thinking and feeling was not without its critics, as can be seen from the proverb 'A young Saint an old Devil'—to which incidentally Tillotson objected. However, such disapproval produced little result.

8. *Education outside the home*

Where more advanced education was concerned parents had, of course, to decide whether it should take place within or outside the home, but the Puritan theoreticians are curiously silent on this point. True, on the whole they seem to have recommended education within the home but they did not, as one might expect, set their faces utterly against education outside it. Even Baxter who briefly examines the question in *Christian Directory* fails to assume a definite attitude in regard to it:

> Therefore let those that are able, either educate their Children most at home, or in private and well-ordered Schools.
>
> (page 546)

And he turns against those parents who expose their children to the most brutalizing influences and then imperil their souls by sending them abroad, possibly into 'papistical' countries, so that they may acquire a worldly polish.

> I would rather let my son, if I had one, become a chimney sweep than deliver him to the Devil in such a fashion.

Milton's father thought it best to let his son visit a London school and at the same time maintained a Puritan tutor for him. He was not alarmed by the possible moral perils of journeys abroad.

It is however quite clear that the habit of educating young people outside the home was too deep-rooted to be replaced by any system of instruction under the parental roof. Later John Locke was to attempt—unsuccessfully as it turned out—to adopt the latter alternative, though he did not do so on Puritanical grounds.

The English habit of clinging to tradition is very much in evidence here. Nevertheless, the practice of letting one's children grow up in the houses of strangers, a practice which in England and in other European countries was already familiar in Anglo-Saxon times and in the High Middle Ages, had a definite idea behind it which can hardly have been peculiar to England alone, an idea which in later times we find continually shaping people's conduct. It was felt that because of the very love they bore them, parents were the least suitable people to be entrusted with the education of their own children.

What is perhaps the earliest description of this practice of handing one's children over to strangers is to be found in the life of Ordericus Vitalis (1075–1142). In it the writer gives a moving description of his weeping father sending away his ten-year-old son ('plorans plorantem tradidit') so that, like Abraham, he should depart from his native country and also from the influence of the father's friendship, so that parental love ('per parentum carnalem affectum') should not impair his preparation for a clerical career (V, 134). Such considerations may well, as far back as the seventh century, have inspired the parents of Bede—who, contrary to popular belief, was probably not an orphan at all—to take their son to a monastery while still a child of tender years.

A fifteenth-century Italian complains that this highly practical procedure (compare *Dinarbas*, XLIV) implies coldness of heart:

> The want of affection in the English is strongly manifested towards their children; for after having kept them at home till they arrive at the age of seven to nine years at the utmost, they put them out, both males and females, to hard service in the houses of other people, binding them generally for another seven or nine years. And these are called apprentices, and during that time they perform all the most menial offices; and few are born who are exempted from this fate, for every one, however rich he may be, sends away his children into the houses of others, whilst he, in return, receives those of strangers into his own. And on inquiring their reason for this severity, they answered that they did it in order that their children might learn better manners. But I, for my part, believe that they do it because they like to enjoy all their comforts themselves, and that they are better served by strangers than they would be by their own children. Besides which, the English being great epicures, and very avaricious by nature, indulge in the most delicate fare themselves and give their household the coarsest bread, and beer, and cold meat baked on Sunday for the week, which, however, they allow them in great abundance. That if they had their own children at home, they would be obliged to give them the same food they made use of for themselves. That if the English sent their children away from home to learn virtue and good manners, and took them back again when their

apprenticeship was over, they might, perhaps, be excused; but they never return, for the girls are settled by their patrons, and the boys make the best marriages they can, and, assisted by their patrons, not by their fathers, they also open a house and strive diligently by this means to make some fortune for themselves; whence it proceeds that, having no hope of their paternal inheritance, that all become so greedy of gain that they feel no shame in asking, almost 'for the love of God', for the smallest sums of money; and to this it may be attributed, that there is no injury that can be committed against the lower orders of the English, that may not be atoned for by money.

(*A Relation of the Island of England*, pages 24–6)

The fact is that those who engaged in this practice were thinking of the child's future and not of their own interest. For by thus severing at a very early age a kind of umbilical cord which ties the spirit of the child and the parental home, parents help to enhance the child's feeling of independence and force it to suppress many emotional impulses which have a kind of tenderheartedness about them. By such action parents themselves make a sacrifice—and at the same time impose a sacrifice on the child—to a rational ideal of life. A real need for such heroic sacrifice could hardly have arisen in a well-organized Puritan family theocracy, but even the Puritan family theocracy was ready to bow to tradition.

9. *The subordination of children*
The process I have just described in which those who could afford it sent their children to what, in effect, were boarding establishments was bound to diminish the importance of the parental home (compare Dressler). The idea of youth in England has thus tended to be associated not with home but with school. The school has already begun to exert its influence when the children are only nine or ten years old. Since families tended to be large, this did not necessarily empty the home and so leave Puritan principles of education with nothing to work on. We find that at a very early stage these very principles become affected by a kind of rigour, for the mediaeval principle of unconditional subordination on the part of the children still held its validity. The prime duty of the child was obedience and, what is more, such obedience had to be clearly manifest. It was, of course, not the obedience of a slave but simply the expression of a reverent attitude. Their meekness, modesty,

docility and patience was to be the product of 'loving-fear or fearing-love'.

The outward evidence of such an inward attitude could take a number of forms, the most eloquent of which was the habit of kneeling, both morning and evening, before the parents as representatives of the divine authority; in that attitude they besought the parental blessing. It is characteristic of a certain dogged persistence with which the English clung to the traditions of the Catholic Middle Ages that this practice, which amongst other places, was also known in Germany, was maintained far and wide—for so long a time—and not in Puritan circles alone, for we hear of it in the life of Sir Thomas More and also in the conduct book of the Catholic Whitforde in 1533. Shakespeare is fully acquainted with it and puts it to effective use while Puritanical writers such as Becon (folio 524b), Stubbes, Gouge and Downame, all seem to have a warm affection for this symbol of the perfect relationship between parents and children.

It is evident from Gouge's writings that as far back as the beginning of the seventeenth century there was already some disapproval of the practice. For all that, however, in Richardson's *Pamela* (1740) the virtuous maiden who has risen from the position of a servant to be mistress of the household, kneels before her father, a simple workman. The custom lasted even longer at the English court; perhaps its discontinuance as a universal practice denotes the end of a certain stage in spiritual development.

Yet such development proceeded very slowly, for everything we read lays on the parents the duty of maintaining their position of superiority over their children and of preserving their dignity before them. Certain fundamental ideas in this matter, which were based on Biblical texts, remained completely unchanged throughout the century. There is something sinister in the words which Tyndale puts into the mouths of parents supposedly addressing their children:

> Yf thou mekely obeye so shalt thou grow both in the favoure of God and Man and knowledge of oure lorde Christe. Yf thou wilt not obeye as at his commandemente: then are we charged to correct thee yee and yf thou repente not and amende thy selfe God shall sley the by his officers or punish ye everlastingly.
>
> (*The Obedience of a Christen man*, folio xlviiib)

A generation later, in 1560, Becon was to produce a variant of *Ecclesiasticus*, XXX, 10–12.

> Laugh not with thy son, lest thou have sorrow with him, and lest thou gnash thy teeth in the end.
> Give him no liberty in his youth, and wink not at his follies.
> Bow down his neck while he is young, and beat him on the sides while he is a child, lest he wax stubborn, and be disobedient unto thee, and so bring sorrow to thine heart.

This injunction to destroy the child's self-will, to hold it on a short rein and compel its respect, are to be found in all subsequent authors. There is scarcely one who does not apply to the relations between parents and children the text of Terence which has virtually become a proverb in England, 'familiarity breeds contempt'. Even Rogers is no exception here, while Baxter (*Christian Directory*, page 543) regards it as an important educational principle that parents should keep their proper distance. Above all, he declares, parents should not make companions out of their children. Naturally, they should in all matters set an example to the child, particularly in the matter of self-control, while at the same time inwardly fettering it to themselves by means of praise and kindness and by making the love they bear it apparent in all their actions. For, although the parents should display earnestness of purpose and a high measure of dignity, nevertheless, mixed with these qualities there should be, as Downame expresses it in *A Guide to Godlynesse*, 'parent-like love, brotherly humanity, and Christian mildnesse and modesty' (page 341). As in the case of the 'subordination' of the wife, this obedience is unlimited save where it would bring the child into conflict with the laws of God. Where a child, shall we say, is forbidden to attend church or is commanded to lie or steal or commit some other evil deed, in such a case the father would be untrue to his office as God's representative.

10. *Punishment in the family*

However the father conforms in a special manner to the duties of his office and assumes all its inherent rights when he punishes. In Becon's *Catechism* the father asks the son: 'What if, the father doing his duty, the children be negligent and will not learn; or if they learn, they will not frame their life according to their knowledge; may not the father with a good conscience correct those children?' And the model child answers: 'Yes, most lawfully. For moderate correction is as necessary for children as meat and drink.'

This view has become well nigh axiomatic, supported, as it is, by numerous Biblical texts that are everlastingly repeated and, in the last analysis, inspired by its analogy to the Christian conception of evil as a divine punishment and visitation. In a piece of writing that dates back to an early period (*The Christian Man's Closet*, 1581) Batty explains in a remarkably naive fashion how the providence and wisdom of God had specially formed the human posterior in such a fashion that it could receive blows without incurring serious bodily injury (page 26). Beatings indeed, seem at that time to have constituted the most essential part of education. So much so, that so delicately minded a writer as Rogers can find no better way of describing the spiritual harmony and agreement of husband and wife than the following:

> (she) holdes not his hand from due stroakes, but bares their (the children's) skins with delight, to his fatherly stripes.
>
> (page 299)

Yet here too one feels that behind such an extension of ancient pedagogic principles there is that unmistakable desire to safeguard spiritual values which marks the whole movement. The Bible's advice, as contained in *Ephesians*, VI, 4 'And ye fathers, provoke not your children to wrath', advice which the fathers, such as Jonas of Orleans, scrupulously observed (*De institutione laicali*, liber II, Migne 106, page 194), is now repeated with increased emphasis. There has been a tempering of the recklessness shown by such men as Robert Mannyng (1345) whose only concern was that there should not be any actual breaking of children's bones. Indeed, so early a writer as Becon advises against over-severity, which might well harden a child's heart and urges that treatment should conform to the individual character of the child concerned since some are as amenable to words as others are to blows. He also insists that, before there is chastisement, the reason for giving it should be explained, nor should a child ever be led to doubt his father's continuing love.

Gouge developed the theme still further. Like Perkins before him, he counselled a sensible middle way that was neither too harsh nor too gentle, and urged that delicate children and those that were too small should not be beaten at all. Actually his system had already begun to assume that pietistic character which was still lacking in Becon. Like every other serious undertaking, the punishment of a child must, according to Gouge, be accompanied by prayer, at any rate, he who inflicts it—who must never labour under any powerful emotion—must 'lift up his heart' and pray for blessing and guidance before he raises the rod. It must also be made clear to the child that in swearing, lying or stealing, he has not only sinned against his father but against God; the punishment can then be regarded—to quote Griffith (1633)—as having been administered 'for the glory of God'. This is really the ancient scholastic interpretation, according to which sin represents the withdrawal from God of an honour which is his due (compare Ziegler, page 260). In *Christian Directory* (page 547) Baxter, who adds little of substance to the discussion, demonstrates that the character of the punishment is designed to bring home to the little offender in a particularly unmistakable manner what God thinks of him. For, before receiving the punishment, the child must read those passages from Scripture on the strength of which it is going to receive a beating. Better still, it should be asked whether it wishes through a remission of the punishment, that injury should be done to its soul. Once it is inwardly convinced that the punishment is just it will draw all the greater profit therefrom. Whereas Bunyan only lets the father do any praying, Baxter insists that after receiving punishment the child should in every case, kneel down and entreat God to 'bless and sanctify' its effects, 'that it may do you good'. Thus the unlovely mediaeval custom that made the child kiss the rod after it had been beaten is translated into religious terms (compare Tillotson, 1694).

11. *The work of revival*

These things however also aid in the great task of revival. Since man is evil both in thought and imagination from youth up, the battle against the natural man becomes necessary from the earliest years and this battle must be fought within the family. Bunyan's advice is to make it clear to children what accursed creatures they are, how through original sin and their own actual sins they are under the wrath of God. By means of threat and reward, by bringing home to them at an early age the lot of the Godless, by describing the inward glory of the pious, children must be set upon the road towards that inward conversion which brings with it the certainty of grace; but this must be done while they are still very young for it is the tender twigs that can still be bent, even as clay and wax can be given a shape while they are still soft (Gouge).

This aim is in part achieved if the parents can explain to the children how God works within the church, within history and within nature. Nature in particular seems almost to have been created in order to be an object lesson of moral instruction, the steadfastness of the stars in their courses, the trustworthiness of fruit trees in the matter of bearing their fruits, are so many lessons to the faithful, for the learning of which it is well worth taking a walk out of doors. But the child must also be encouraged betimes to discern the deeper symbolic significance of the events of ordinary life. For instance, when it wets its hands and face in the morning—a more intensive ablution was not yet customary in 1600—its thoughts should be directed to the cleansing of its own soul through the redemption which is made effective in baptism (Stubbes, 1592). When it partakes of bodily food, it should think of the food of the Spirit (Gouge), while the crowing of the cock should call to mind the shrill trumpet of the last judgment (Downame, Bunyan). These are very old ideas which derive from patristic literature which have here come to life again and found expression.

12. *The cultivation of industry and simplicity*
In this way the soil is prepared for the growth of that unworldliness which is the main aim of Puritan education and leads to moderation in eating and drinking, simplicity in dress and unpretentiousness in one's whole bearing and way of life. From childhood up the young person should be trained to regard riches and display as being worthless in the sight of God and contemptible in themselves. How vigorously this idea lives on in Puritanism is made very clear when Milton, almost against all reason and relevance, uses the opportunity provided by the angel's appearance in *Paradise Lost* to have a dig at what he calls the 'tedious pomp that waits on Princes' (V, 353).

Very much in line with all this is the stress laid on humility and the repeated insistence that all pride and boastfulness should be suppressed. It is, however, all too easy for such humility to degenerate into a contempt for the courtesies of social intercourse which the growth since the end of the sixteenth century of the aristocratic spirit and outlook had so luxuriantly brought in its train.

The Puritan set his face against the more extravagant manifestations of this trend. Nevertheless, he taught his children that good manners and firm religious principles are by no means mutually exclusive. Education to unworldliness most certainly did not imply a turning away from the world; on the contrary, the world is there for the children of God to conquer and every individual is a soldier in the great army. To see the matter in this light is to postulate for everyone the qualities of leadership—resolution and clarity of aim, even though these are qualities which the individual is not normally called upon to display. The essential Puritan attitude towards life was not one of mere passivity. It was indeed the opposite.

Closely associated with all that has just been said is the stress laid on industry. I shall later (page 106) have occasion to speak of the great weight which the Puritan attaches to the moral value of work, but this concept is also something very old, an ancient inheritance which now attains new splendour. Indeed so early a writer as the mystic Rolle von Hampole regards the dignity of labour as that of a form of worship (compare Hittmair, page 216). This idea has a particularly decisive part to play in the thinking of Langland. Another work which devotes a significantly large section to it is John Watton's *Speculum Christianorum* which was widely read towards the end of the Middle Ages (*De labore*, B, IV). Small wonder then that, during the Reformation, Latimer's sermons should have inculcated the duty of work, a duty from which no man could escape, or that his pupil Becon (folio 522b) should have taken this teaching so seriously.

This duty continued to be recognized by the Puritans in those later years, though the animating spirit behind it was somewhat different. Indeed, we can already faintly discern behind their insistence on the value of time the 'time is money' of a more recent age. Practical and moral considerations had begun to unite with each other. But this made the thought unbearable that any creature should be idle who could be considered worthy of reverence—indeed, on at least one occasion Downame makes a special point of acquitting the blessed in heaven of the imputation of idleness on the ground that they are unremittingly busying themselves with songs of praise. Tillotson (1694) goes even further and can find even the devil admirable, not to say exemplary in at least one respect, namely in the diligence with which he goes everlastingly around, 'seeking whom he may devour'. It is to that diligence that he owes his success. This being so, it is not surprising that the judgment passed on the prevailing educational system and particularly on that provided for women of the upper classes should be a devastating one. Such women spent their whole lives in idleness, and indeed, Baxter vehemently criticizes the arrangement which causes their education to have no other object than to train them to occupy their leisure hours. Even their bodily training is so inadequate that it is insufficient to keep them well and the result is that women, like the sick, spend that part of the day in bed which they should be devoting to some useful occupation. The greater part of their life is made a misery by illness and they are out of breath as soon as they have but to use their legs to carry them into a room. As a result, few of them live much more than half the span of time allotted them by nature.

The correctness of Baxter's observations, I might remark, is confirmed by the high mortality rate of women, which in its turn explains the fact that so many men married more than once. We keep reading about men who married two or three times and it was certainly this which in its turn produced the searching disquisitions of the conduct books on the relations between step-mothers and step-children. (One of the conclusions arrived at in these is that when step-mother and step-children fail to agree, it is the duty of the husband to remove the children from the house.)

13. *Parental concern in the choice of profession*
The encouragement of industry is likely to lead, sooner or later, to the choice of a profession. That parents in making this choice should respect the special characteristics and aptitudes of their children is hardly to be wondered at. What is remarkable is the unquestioning conviction that in this parents are performing a function which not only serves the interests of their children but also those of the State. Dressler has rightly stressed this 'State-mindedness' in Puritanism and indeed, nothing can more strikingly prove the error of that policy of suppression which Queen Elizabeth carried out against the Puritans than the unconditional loyalty to State authority which animated Puritan writing for as

long as it was possible to do so. How scrupulously, too, so many of the conduct books continued to assert the duty of praying for the queen. The common good, however, is never lost sight of, and it is typical that Gouge (Treatise 6, section 52) should declare it to be a cancer both in Church and State that so many people managed to secure administrative posts for their children who were quite unfitted to hold them. One can find other examples elsewhere. Richardson, in one of his novels, causes the heroine to refuse to purchase smuggled lace because this would constitute a wrong against the State.

14. Parental role in marrying the children
Even more important for the life of the family than the choice of a profession is the marriage of their children. This is quite specifically a parental duty. Perkins for instance, sums up the duties of parents under the two headings: educating the children and marrying them off. Needless to say the moralists would have nothing to do with child marriages, though these were to continue for many a year and often took place even before sexual maturity had been attained; relatively little however was said against the mediaeval custom of early marriages. What came later to be regarded as an essential precondition for a sound marriage, namely economic independence and ability to sustain life, was far from being invariably required, even though Becon insisted on it (compare Fripp, page 23). However, that condition could hardly be fulfilled if respect was to be had for Defoe's insistence that the devil should be deprived of his head start; for the devil's most formidable instruments are the senses and it is the senses that would play the decisive part, so it was felt, if youth were left the time to choose; at best there would always be the danger that young people would let themselves be deceived by them and would utterly ignore those considerations which it was essential to take into account when contracting a marriage.

Parents therefore should teach their children—indeed Tyndale in 1528 specifically laid this down—that it is the children's duty to ask them to grant a marriage, and those same parents must, at an early stage, make a choice on their children's behalf. This seems actually to have been the normal procedure. In the prudent counsels offered by Thomas Lupset, one of the early English humanists, in his *An Exhortation to yonge Men* (1530) he advises the said young men to practise continence, for it will not be long ere 'your frendes'—by which he obviously means the family—'will provide you of an honest mate'. Parents therefore must not just wait upon events, to quote the words of Rogers:

> Parents, I grant, should not only hearken to, but runne and ride to seeke out good matches for their children, if any occasion be offered.
> (page 80)

In this they must of course respect the prudent wishes of their children, for even God—as we read with a certain amount of astonishment—first presented Eve to Adam before she became his wife. In a word, mutual liking is most certainly desirable, but we know only too well that just in this department of life the dispositions of the human spirit are highly complex so that no simple formula can provide a solution to the problems involved. That is why the people in those days paid great attention to the relations between parents and children in all matters pertaining to the marriage of the latter. It was, indeed, one of the central problems of life and for that very reason was constantly under discussion (compare Howard, Gairdner and Martin).

15. *The unqualified necessity of parental consent*
One iron rule remains inviolable: children, when they marry, need the counsel or, at the very least, the consent of their parents. Here we come upon one of the most characteristic qualities of English civilization, namely a tendency to cleave with quite remarkable strictness to the principles of the very oldest ecclesiastical law, which tends to follow Roman law. For to offend against the aforesaid principle is regarded as the blackest ingratitude, the very worst kind of disobedience of which children can become guilty. It is only when parents have definitely been at fault themselves, when, that is to say, they have allowed matters to take their course under their very eyes, when their silence appeared to give consent, when they have failed to make their wishes known—it is only then that they lose the right to see those wishes obeyed.

There is one other occasion on which marriage becomes obligatory, whatever the parents may think; that is where sexual intercourse has already taken place and the child has thus proved itself unworthy of its normal relations with its parent.

When parents refuse to give their consent to a proposed

marriage, the children, while strictly following the forms of affection and obedience, must first attempt to bring about a change of heart within them. If they fail to win their parents over, they may invite the mediation of friends and relatives. If this too proves vain and if there has really been a misuse of parental power, it is well to appeal to higher authority, either lay or ecclesiastical; if this also proves abortive, they must reconcile themselves to their ill-fortune, treating it as a visitation and hoping for God's help in the matter.

It need hardly be said that this rigorous advocation of obedience finds no support whatsoever in Catholic teaching which has successfully defended the claims of the individual—even against feudalism. Thus, for instance, *Dives et Pauper* declares that though the counsel and consent of parents and friends is much to be desired in a marriage, nevertheless 'in things that long to kind of body, as in substance of the body, in bringing forth children' (folio 152b) all men are equal and the servant has as little need of the consent of his master as the son that of his father (compare page 96). Luther too takes the view that 'the rule of the parents ... neither makes nor mars a marriage'.

It is however with Calvinism that the English view most sharply contrasts. In Geneva the father's concurrence was obligatory only up to the age of twenty in the case of a son and of eighteen in that of a daughter. Children could even start an action and compel the father to produce a dowry if he opposed a marriage on insufficient grounds. In England, however, as early a writer as Tyndale sets up the thesis that marriages which lack parental consent are invalid, and in the approved form of marriage contract express mention is made of parental consent as a condition that has been fulfilled. This view therefore extends far beyond Puritan circles, a fact evident in the book *The Whole Duty of Man*, a work which had a well-nigh limitless circulation and earned the warm applause of Archbishop Tillotson. This book declares that a marriage contracted by children contrary to the wishes of their parents is unpardonable and, since children are the property of the parents, constitutes 'a kind of theft' (compare Gairdner).

16. *Force and influence on the shaping of the will*
Whereas therefore there can be no kind of doubt as to the necessity of parental consent, the question of whether parents can actually

force children to marry against their will is not a simple one. This has always been a most rewarding literary theme, and one which has merely to be stated for the reader to realize immediately how the problem can be resolved. Indeed the halo that surrounds the head of dead Juliet, the tears that flow from the eyes of Imogen, show clearly that all doubts as to the correct solution have long been dispelled.

Nevertheless, it is all too clear from Puritan literature that these disputes were by no means such anachronisms as many popular writings and certain humane dramatists of the seventeenth century might lead us to suppose. Of course, the wonderfully enlightened Puritan view that perfect spiritual harmony between husband and wife constituted the very essence of marriage should have utterly precluded a relapse into so barbarous a conception of parental rights as that underlying the enforced marriage of their children, and indeed no Puritan wished, as Capulet (*Romeo and Juliet*, III, 5), to drag a child to the altar. Actually, strong exception is taken to children being forced into a marriage. Despite this, however, where an actual conflict occurs, sympathy seems to incline towards the parents, if only because in the vast majority of cases the quarrel with youth represents the conflict between *ratio* and *passio*, and parents are often only considered to be in the wrong in so far as they have allowed a conflict to arise at all, instead of making prudent provision in time (compare Cleuer and Dod).

Moreover, the law of competing duties, to which reference has already made, holds good here too. Certainly, parents must not use force to compel their children to contract a marriage: as against this however, the duty of obedience incumbent on children demands that they willingly submit to the wishes of their parents in this as in other matters. Only the very gravest reasons—and among these no one has included a liking for another person— could furnish a just cause for opposing the parental will, and needless to say, a daughter was considered to have even less right than a son to a will of her own. Moreover, it would almost seem as though the spread of pietism had caused ideas about children's rights to become not more liberal, but actually narrower. While to Becon (1560) it was still a matter of the utmost importance that there should be a full concordance of wishes between parents and children, there were soon to be plenty of others to whom the free assent of children was of negligible importance. Jeremy Taylor was not a Puritan himself but his moral teaching, despite certain differences in theory, follows the Puritan line in all important matters with great exactness. The following utterance may be regarded as typical of his basic feeling on this point:

> if a father offers a wife to a son, or a husband to a daughter such as a wise or a good man may offer without folly and injury, the child is not to dispute at all, but to obey, if the Father urges and insists upon the precept.
>
> (*Rule of Conscience* III, V, viii, 32)

On the other side of the account, there seems to have been pretty general agreement that parents had a moral duty to save money on behalf of their children wherever this was possible and—this held good whether it was the matter of a son or a daughter—to alleviate the difficulties of married life by making a decent marriage settlement upon them. This point of view had been far from universal in the Middle Ages (compare Robert Mannyng of Brunne).

17. *The examples of Hutchinson and Cromwell*

It would seem that the Puritans shared these sentiments in a general way with the majority of their compatriots. We find evidence of this both in the facts of the real world and in imaginative literature.

A very strict conception of the subjection of children however may indeed have been accepted in principle, yet in the give and take of family life it was inevitable that a less rigid interpretation should prevail. I will quote only two highly characteristic examples that illustrate my point, though I could find a good many more. One is the marriage of the man who later became Colonel Hutchinson. His wife in her memoirs considers it greatly to her father-in-law's credit that, though being ignorant of the attachment to the writer which his son had formed, he had already concluded a bargain for a much more profitable match and one which was in every respect more advantageous, he nevertheless respected his son's inclinations and refused the sacrifice which the latter declared himself ready to make.

The other example is the behaviour of Oliver Cromwell, whose letters show him to be indefatigable in matters relating to the marriage of his children. On one occasion we discover him seeking and finding a wife for his son, Richard, having refused a more profitable match because of the lady's lack of Godliness. He struggled for two years to get more advantageous terms from the father of the lady of his choice, yet made the final decision dependent on the young people's liking each other. It would appear that in the end such a clause became standard practice, for we find that somewhat later there is an allusion to this in Defoe:

> do we not always, when we make Proposals one to another for our Children, make this Condition, *viz. if the young people can agree?*
> (*Religious Courtship*, I, 3)

When however the marriage had taken place, he not only shows himself very generous towards his opposite number, whose performance lags badly behind his obligations, but adopts towards his daughter-in-law a tone so warm and respectful that the nature of his purpose is clearly apparent: it is to convince her that a son- or daughter-in-law can command his heart just as much as his own children. The conduct books, I might add, point out again and again how necessary it is that a son- or daughter-in-law should be so convinced.

18. *Reasons for the discomfort in family relationships: suppressed position of the mother*

Needless to say, parental authority did not always respect emotional and spiritual needs in quite so enlightened a manner. And indeed, if it were to do so, there would have had to be a much greater intimacy between parents and children than was usually to be found at this time. In general, the reasons for this situation are to be sought in the depressed position of the mother. The family in so far as it is a temperamentally harmonious whole, receives its characteristic imprint from the mother—as later ages were clearly to show. The mother's tenderness is the oil which calms the frictions in everyday life, it is the mother's understanding which bridges the gulf between characters that are hopelessly and unavoidably incompatible and binds together those who would otherwise break irremediably apart.

It is essential that the mother should have a special place in the family and that the unique value of the quality of motherliness should be appreciated. There is, however, a mass of evidence to show that, in the period under review—and for some time to come—there can be no question of anything of this kind. No fine literary feelings can disguise the fact that the ideal of cultured people was that of masculinity whose rough nature had little understanding for the loveliest features of the feminine character.

No better example can be found of this distorted vision than the lines from *Julius Caesar* when Cassius says:

> But, woe the while! our fathers' minds are dead,
> And we are govern'd with our mothers' spirits;
> Our yoke and sufferance show us womanish.
>
> (I, 3)

When in *Coriolanus* Shakespeare sets himself the task of showing us the influence of a mother on a wild and unruly character, he does not draw the picture of a motherly woman whose mollifying manner and wisdom of understanding melts the steely hardness of the man she is seeking to move. He shows a Spartan and thoroughly masculine type who triumphs in a violent collision with a son who is no more than a replica of herself. In many cases, however, the dramatists of the day when representing the family contrive—in a manner that to ourselves would be incomprehensible—to do without any mother at all.

In *The Tempest*, for instance, Prospero strands the court of the King of Naples and the Duke of Milan on a magic island but though they have come from a wedding in Tunis not a single woman is to be found on that wrecked ship—the ladies apparently being nervous of any such voyage—and the same is true of the accompanying vessels which have disappeared. Again in the long introductory speech of the same play Prospero is telling his daughter the story of his banishment from Milan. The daughter listens spellbound. She then begins to question him on all the various details of the affair, but it never once occurs to her to enquire about her mother. Only once when Miranda asks Prospero whether he is her father is there a quite casual mention of that mother in Prospero's most cautiously framed statement:

> Thy mother was a piece of virtue, and
> She said thou wast my daughter.
>
> (I, 2)

This is surely an astonishingly brief description. Yet if we examine imaginative literature up till well into the eighteenth century we shall find a remarkable number of cases in which an equally casual attitude towards the mother can be observed. In Johnson's *Rasselas* and its continuation *Dinarbas* we have fathers and sons, even brothers and sisters and not a word is uttered about the mothers of the heroes.

That the mother is essentially an unimportant person is something which the historical evidence of these centuries makes plain wherever we look. That is why, in the case of the earlier biographies, anyone wanting to learn something about the subject's relation to his mother is liable to be disappointed.

Thus we do not get so much as a mention of the mother of John Locke, we do not even know how long she lived, though a friend of his claims to have heard him say that she was loving and pious, but that is absolutely all, though we know some highly individual details about his father. Similarly we know nothing of any significance about the mother of Addison and the same applies to Fuller, Steele, Cibber and Dr Joseph Warton. It is strange that artists, of all people, should tell us so little about their mothers, for studies in heredity have shown how often it is the mothers from whom their gifts derive.

It is much the same where the Puritans are concerned. How little—to take but one example—do we know of Milton's mother! When Baxter describes the day of his youth in his *Reliquiae Baxterianae* (1696), he speaks only of his father.

In view of the improvement in the position of women under Puritanism this may seem surprising. Yet such improvement was necessarily limited by the prevailing circumstances. It is true, as we have seen, that women played a more important part than before in their children's education, in so far as they were expected to instruct the latter in the catechism. Special 'mother's catechisms' were produced for this purpose. One of these was divided into twenty lessons, which, by means of question and answer, imparted the most necessary elements of the 'knowledge of God, of themselves and of Holy Scripture'. But the effects on the wife's position of such deputising for the husband were slight, and we must remember that her duties were only concerned with very small children. Certainly the performance of such duties did not suffice to get her wishes respected in any matter of principle, if they conflicted with those of her husband. The image which was so frequently used, which compared husband and wife to sun and moon, is very illuminating and shows clearly what position the mother really occupied within the family. As the moon obtains its light from the sun, so in the family the mother receives her authority from the father.

Even the most advanced minds did not dare to question such a view. How firmly it was held is shown by the way in which the duties of children tended to be defined when a prospective marriage was under consideration. It was laid down again and again that it was a sin to marry without the parents' consent. Yet we are told from time to time—somewhat surprisingly in the circumstances—that the really important task is to overcome the resistance of the father (Rogers, page 81). If the mother alone persists in her objections the children may marry with a good conscience. Gouge, with his characteristic perspicacity shows himself aware of the scant regard the mother enjoyed in the eyes of her children and is thoroughly indignant about it (Treatise 5, section 55). Surely he is right to say that this derives from her subordination to the father. Indeed, as far as it goes, such a conclusion is inevitable. What is really important is that he puts part of the blame on the mothers themselves, on the grounds that they are too gentle and forebearing with their children. Elsewhere he sharply condemns the disastrous influence that most mothers have on the bringing up of their children, in so far as—unlike that ideal wife described by Rogers, who actually helped with the thrashing of her children—they endeavoured to prevent them from being thrashed at all and even begged the teachers to whose care those children were entrusted to refrain from beating them. Similar criticisms of mothers are made by the Anglican Tillotson, a much milder man (1694).

We see here how the iron strictness which was still the real basis of all family relationships, together with the prevailing basic principles of education made it impossible for true motherliness to have any appreciable influence, and hindered its expression at every turn. Both the poor estimation in which so many children held their mothers and the foolish fondness which so many of the latter displayed towards the former—Gouge castigates both extremes—was clearly connected with the quality of women's education, with their lack of culture and with the consequent damage to the whole personality. Yet a long time was to pass before anyone became even dimly aware of these facts.

PARENTS AND CHILDREN UNDER PURITANISM

19. *The relations between the children in a family*

The negligible role of motherliness is surely only one among a number of reasons for the lack of sincerity and depth in the feelings between the family members.

Another and somewhat similar defect arises through the rather peculiar mental attitudes of the various children in a family towards one another. It is strange that the conduct books, which subject the smallest details of family life to critical examination, have hardly a word to say about the conduct of children towards each other. Occasional reference is made to the excessively exalted position of the eldest brother (Gouge, Treatise 3, section 23) and, as usual, precedent for this is sought in the Bible. We are also told that a younger daughter, if married, takes precedence over her unmarried sister, but we hear nothing of the privileged position of the eldest daughter, which in England is in some cases acknowledged even today.

The conduct books consistently fail to make any mention of the feelings which the children of a family may be expected to entertain towards one another. In this we can see the effects of a very characteristic notion of that time which rejected the idea of a natural community, of a comradeship among siblings and of any rules governing such a relationship. The only relationships which the family accepts as being of any significance at all are those between parents and children. When these have been defined, everything has been done.

Such a book as Defoe's *Religious Courtship* illustrates all this very well and makes us realize how remote were the then prevailing attitudes from the ideas of a later age. Here we find a daughter engaged in a violent dispute with her father. But although she is in the right and profoundly unhappy, she receives from her sister, who secretly sympathizes with her, none of the support which we today would have regarded as that sister's self-evident duty to give. When appealing to her in her need, all the unhappy girl receives is a somewhat negative reply, 'It's hard for a daughter to make herself judge between her father and the rest of his children', and that of course was the view of Defoe himself (page 30).

One sees from this very typical example how the rigidity of family discipline rendered any personal relationship impossible. In Defoe's *Family Instructor*, moreover, when one of the children is represented as being in the wrong, the conduct of the others is marked by a degree of Pharisaical self-righteousness, by a 'holier-than-thou' attitude which to our own age would appear completely insufferable. If we examine the historical evidence, such as letters exchanged between brothers and sisters, we note with some surprise that a certain tradition of a very similar character has developed, a tradition which causes children of the same family to follow the custom of the time and write 'educational' letters to each other—precocious and grandmotherly exhortations to virtue, designed without exception to remain completely impersonal. It is clear that these letters are something more than mere stylistic exercises and are really examples of the duty of which we can read in Baxter, the duty incumbent both on servants and children to stand by each other when in danger of temptation and sin and urge each other to follow a pious way of life.

That such educational duty was a very old one is evident from the moralizing advice and encouragement that Laertes and Ophelia feel impelled to offer each other. Laertes, although himself still young and very much in need of guidance, as the wise counsels of his father clearly show, dilates on the special moral dangers that threaten their youth and thus moves his sister, who, if anything, inclines to reticence, to repeat these lessons to him after her own fashion.

The idea of the family as a school of virtue, and of the brotherly and sisterly relationship as the providential opportunity for moral instruction, is one which is still apparent in Richardson. In his *Letters Written to and for Particular Friends*—the book from out of which *Pamela* was born—he includes a number of model letters in which an elder brother imparts moral instruction to his brothers and sisters.*

I might remark that Erasmus Darwin appears to have viewed his task as a brother in a rather more light and fanciful fashion—one of his sisters once sought his moral confirmation of an opinion she had formed on the question of whether it was lawful to eat pork at a time of abstinence. The sister had in this case already had the question answered in the affirmative by a clergyman. She had been told that since the Devil had got into the swine and they had rushed down into Lake Gennesaret, they should be regarded as aquatic creatures. (Hog's flesh is fish.) Young Erasmus, who was

* Cf. Lessing's letter to his sister, 30 December 1743 and Mary Cromwell's to her brother, 7 December 1655.

seventeen at the time, replied that during times of abstinence he regarded all meat as a form of vegetable, for the Bible had declared that 'All flesh is as grass'. Such jests must of necessity have been infrequent. There were still too many things that hindered the emergence of that natural comradely relationship which later contributed to the creation of the typical family atmosphere.

20. *The ultimate religious purpose of the family: attitude to life*
It is obvious that we are here dealing with very widespread habits. In a certain sense, of course, the Puritan family was under the influence of special circumstances. On one hand those preconditions of a deep inward relationship were present in the intensive spiritual preoccupation with the children. But if indeed close human relationships were in many instances thus created, such effects were really only secondary ones. For, as was made very clear at the end of the chapter on Puritan marriage, the ultimate purpose of the close association between husband and wife—or between members of a family—and the highest happiness attainable therein, consisted not in a sharing of any purely human experience, however profound. It would be truer to say that the primary function of so close a spiritual relationship as that entailed by marriage—or by that of the family—was to yield a different kind of fruit. Its purpose was to provide mutual help in achieving rebirth and in remaining constant therein afterwards. More than anything else, members of a family were travelling companions on the road to the next world. They assisted each other in warding off anything that might obstruct their progress. Family life, therefore, provides a common bond designed to help in the struggle against sinful impulse.

In the final analysis family relations are a matter of duty and nothing else. It is true that so early a writer as Becon sincerely talks about the human joys which children can bring, and a hundred years later Jeremy Taylor was to describe the peculiar charm of a little child in a fashion that is quite enchanting—although he did remark that, 'To dye without a natural heir is no intolerable evil' (*Holy Living*, chapter 2, section 6) but what a chill goes down the reader's spine when he reads—again in Baxter—that childless couples should give thanks to God for all the toil and trouble, the worry and the care which they have been spared

(*Christian Directory*, page 548). Later Richardson expressed the same idea:

> The man who has passed all his days single, is not always a loser. Children are careful comforts, though good, Daughters when marriageable, especially.

What such utterances show is not so much a lack of understanding for the joys of domesticity (a lack of understanding which is at the root of the remarks made by such people as Lord Chesterfield). What is behind this attitude is that basically Christian pessimism concerning all that pertains to this world, a pessimism that was taken over as part of the heritage of the Middle Ages and caused a man like Rogers—despite the fact that in one passage he most vigorously urges us to rejoice—to make it all too plain in another that he is enclosed by prison walls. Even Milton lets the Archangel Gabriel say to Adam, 'Nor love thy Life, nor hate' (XI, 353). This is scarcely an affirmation of the joys of life.

21. *Asceticism and hostility to youth*
Since the whole value of life resides in the possibility of sanctification which it provides, it is essential that we should keep our eyes fixed on the road—and on that alone—by which the family is jointly seeking to travel to that goal. While the family is thus engaged, little attention is paid to the children *qua* children, and that in particular means that little regard is paid to the stage of spiritual development which they have reached—as indeed we can see from the fact that religious instruction is begun at a ridiculously early age—'from the cradle on', in fact. When we take note of the meticulous delicacy of psychological insight into the inner life of women which Puritan writers such as Rogers display, the lack of understanding for the mental processes of childhood seems astonishing. They have the sense to see that work must be interrupted by leisure if the child is to remain vigorous and healthy both in body and mind, but even Becon already stipulates that children's games should not lack that 'gravity and modesty' which should ultimately govern the whole of their lives. Even later writers such as Gouge, Downame, Rogers, Baxter and others never question the necessity of games, though nearly all insist that indulgence in them should remain within sensible limits. Baxter, incidentally, is particularly emphatic in insisting that those games are the best

which provide vigorous exercise for the body (*Christian Directory*, page 546). Of course such a use of time must never interfere with that set apart for religious duties. Not only on the Sabbath but on feast days too, there must be no games or conversation of any kind, this being a concession to the prescribed 'humiliation'. Finally in all games the element of pleasure also plays a major part and everything that goes beyond mere utility runs the risk of being tainted with evil in so far as it diverts our thoughts from sanctification.

Of course this asceticism had a wide variety of shades and it is by no means easy to say what was typical but it is illuminating to learn from Mrs Hutchinson who as a child was completely immersed in the Bible—'the book', as the Puritans liked to call it—that she was in the habit of tearing all her little playmates' dolls to pieces whenever they paid her a visit. If such a thing was possible in a distinguished home that had some regard for traditional cultural values, what was to be expected from people of the middle classes where the essential supporters of the Puritan movement were to be found?

We can, moreover note the intensification of certain tendencies which have actually been present from the start and now begin to assert themselves. We can see this in the sanctification of the Sabbath. According to Lewis Bayly in his *Practise of Pietie* (1613):

> The *conscionable* keeping of the Sabbath, is the *Mother* of all Religion.
> (page 513)

This, in itself, holds high potentialities for family harmony, though its effects are sometimes not so pleasing. In the main Puritanism, in this as in other matters, was far from invariably destroying the graces of life. Colonel Hutchinson's Puritan opinions, for instance did not interfere with his interests as an art collector or lessen his love of music, while Oliver Cromwell can claim the credit of having saved Raphael's cartoons for England. But the fanatical Puritan in Swift's brilliant satire *The Tale of a Tub*, which belongs to a somewhat later date (1704), carries stones about with him in his pocket to hurl at painted inn signs.

How lively was the interest in music in the comfortable house of Milton's father! (see Davey). It was moreover the family that in those days kept alive the art of part-singing in cultured homes, 'the madrigals being sung by a few friends sitting round a table'. We can see traces of this in Shakespeare's sonnet 8:

> Mark how one string, sweet husband to another,
> Strikes each in each by mutual ordering;
> Resembling sire and child and happy mother,
> Who, all in one, one pleasing note do sing:

Even by the second half of the seventeenth century these interests in the arts had not died out—as we can see from Pepys' *Diary* (1659-69). But the Puritan was increasingly inclined to put them out of his mind and the only outlet which his love of music could find was the singing of Psalms, an exercise that was practised collectively by the family with great earnestness and deliberation. The history of music tells of numerous publications during the reign of Cromwell and this shows that musical life was at that time by no means dead. But the spirit which forbade all profane music on the Sabbath, on the very day, that is to say, on which the amateur might have had the opportunity to indulge in his art, could only have had disastrous consequences.

Home life, as depicted in Defoe's *Family Instructor*, shows no trace of any such enthusiasms, in fact it shows not the faintest sign of any cultural interests whatever. Whereas a man like Downame could speak with real warmth of the recreation of mind and body by means of blameless art, games and the chase, the view of the pietists, as exemplified by Defoe a hundred years later, was that 'recreation is the meanest lawful thing that can be done' (I, 103). All worldly art was in greater or less degree regarded as the devil's handiwork and a reformed daughter showed the completeness of her conversion by throwing all songs, plays, tales, novels and the like into the fire—including presumably those of Defoe himself. No affectionate word is ever spoken. Social intercourse between families, such as one could have found among the unconverted, is now something wholly unknown. The principal visitor is the minister. Reading aloud, once a very popular pastime is in this now very widespread type of family confined to the Bible, to religious works, conduct books and collections of sermons specially designed for home use.

Such conditions are scarcely favourable to the growth of pleasant human relations. In so cramping and oppressive an atmosphere, in circumstances where such continual pressure is applied to force all mental life into exclusively religious moulds, natural human bonds, so far from being strengthened, are burst asunder. If there is to be friendship and mutual liking, if intimate human relationships are to develop, it is essential that there should be freedom. Only where freedom exists, only where characters are strong enough not to allow their humanity to be utterly suppressed by their religion, can the Puritan family provide an opportunity for a real understanding between its members. Yet while we reflect upon the cruel torture which for many this kind of life entailed, let us not forget such cases as that of Oliver Cromwell, who so loved his daughter Elizabeth that her death was one of the causes of his own.

III

Masters and Servants

1. Servants as part of the family

A very characteristic feature would have been omitted in the picture of Puritanism that has just been drawn if nothing was said of the relation between master and servant, for this was a part of domestic life that was of sufficient importance to claim a very considerable degree of attention from the Puritan theorist.

Here too we can observe the persistence of a mediaeval tradition which treated servants as part of the family. Of course there is no thought of making so great a concession to religion as to wipe out all those divisions between classes which are part of the ordering of this world. That ordering, and all that it implies, does not simply disappear because all men are equal before God. The fact that in practice the Baptist sects drew far-reaching conclusions from this caused very palpable offence. In 1618 Daniel Dyke lets us know his opinion by pointing out the fact that, as Paul recognized status, he was not of the Anabaptists. As against this Singer rightly claims that no such injunction could ever appear in Puritan writing as John Locke's warning to parents not to let their children associate with servants, since the company of the latter might well prove dangerous to their morals and character (Locke, § 59). And indeed such ideas belong to what is, sociologically speaking, an entirely different world. Obviously there can at this stage be no case for erecting social barriers. To do so would create difficulties in the house of a merchant or an artisan and a large part of the body of Puritans was made up of just such people. The acceptance as apprentices of the sons of business friends, a practice which usually entailed the payment of a premium and so brought a small increase to the master's capital, caused a kind of 'greater family' to come into being. Elizabethan dramatists have already introduced us to the stage-struck apprentice who, left in charge, silences his master's unruly children with bombastic passages from such plays as *The Spanish Tragedy* (Thomas Kyd, 1587). According to Defoe, it was customary among shopkeepers and wholesalers up to the end of the seventeenth century for the apprentice to clean shoes, carry water, wait at table and carry the master's prayer book before him when going to church.

The prevailing circumstances, as far as servants were concerned, were essentially patriarchal. An old proverb speaks of England as being a paradise for women, but in the same breath describes it as hell for horses and purgatory for servants. This seems to suggest that at one time the servants' lot had been a hard one. Perhaps it was for this very reason that the Puritans laid down precise rules governing their treatment.

2. Duties of either party

Here, too, Biblical precepts were followed:

> And that servant, which knew his lord's will, and prepared not himself, neither did according to his will, shall be beaten with many stripes.
>
> (*Luke*, XII, 47)

Such principles remained unchanged for centuries. Becon's teacher, Latimer, had already developed a theory of service according to which it was directly due to the master but indirectly to God Himself. But since God must be obeyed rather than man, no doubt is left as to where the limits to a master's power to command are to be found.

> Masters, give unto your servants that which is just and equal; knowing that ye also have a Master in heaven.
>
> (*Colossians*, IV, 1)

The principle that Calvin had worked out with great exactness— Calvin was in this particular in agreement with Luther—that children must regard their parents as strangers immediately they seek to make them transgress God's commandments is valid for the Puritan servant's duty towards his master. This question became highly relevant in the matter of Sunday labour and here there were many who sought to calm the servant who had been told to undertake it by saying that if indeed a sin were thus committed, it was a sin on the master's conscience and nobody else's. But this was something that the Puritan could not possibly accept, for none can be exempted from the dictates of his conscience through the command of another.

Most important is the servant's attitude towards the master, and we would do well to note how seriously his task is viewed. As in marriage the duties of husband and wife cut across each other, so here in many matters both master and servant are each held to have their own responsibilities. But it is the master who has the greater share of responsibility. Attention is paid in this connection to the lessons of antiquity and particularly to those of Seneca. But instruction also proceeds by means of parables from ordinary life. Thus the worthless servant is compared to an unreliable watch, and we are told that if the master does not set a good example, it is as though the principal clock in the house were wrong (Gouge). It is the master's duty—as far back as Becon (1560) the duties of masters have been firmly laid down—to safeguard the morals and religion of his servants, to treat them with humanity and justice in apportioning their work and to teach them that the religious obligation is the most important and the one which holds men's attention over the longest period of time.

It is this obligation that people had in mind when they declared, as they often did, that servants only differed from the children of a household in a very slight degree. Tyndale for instance, enjoins us to 'nurture' them as we do our own sons in instruction concerning the Lord (*The Obedience of a Christen man*). Jeremy Taylor, Downame, Bunyan and others write in a similar vein; not only must masters make sure that their servants attended church, they must hold themselves responsible for the latter's religious life as a whole in exactly the same way as they watch over the religious life of their children.

This means that not only children, but servants too, must be catechized by the head of the household and examined to see whether they have fully understood the sermon. This is a duty in which no less a one than the Patriarch Abraham sets us an example and a formidable example it is, for as Lewis Bayly points out in his *Practise of Pietie*, the most widely read book of devotion which the seventeenth century produced, Abraham performed this duty in most punctilious fashion towards no less than 318 manservants, and it is a duty from which a master cannot be absolved. Closely connected with this duty is that of consideration for servants on Sunday—as the decalogue demands. As to the care for the moral welfare of servants, as early a writer as Becon had already enumerated a number of rules of an essentially pietistic character. The master must forbid the singing in the kitchen of 'filthy balades and songs of love' and get those so engaged to sing the psalms of David instead, he must settle all quarrels between the servants and when the grounds for such have disappeared he must re-establish among them a friendly attitude towards one another. This presupposes a human relationship and indeed this is something to which great weight is attached. That one must be patient and considerate with servants, and must not treat them as though they were either slaves or cattle is a principle with which the Stoics were already familiar and one to which reference is made again and again from Bullinger-Coverdale onwards—Tyndale alludes to it too. Becon goes so far as to give practical instances of its application by enjoining masters not to throw pots and plates at their servants' heads. Later the insistence tends rather to be on the moderation of punishments. Since corporal punishment was quite the normal thing in the case of children, it is easy to understand that servants should not have been immune from it, and so we find Tyndale treating the thrashing of servants as the most natural thing in the world. All that he asks is that the word of God should be invoked, that revenge should not be a motive and that, if a master exceeded the just measure, he should show mercy on some other occasion.

Nearly a hundred years later Gouge was to give very precise directions about this and among these we should particularly note the one which enjoins that the chastisement of male servants is to be undertaken by the head of the house while that of females is to be administered by his wife—actually St Chrysostom had already made this point—and it is only when the wife is physically too sensitive or when she is sick or pregnant, that the husband may take her place. By their silence on the master's right to such forms of disciplinary power, later writings such as those of Gouge and Baxter reveal that people's views on these matters were no longer quite the same as they had been at the beginning of the century.

Circumstances had changed. Addressing himself to the servant, Tyndale had defined the latter's relation to the master in the words, 'Thou art his good and possession, as his ox or his horse'. But in a later age a different note had to be struck. Even the doctrine (Gouge, Treatise 8, section 17) that a master might not marry off his servant had ceased to have much relevance. Much was now revealed as a mere dictate of utility which had once been paraded as a command of morality. Tillotson admits at one point with refreshing frankness that:

> it is really of our service and advantage that those that belong to us should serve and fear God; Religion being the best and surest Foundation of the *Duties* of all *Relations*.
>
> (*Six Sermons*, page 73)

Gouge enjoins masters to make no inordinately high demand on their servants and not to endanger their health by putting over-heavy burdens upon them or injure them by subjecting them to bad conditions of work. Of course, such demands admitted of widely different interpretations. In the matter of sleep, for instance, Gouge declared five hours to be a minimum and seven a maximum requirement (Treatise 8, section 29). We must, however, not overlook the fact that people were thoroughly alive to their duty of caring for their servants in sickness or when they were no longer capable of work and of making the necessary dispositions in the event of their death.

> Know that it is thy duty so to behave they self to thy Servant, that thy service may not only be for thy good, but for the good of thy Servant, and that both in body and soul.
>
> (page 60)

So wrote Bunyan in his *Christian Behaviour* and this idea is to be found in all descriptions of the master-servant relationship. Even Becon declares that a master should be concerned for the future welfare of his servants, and that he should be grateful to them for their services. This last was somewhat expanded by Downame who held that after the end of his service a servant should be regarded as a friend. As long as his service lasted however, he remained a member of the iron theocracy of the Puritan family.

The catalogue of servants' duties as set forth by such writers as Gouge is extremely long and certainly affords an insight, as does no literary testimony, into the inmost heart of an English household of the seventeenth century, but it certainly shows that the sense of community created by the religious bond has on the whole not diminished the demands made upon the servants.

3. *Change in views and circumstances*

To understand what happened we must go back quite a way, for it is the seventeenth century which brings the sweeping changes, and of course these do not leave the family unaffected. For instance, the relation of the apprentice to his master becomes an entirely new one. The apprentices have turned into young gentlemen whose premiums represent a considerable amount of capital. They no longer perform any menial duties but are actually waited upon themselves. Even the servants did not remain unaffected by the social upheavals of the time; their feeling for personal dignity rose perceptibly with the spread of democratic ideas. The skill they displayed in applying the grand idea of freedom, of which they had heard so much, to their own affairs was sufficient to evoke many a sigh from their masters. Defoe gives many instances of such awakening among servants of a sense of human dignity. It is evident that such things formed a prominent feature of discussion. Bishop John Tillotson said, not wholly without reason:

> For when *publick Laws* lose their Authority, it is hard to maintain and keep up the strict *Rules* and *Order of Families*.
> (*Six Sermons*, page 79)

This social battle is reflected in the amusing title of Defoe's work of 1724—*The Great Law of Subordination consider'd or, the Insolence and unsufferable behaviour of Servants in England duly enquir'd into* (cf. Aitken, vol. II, 163 ff.).

Complaints about servants, of course, are anything but new, but never had they been so fierce as now, for now amongst others the economic factor was at work; labour was being drawn off into the growing wool trade and was leaving the land. This created a peculiarly critical situation. It caused a loosening of the old patriarchal bonds. Where, however, they still remained, as they did in the Puritan family, the servant—rightly or wrongly—gained the impression that this curtailment of his rights, which was so little in accord with the times, was the result not of religious considerations but of simple egotism.

That is why, as we read, amongst others, in Bunyan that heretical views had begun to be voiced among servants according to which they were fundamentally better off among the 'carnal' than among the saints, while the masters, despite their determination to have none but religious men and women handling their brooms and their pots and pans, agreed amongst each other that religious servants were often impertinent, self-opinionated and demanding (compare Defoe, *Religious Courtship*, Appendix III, 2). The supposed patriarchal relationship, which till then had only been hesitatingly called in question, was later revealed in the dazzling brilliance of Swift's *Directions to Servants in General* (1745) as a sheer travesty of reality. (See also Defoe's *Everybody's Business is Nobody's Business*, 1725 and Jane Collier's *An Essay on the Art of ingenuously Tormenting*, 1753, the latter stating the opposite point of view.)

IV

The Image of the Puritan Family in Literature

(a) MILTON'S CONCEPTION OF MARRIAGE

1. Paradise Lost *as a conduct book*
Among the proofs of the dignity and sanctity of marriage adduced by Puritan writers, especially among those used to refute the Papists, it was rare for the argument to be omitted that God Himself had ordained the first marriage which was that between Adam and Eve. With that engaging simplicity which characterized the early masters people thought of Adam as a good Puritanically-minded head of the household who instructed his family in the catechism ('Adam catechized his family', we are told by Philip Henry, 1631-96) and pictured his life very much after the pattern of their own. It is in many ways instructive to note that even for Milton the Puritan way of life is in many respects the model on which he bases the descriptions in *Paradise Lost*. Indeed in certain parts of the great epic we feel that we have a kind of poetical conduct book before us which actually anticipates certain artistic forms with a similar content. Most certainly in its portrayals of married life the work breathes the spirit of the Puritan book of marriage. Again and again Adam's relation to Eve is deliberately spoken of as a marital one and the frequency with which the terms 'matrimonial love' or 'conjugal love' are used shows clearly—as does the phrase 'domestic Adam'—what system of ideas makes up the background of such scenes.

It may perhaps be objected that the general atmosphere of the poem which in many places is saturated with eroticism to some extent contradicts what I have said, and indeed those passages are generally considered among the finest in the poem in which Adam is described as being positively drunk with sensual desire when God brings Eve into his presence, a creature already skilled in love. Again and again the poet dwells on the captivating charm and bodily grace of the naked woman and paints his picture in glowing colours. He makes certain that we are in no doubt as to their effects, which do not even leave the tempter himself unmoved (IX, 444 ff.).

All this strikes us as anything but Puritanical. But we must realize that the atmosphere which these parts of the poem are intended to call to mind is that of the honeymoon.

> Nor gentle purpose, nor endearing smiles
> Wanted, nor youthful dalliance as beseems
> Fair couple, linkt in happy nuptial League.
>
> (IV, 333 ff.)

I have already explained that Puritanism was much too rational not to recognize the justification of the physical side of love in marriage, that of the 'undefiled bed'—indeed it is significant that this expression which is so frequently used, occurs, amongst other places, in this particular passage (IV, 761). In saying this we can ignore certain secondary trends associated with the Reformation, against which Calvin himself had already set his face. Gouge expressed his indignation in *Domesticall Duties* (Treatise 4, section 42), where he inveighs against the shameless who follow the example of Isaac and Rebecca:

> And it came to pass, when he had been there a long time, that Abimelech king of the Philistines looked out at a window, and saw, and, behold, Isaac was sporting with Rebecca his wife.
>
> (*Genesis* XXVI, 8)

It is more to the point that we should note such a passage in which Daniel Rogers speaks of the *Song of Songs* and refers—admittedly with great caution—to the beauty which a woman has in her teeth, her forehead, her lips, her bosom, her thighs, even in her walk. Therefore Milton here is above reproach for in this case he has not departed very far from the standards prevailing in such matters, though the forceful and deliberate assertion of the right to shared erotic experience may in some cases have provoked a certain feeling of discomfort.

2. *Intellectual and spiritual communion*

However that may be, Milton was wholly in line with the ideas of his time when he described the sharing in marriage of spiritual and intellectual experience. The picture which Milton draws of Adam as Eve's teacher is very similar to that set forth more or less uniformly in the conduct books of the good husband and head of the household. For it is the husband's duty to awaken in the wife a thirst for religious knowledge and to satisfy that thirst. Adam instructs Eve in much the same way and answers her questions about the stars and explains on the basis of his own scientific knowledge the real nature of her dream and of dreams in general. Here, as in the case of the angel's expositions, she is represented as being fully capable of understanding what she is told.

In yet another passage Milton lets the woman show herself more adept than the man in the running of a home, though the poet unhesitatingly treats her superiority in this particular as something exceptional. This view does not derive from Plato (compare A. H. Gilbert); it is a commonplace in Puritan writers.

Another point of similarity between Milton's picture and the Puritan home is the practice of joining together in religious exercises. Exactly as in Puritan households, the day begins with a hymn of praise 'either in prose or verse', extolling the Creator's work in nature, while a night prayer is recited in unison before both retire to the couch of love.

3. *The sharing of work. The duty of living together*
Even more indicative of the general trend of ideas in the light of which the poem must be read is the need to which it bears witness of work undertaken in common. Despite the fact that the fortunate inhabitants of Paradise are assured of the satisfaction of all their needs, they nevertheless find the thought of idleness intolerable. The daily portion of labour both for body and mind which is allotted to man is a sign of his dignity. That is why Adam in the Garden of Eden busies himself with the work of a gardener and checks the wild natural growth of bush and tree, an activity which accurately reflects the seventeenth-century attitude towards nature and the gardener's task; Eve shares in this work by tending her flowers.

In all this the emphasis is very definitely placed on the fact that creative activity is shared, that it is the work of 'joint hands', all of which really repeats what is to be found in the conduct books, where the wife is pre-eminently the helper of the husband (Rogers, page 303). It is entirely in accordance with the very emphatic and repeated warning given by these books that one of the chief reasons for the disaster which overtook our first parents should have been the circumstance that the woman, though not compelled to do so, kept herself at a distance from her husband and worked by herself. It was this that gave the tempter the opportunity to approach her when her husband was not at hand to lend her his aid.

The following words are put into the mouth of Adam:

> The Wife, where danger or dishonour lurks,
> Safest and seemliest by her Husband stays,
> Who guards her, or with her the worst endures.
>
> (IX, 265 ff.)

This is in harmony with the teaching of such a writer as Gouge, teaching which he develops in long spun out arguments (Treatise 2, part 2, sections 14-17) on the necessity for husband and wife to avoid separation from each other. All treatises on marriage set forth this view in great detail and condemn any kind of spatial separation whether by night or day—separate bedrooms, for instance. They frequently complained that the evil practice of married couples living apart from one another was becoming ever more common—often as a result of demands by the wife—a fact that seems to show that Shakespeare's solitary life in London was at that time nothing unusual (compare Fripp).

This conception of work as the foundation of human dignity makes the Biblical conception, which regards it as a curse which is closely bound up with the expulsion from Eden, somewhat difficult to entertain. Indeed Adam deals with the latter notion in a distinctly heretical way:

> With labour I must earne
> My bread; what harm? Idleness had bin worse;
> My labour will sustain me;
>
> (X, 1054 ff.)

4. Sharing of pleasures. Hospitality. Picnic with the angel
But of course labour is not intended to make man unhappy. That would go contrary to his divinely appointed end which is happiness.

> Yet not so strictly has our Lord impos'd
> Labour, as to debarr us when we need
> Refreshment, whether food, or talk between,

Food of the mind, or this sweet intercourse
Of looks and smiles
                                                    (IX, 235 ff.)

This too is a thought wholly in keeping with the contemporary system of ideas. Now among the ideal pleasures of the married state that of hospitality ranks very high. It is a virtue on which the conduct books, basing themselves on *Romans*, XII, 13 and *Hebrews*, XIII, 2, insist again and again, a virtue that it is particularly necessary to display towards co-religionists, towards the 'saints' (Gouge, Treatise 2, part 2, section 42). Even the old Church Fathers (see Jonas of Orleans, liber II) could not praise it too highly.

In the relevant Biblical passages we hear of shelter being given to angels and perhaps it was this that put the idea into Milton's mind of letting the angel Raphael be the first guest to be entertained in Adam and Eve's household. This scene is in many ways highly informative, for there is probably nothing in all the narrative literature of the seventeenth century that comes so close to the spirit of bourgeois art of a slightly later time. As we read of this picnic, partaken on mossy seats, the picnic at which the 'winged saint' is the guest—Defoe was later to take severe exception to such description of an angel (see *Political History of the Devil*, page 69)—as we read this, we seem to be transported into the world of *The Vicar of Wakefield*. Eve busies herself on behalf of her husband and his guest and shows how, despite the simplicity of the 'rural repast', she has mastered the art of providing variety in the dishes ('not to mix tastes'). We seem to be watching Deborah Primrose displaying her housewifely gifts. Yet when we read this charming and idyllic description of women's domesticity, we are immediately struck by a thought that so patently inspires much bourgeois art, namely that it is in just such doings as these that woman develops a quite peculiar charm and one that makes it easy to see how a man might lose his heart to her.

All this is but a great song of praise for spiritual and physical community in marriage. Its summit is that Augustinian 'household peace' (X, 908) which according to the conduct books constitutes the very essence of human happiness. Indeed, so meaningful is this love that it 'is the scale by which to heav'nly Love thou may'st ascend' (VIII, 591 f.).

This last, incidentally, is an image which need not immediately recall the name of Dante, as A. H. Gilbert seems to think, but is much more readily intelligible if we relate it to the idea of the 'mystery of marriage' which is an ancient inheritance of Catholic doctrine. Amongst others the author of *Dives et Pauper* (folio 197b) seems to have something of this sort in mind when he declares that the love between a man and a woman 'betokeneth the love that we owe to God that is our ghostly husbande, to whom we be all wedded in our baptysm'. Again in Bunyan the idea of a deeper significance being implicit in marriage finds expression in the thought that one of God's chief purposes in the institution of marriage is that Christ and His church should be symbolically present wherever there is a couple which has received the grace of faith. The teaching of the mediaeval theologians, as von Eicken shows (page 450), followed almost exactly these lines.

Gouge (Treatise 2, part 1, section 26) gives the idea a slightly different twist when he adopts a more rationalist tone and declares that even as parents, through the love they feel towards their children, have a better understanding of the love of God, so the happily married are better able to understand the nature of Christ who is married to the soul of every believer.

There is something very profound in this idea that we find our way towards heavenly love through its earthly counterpart. We can detect more or less the same thought in Goethe's *Faust*; indeed there is something distinctly Faustian in the actual architecture of the poem through the contrast between its main action on the one hand which is concerned with the destiny of the world as such, and affords perspectives into immeasurable aeons, and the idyllic story of a pair of lovers, on the other, with all its wealth of homely detail. This similarity between Milton's epic and *Faust* is more than merely fortuitous. For Milton, as we have seen, is the child of a new age which, thanks to its incipient bourgeois character, has begun to realize that the happenings of ordinary life, if rightly regarded, need by no means be wholly trivial in themselves. That is why Milton can discern poetic qualities in the domestic idyll as much as in the gigantic design of the battle between heaven and hell which corresponds more closely to the traditional notion of the poetic. In a later age when the bourgeois values in art had begun more effectively to assert themselves, Goethe, basing himself on a very similar conception, combined the idyllic Gretchen theme with the mighty problems of *Faust* proper.

THE IMAGE OF THE PURITAN FAMILY IN LITERATURE

5. The reasons for the catastrophe. Eve as a representative of womanhood. Her weakness

Yet why does the happiness of Paradise come to such a pitiful end? I have already indicated the essential lines along which that question is to be answered. There are however yet other reasons and these are to be found in the whole relationship between man and woman. Looked at thus, the story of *Paradise Lost* is basically a treatise on the problem of marriage, for there can be no doubt that Adam and Eve are each intended to be typical of their sex. The decisive element in this problem is the way in which woman is conceived.

Now how does the image of woman appear to Milton's inner eye? In a sense the answer to that question throws light on the character of an entire new literary era. Woman is above all else the possessor of infinite external charms, she is so beautiful that Satan himself is seized with sensual desire for her (IX, 469). Milton lays bare all his artist's heart, that heart which delights in sensual joys, as he gazes enraptured on her naked beauty. She comes before us in all her natural chastity and dignity, and her whole being radiates charm and love for her husband. An air envelopes her that is full of true delicacy of soul. She is so sensitive that an oppressive dream brings tears to her eyes. So far we are dealing with an ideal figure which betrays its origin in the conceptions of the seventeenth century by the emphasis placed on sensual charm and on sensibility. However this picture also displays certain features that express specifically feminine weaknesses, weaknesses which are palpably intended to contrast her character with that of her husband.

There is something engaging in her action when she deserts the company of her husband and the Angel Raphael because the angel talks so much and she prefers to listen to her husband—especially when he interrupts his scientific expositions with kisses and caresses. Her conduct becomes more questionable however when, apparently obeying some irresistible urge in her nature, she listens at the door (IX, 277). Nor are we edified when we are told of certain petty instances of dishonesty in her conduct—as when, having herself eaten without Adam's knowledge of the forbidden fruit, she deliberates whether she should not conceal the whole matter from him and, having become his equal by the wisdom she now has gained, continue simply to live by his side. Afterwards when, despite this, she has told Adam what she has done, she gives the astounding excuse that it was for his sake that she had carried out the experiment (IX, 877). Clearly there is an element of deceit in her love. It is also very apparent that she is easily irritated and easily dissatisfied. When her husband very properly remarks that Satan's cunning must be guarded against, she sees in this an insulting lack of confidence and insists on an explanation.

Adam on the other hand on this occasion shows himself capable of all that could be expected of him as a married man, for 'in his care and Matrimonial Love' (IX, 318-19) he displays that virtue of 'family patience' which the conduct books say is like a pack of loose wool which, if necessary, can stop a cannon-ball; he doubles his tenderness, he finds 'healing' words of a very flattering nature yet completely fails to overcome that spirit of contradiction which is all too apparent in his wife.

The realism displayed in this scene almost makes one feel that one is reading a passage from Defoe's *Family Instructor* such as the scene (Book III, dialogue 3) which shows us the irritated wife with her spiteful tongue attacking the husband who remains conspicuous for his iron self-control. (It is worth noting that, just as in Defoe, the husband, despite all his wife's provocations, continues to preface all his remarks with the words 'my dear' without eliciting any corresponding response, so here the excited Eve, unlike her husband, no longer feels constrained to utter any friendly word when addressing him.) Lacking in understanding as she is, she contrives to assert her will; she works alone and so provides Satan with the opportunity which he desires. Satan sets about tempting her and prepares the way for this by skilful flatteries, to which Eve very readily succumbs. After the disaster when the pair realize its extent, Adam makes a very natural remark:

> Would thou hadst hearkened to my words, and stay'd
> With me, as I besought thee.
> (IX, 1134-5)

To this however Eve makes a very ill-tempered reply. Did Adam expect that she would never have parted from his side. If that were so, she might 'As good have grown there still, a lifeless rib'. She then adds a remark infuriating in its injustice:

> Being as I am, why didst thou not the Head
> Command me absolutely not to go . . . ?
> (IX, 1155-6)

Since Adam did not do this, everything that had happened was, according to Eve, his fault. In this way a great and tragic destiny is reduced to the level of a petty squabble. When at length Eve falls at Adam's feet and begs his forgiveness, her previous conduct robs this act of well nigh all its pathos.

6. *Milton's Strindbergian conception of woman*
As is very apparent, this Eve with her little weaknesses that are very sharply observed and very convincingly portrayed, is the product of a new trend and a new age, an age whose character has already been made evident in the quotations I have given from Baxter and Defoe which so strikingly recall corresponding passages in the poet. Her character is conceived in that spirit of rationalism which everywhere lies at the bottom of Puritan thought. It is a spirit that always cleaves close to reality—and it does so in the present instance. This woman has, as it were, emerged from the chapter headed 'Feminine Weaknesses' in the conduct book and she is therefore very genuine and true to life; there is however about her a certain pettiness and banality that is bound to prove disastrous in any of the great crises of life.

Yet the subject matter of the story by no means necessitated a character of this kind. As far back as the ninth century the great Low German poet who told the story of the Fall in so masterly a fashion in the so-called *Genesis B*, portrayed the conflict between Adam and Eve in a quite different fashion. In this version Adam cries out in his despair, saying that he wished he had never so much as caught sight of Eve, whereupon Eve disarms him with the words: 'Thou mayest well upbraid me, Adam, my friend, but thou canst not be more unhappy than I'.

Milton's Eve is not so magnanimous nor so free from any petty and personal ill-feeling. Of course, at the very end she says some fine words about love and declares that to go with Adam is to remain in Paradise, but this scarcely modifies our general impression that this woman is lacking in any real stature. What an enormous gulf stretches between such a world as this and that of Shakespeare, who builds up his loveliest female characters on their capacity for infinite devotion, for whom the ideal of womanhood is, in the final analysis, synonymous with readiness for sacrifice, with understanding and boundless compassion. We should not however lightly assert that this great gulf implies a kind of divorce between Puritanism and humanity as such, for we have discovered a much higher conception of womanhood not, it is true, in Baxter, but in Rogers (1642) who is most certainly a Puritan writer.

This attitude is peculiar to Milton. It is even more undisguised in his later work, *Samson Agonistes*, where the impersonal chorus erupts with almost Strindbergian hate for womanhood. A woman does not love virtue and excellence. Moreover, she is provided so richly with external gifts only in order to hide her inner lack and imperfection. She deceives at first with gentleness and modesty, but that is her cunning: once she has caught a man in marriage, she recklessly destroys his moral fibre.

7. *Milton's Adam a prig*

This idea is supplemented by the figure of Adam as the typical man: he is another Samson. His tragedy is that he is too dependent on the woman's charms. When he becomes aware of his own guilt he is not portrayed unsympathetically, but imperfectly. For this Adam has a pronounced trait of that type of moral self-protectiveness and false superiority which later his descendants in England called priggishness. Even when speaking of Eve with the greatest passion, he never forgets, for instance, to mention how very much she is spiritually inferior to him. He insists how well he knows that he is much more like God than Eve, and it seems to be one of his paradisial joys to get her to acknowledge this and to listen to statements from her lips declaring his own superior worth (IV, 442 ff., 489 ff.). The conduct books declare that women should be handled gently like pieces of Venetian glass and Adam, for so long as they both are happy, certainly follows this advice. He speaks to Eve...

> ... then with voice
> Milde as when Zephyrus on Flora breathes,
> Her hand soft touching,
>
> (V, 15-17)

and while she is absent weaves a garland for her locks. As soon however as her recklessness has brought disaster upon the pair, he becomes thoroughly offensive, calls her a snake and speaks of her as 'this fair defect of nature' and when God calls both of them to account, neglects the elementary principle that both parties to a marriage should support each other against any third person.

After so many human failings not only on the part of Eve but of

THE IMAGE OF THE PURITAN FAMILY IN LITERATURE

Adam too we cannot help feeling that the plea for mercy by the kneeling and repentant Eve and Adam's forgiveness of her, which he grants with so superior an air, fail somehow to restore the moral balance, while the moral so clearly set forth in a number of places (IX, 1182 ff., X, 144 ff.) that the fault of Adam who had been given so many advantages over Eve, was that he had failed to take account of his position and had failed to exercise that complete authority over his wife which was necessary for her, hardly seems to accord with the facts.

We have however something very similar in *Samson Agonistes*. Here too the blame falls on the woman, Delilah. Yet Milton does not seem to mind Samson confessing that he had married her in order to 'find some occasion to infest our foes'—an intention which, despite the commendable patriotism behind it, could hardly be accounted a sound basis for marriage. Yet in this case too the divinely ordained panacea is the 'despotic power' of the husband over the wife.

8. *Puritanism and the unpuritanical in the relations between the sexes in Milton*

Such a conception as that described above is very far removed from the 'subjection' which we encountered in a previous chapter. Subjection implied the enforcing of the husband's will by persuasion and not by brute force and the avoidance of any domineering gesture; it implied sympathetic understanding and the showing of all possible consideration. Surely Dr Johnson was not so far out when he spoke of Milton's Turkish view of women, though this does not tell us where it was that Milton's ideas on the subject originated (compare Haller, page 122).

Milton was a pupil of Spenser's but he was also a pupil of Puritan preachers such as Gouge and Dod. Mediaeval romantic idealization of woman, an idealization that Spenser transferred from the sphere of extra-marital relations to that of marriage, was combined by Milton with the Puritanical and religious idealization of marriage and of woman as a wife, the result being the classical picture of Puritan marriage that we find in *Paradise Lost*. This enables us more clearly than is the case anywhere else to appreciate the contradictory elements in Milton's make-up. In his general feeling about the institution of marriage, as exemplified by the paean of joy which the subject inspired ('Hail, wedded love,' IV,

750 ff.) he is wholly a Puritan and his writing is attuned to the sentiments of his readers who had been taught and grown accustomed to see in marriage the greatest happiness in life. In regard to woman *qua* woman however, his views derive, if anything, from the worldly outlook of Renaissance society.

These contradictions between the man of the Renaissance and Milton the Puritan cannot however be resolved. A marriage in which the husband has complete dictatorial power is no marriage at all. The side to which his heart really drew him is shown by his writings on divorce, writings that brought him near to demanding free love—a fact that caused Defoe to declare him unintelligible. His unhappy domestic circumstances, his lack of love for his daughters and the latters' contempt for the wishes of their blind father show clearly how far he was removed in his heart from the spirit of the Puritan family.

(*b*) THE FAMILY IN BUNYAN AND DEFOE

1. *Bunyan as husband and father*

However explicitly the relation between Adam and Eve in *Paradise Lost* may present itself to us as that of a married couple, there was too little correspondence between Milton's complicated personality on the one hand and that ideal human type on the other on which the Puritan sought to model himself, for the Puritan attitude towards life to find full expression in his art. Above all else his own temperament was to such a marked degree *un*-bourgeois, his talent for a normal domestic life so exiguous that his art could never give truly effective service in glorifying a way of life to which he was so imperfectly suited.

The case with a man like Bunyan was very different. Bunyan stood far below Milton both as an artist and as possessor of a cultivated mind. Yet Bunyan's manner of life was far closer to the ideal which I have endeavoured to set forth in the foregoing pages. Milton, the married man, became the victim of catastrophe for which his own character was at least as much to blame as any external circumstance and it was the same cause which made him live in a state of strife with his children which could assume quite terrifying proportions.

Bunyan however, the lay preacher, poor and for the greater

part of his life socially suppressed, contrived while in the worst kind of material distress to enjoy the closest spiritual communion with his good wife. When her husband lay in prison for unauthorized preaching, she did not hesitate to take up the battle with stern authority on his behalf.

As to his relations with his children, we know enough about the circumstances of his life to say that he was a most affectionate father. Indeed we are even told—and after what has been said on the subject the information should hardly surprise us—that those who shared his religious beliefs reproached him with weakness and excessive consideration for others. Small wonder then that we find traces of this in his works, and nowhere are such traces more in evidence than in the second part of the book on which his literary fame chiefly reposes, *The Pilgrim's Progress* (1678).

2. *The basic idea behind the second part of* The Pilgrim's Progress
The literary critics have, of course, tended to ignore this second part (1684). Froude, for instance, treats it as nothing but a pale shadow of the first. He feels that Bunyan had really nothing more to say and, as happens in most continuations of famous literary works, is merely serving up matter that is superfluous and second rate.

In so far as it merely deals with the book as a work of art, this estimate may be incontestable. It nevertheless betrays a complete inability to grasp the basic idea behind the whole work. What drove Bunyan to compose this second part is quite obvious when we take the basic Puritan attitude into account. In *The Pilgrim's Progress* he had portrayed a soul which, driven by a terrible fear for its eternal salvation, leaves all that is dear to it behind and in a series of tremendous struggles, depicted in vivid allegories, overcomes all weakness and all repulsion and in the end wins the gift of Divine Grace and so, leaving all that once held it prisoner far behind, enters into everlasting happiness. In this system of ideas —and indeed in the whole attitude of the Puritan—a great deal of mediaeval man continues to live on. Indeed the spiritual features of Christian, the pilgrim, show a strong family likeness to those of the hero of the morality play, *Everyman*, for he, too, having been stirred to the very depths of his being, bids farewell to all on which till now his worldly heart has hung, and, after many desperate battles, seeks blessed death, the way from the transitory to the eternal, from earth to heaven.

But the differences between the reforming seventeenth-century sectary and the mediaeval poet of the fifteenth are nowhere more apparent than in the attitude displayed towards wife and children. In *Everyman* the family plays no part at all. Only the 'kindred' do, and these are to be counted among those false friends to whom Everyman turns in his terrible distress and who in the end contemptuously desert him. The mediaeval poet simply did not know how to treat his wife and children. The rigid individualism of mediaeval religion made it impossible to bring about any kind of fusion between such trivial human relations and the divine ones. It is this that Coulton has in mind when he speaks of a religious *sauve qui peut* prevailing in the Middle Ages, and one could find justification for such an expression in the most widely-known poem of the early middle English period, the *Poema Morale*, which contains the following lines:

> Nu lipne noman to muchel to childe ne to wiue
> þe þe him selfe forgeit for wiue other for childe,
> He sal cumen on euel stede bute him god be milde*
>
> (24–27)

The Puritan, however, no longer felt like that. Bunyan's hero finds it hard indeed to part from his wife and children and only does so because the pressure of conscience has become irresistible. Moreover, he first endeavours to convince his wife that she, too, would benefit by following the course that he himself intends to pursue. But he urges her in vain; she is too attached to the delights of the world, while the children are too absorbed in the pleasures of youth, and so he goes on his weary pilgrimage alone.

All this might quite possibly have been said by a mediaeval writer, but Bunyan goes somewhat further. We realize this once we have grasped what earlier chapters have shown, namely how intensely the believing Puritan felt himself to be a member of a family community in which each was responsible for his fellow members. We must, in fact, understand the nature of that process of spiritual growing into one another which in this context may be regarded as the essential characteristic of marriage.

Christian is saved, but what becomes of Christiana? Christian

---

* Let no man trust too much to child or wife;
  For he who forgetteth himself for wife or child,
  Shall come into an evil place, except God be merciful to him.

is an allegory of the human soul as such but does the human soul have a sex? Surely the story of Christian's battles in the story are meant to signify the experiences not of man alone but of woman too. Can there be any question that this was Bunyan's original intention. Yet it was natural that doubts should at some time have begun to enter the writer's mind and that he should have asked himself whether his symbolism with its imagery of physical combat and the like did not tend to reflect an essentially male experience. Further it was of the very essence of his particular creed to regard the bond between husband and wife not only as indissoluble but as a special aid to sanctification. That being so, the very notion of that bond actually being severed, in the life of his model Christian must have struck him as a very grave moral flaw in his work. Thus it was that he came upon the idea of creating in the pilgrimage of his wife, Christiana, a kind of counterpart to Christian's enterprise.

3. *The conjugal love of the Christian woman*
In this fashion the imperilled idea of marriage was brought back to a position of honour. For now Christiana is overcome by a heavy sense of guilt; she now knows that she has misjudged her husband and has mistaken for foolish fancies and for the morbid product of 'melancholy humours' what was in effect the deepest need of his soul. She realizes that she had not comforted him or even hearkened to him but had hardened her heart against him. Suddenly all his words begin to sound once more in her ears, she pours out her heart to her children and the children join their tears to those of their mother. Since they tenderly cherish the memory of their father, they urge their mother to follow him in company with themselves. And that is what happens. Then a young girl called Mercy joins them who is so impressed with Christiana's new-found determination to follow the road she must travel that she too leaves home and friends in order to reach her eternal goal. She becomes a servant to Christiana, but those of the Baptist persuasion, a creed which the Puritans vehemently rejected and to which Bunyan himself subscribed, held that all distinctions between masters and servants were un-Christian. This being so, it was natural that Mercy should be treated not so much as a servant but rather as a sister or a friend.

The fact that Bunyan created this secondary figure to accompany Christiana makes what was in his mind particularly clear. It was meant to show that not only man but woman too, whether married or not, had to fight her way to eternal salvation independently and that in this endeavour, in which she can and must engage, sex was no hindrance. Bunyan however could not command the artistic genius of a Milton for his subject. He therefore confined himself to describing the sensitiveness of women, their propensity to blush, tremble and shed tears, their fear of dogs and the like, their thoughtlessness and lack of caution. In short, certain external weaknesses which he regarded as peculiar to women he depicted but which never even for a moment were seen to lessen the determination of the woman here concerned to pursue to the very end that which their conscience told them to be right. Nor did these feminine weaknesses prevent the pilgrims from behaving in difficult situations with prudence and fortitude. The fundamental idea here is that God is mighty in the weak.

4. *Themes from family life in Bunyan*
Here then we are shown a little company whose leader is happy to experience over again the trials and sufferings which her husband has already undergone. The family excitement mounts as on their difficult trail they find faint traces of their dear father's footsteps. All this is told with much feeling and Bunyan is clearly endeavouring to give us a picture of family life, the first such attempt to be made. We are now permitted to see how admirably the mother cares both for the bodies and souls of her children, we note how thoroughly she catechizes them and how she worries about them when they are ill.

Of course, to understand the kind of thing that I have just described we must recognize that it has a certain symbolic depth; indeed, as we have already seen, this was a practice in which the Puritan indulged with the utmost boldness when dealing with the most trivial objects. Not even the processes of digestion were spared from undergoing such metaphysical interpretation. Thus, when the eldest son has disobediently eaten the fruits from Beelzebub's garden that were hanging over the wall, he falls ill. The physician is summoned and, thanks to the younger brother's confession, makes a correct diagnosis. A purge is prepared as directed by certain passages in Holy Scripture, but proves too weak and a new one is made 'de carne et sanguine Christi'. This the little patient only swallows after his mother has laid it upon his tongue, declaring it, as she does so, to be sweeter than honey and adjuring him, by the love he bears towards all the members of his family, to refuse it no longer. The patient grows hot and begins to sweat and recovery begins.

Such a mixture of dogma and pharmaceutics accompanied by long allegorical explanation may not suit our modern taste; the passage is nevertheless remarkable as a charming little domestic picture of family life seen through wholly unsentimental eyes, a picture in which the close relationship between the various members of the family is clearly discernible.

There is however yet another passage in this work which, in view of certain later developments in literature, is of peculiar interest. I refer to that describing the wooing of Mercy. Here we have the first vague sketch of the ideal Puritan maiden, a picture whose full development we find in Richardson. Since she is pretty, well-mannered, modest and indefatigably industrious—as from times immemorial young women were expected to be (Becon, folio 536b) —she receives the homage of a young man named Brisk, who admires her virtues. She is however very far from throwing herself away on him then and there, but seeks diligently to learn something of his character and for this purpose enquires of the girls in the house. What they tell her causes her to withdraw. It is hardly necessary for her explicitly to reject her suitor however, since the latter's ardour begins to cool when he sees that she gives away the proceeds of her labour to the poor. The girl is not greatly upset by this since she only wants to marry a man who is in complete accord with her in her beliefs. She is too mindful of the unhappy experience of her sister Bountiful, whose marriage failed through similar discrepancies. The same theme and the same character which is here exhibited in its embryonic form, was fully developed when Defoe came to treat of it. Of course the latter had a much better understanding of something which Bunyan did not yet trust himself to describe—the emotion of love.

Christiana is an exemplary mother in yet another respect; following the advice of a prudent friend, she takes an early opportunity of arranging for the marriages of her children and so it comes about that the sometime consumer of unlawfully gathered plums, though still little more than a child, is with singularly little ado joined to Mercy in holy matrimony.

We are now told of Mercy's pregnancy, a condition which

provides her family with the opportunity of practising the particular kinds of consideration prescribed by the conduct books for such occasions. Mercy takes a fancy to a rather special kind of mirror which hangs in the house where the pilgrims have sought shelter. She expresses the fear that unless she can obtain one she will have a miscarriage, whereupon the mother-in-law, not the husband as laid down in Gouge's 'Duties of Husbands' (Treatise 4, section 50), dutifully hastens to obtain the desired object.

The problem of portraying family life as one aspect of the pilgrimage to eternity is tackled in a rather curious way. But we can see how intensely it occupies the author's mind and how warm a feeling he has for the happiness of the domestic community. Daniel Defoe approaches the subject from much the same angle but with greater talent for realism.

5. *Defoe as a eulogist of marriage: its glorification in* Robinson Crusoe

The author of *Robinson Crusoe* (1719) had wanted to be a Nonconformist minister and throughout the many changes in his life he remained a theologian. He was also a literary businessman who owned a large and 'well assorted' stock to meet every requirement.

We can therefore obtain information from his works concerning the most contrary trends in philosophical thought and literary taste. This makes the fact that his attitude towards the family never changed all the more noteworthy. Defoe is a positive enthusiast for marriage. In his treatise of 1727 he explains in some detail that contempt for marriage is not due to wickedness but to folly, to a vague fear of it, and that

> all that can be called happy in the Life of Man, is summ'd up in the state of Marriage; that is the center to which all the lesser Delights of Life tend, as a Point in the Circle; (page 96)

The ship of human existence is ever storm-bound until it has found this safe passage and can at length ride at anchor.

Now of course the plan of this great masterpiece *Robinson Crusoe* did not allow him to develop these ideas in artistic form, so he immediately set about producing a second volume in order to exploit the success of the first. He then became involved with the problem of marriage, the nature of the story affording the requisite freedom to introduce the subject. In this second volume Defoe describes a second visit made by Robinson to the lonely island on which, by agreement with himself, a number of highly respectable and intelligent Spaniards had established themselves together with some Englishmen, some of whom were of the scum of the human race.

There was in particular a certain man called Atkins, a thoroughly bad lot who had been spared the gallows only through the patience and generosity of the Spaniards, though his attempts at murder and other violent and brutal acts made it very clear that he richly deserved such a fate. Yet, thanks to a quite unexpected turn of events, this man's character was destined to undergo a most remarkable change. He was journeying with two companions who were little better than himself in an endeavour to reach the mainland. They only managed to reach another island, however, whose inhabitants were cannibals, though otherwise kind-hearted people. They made the newcomers a gift of a number of brown-skinned men and women who had been reserved for slaughter. When the company had returned to their original island, the women were distributed by lot among the English settlers. The Spanish would have nothing to do with any persons unbaptized, but the conscience of the English being less squeamish, they accounted themselves fortunate at one stroke to acquire both servants and wives. From this point onwards, however, a spiritual change began to take place in Atkins, a change which plainly showed how the elevating influence of family life, to which the conduct books attached so much weight, could produce its beneficent results even where that life was of the most primitive kind.

All this becomes particularly clear when a shipwrecked 'Papistical' French priest arrives on the island. Needless to say, his clerical conscience cannot tolerate anything so sinful as this 'open immorality' and he earnestly begs Robinson Crusoe, the lord of the island, to guide these immortal souls which, thanks to intensive propagation, now number thirty-six, along the road that leads to everlasting salvation. The regularizing of the various unions now begins to be planned and marriage services are conducted by the priest. The brown-skinned wives recognize the importance of the service with surprising speed and the pleasure with which the old pirates show themselves ready to play their parts makes it plain that, despite everything, their finer instincts are not yet dead. But if the ceremony is to have a deeper meaning it is necessary for those about to become wives to gain some familiarity with the truths of the Christian religion, and the imparting of such truths is a task which, as the conduct books show, should, wherever possible, be undertaken by the husband.

This causes Atkins' long-buried better nature suddenly to break through to the surface. The task which faces him not only stirs him to repentance and begets a desire in him to save his soul, it reveals the presence within him of pedagogic and catechetical gifts which till then had been unsuspected. It was not long before his pastors were watching with ill restrained emotion his breathless efforts to convert the brown-skinned mother of his children, who scarcely understood his language, into a faithful Christian. Actually this was no mean task since the woman confronted her husband-to-be with a number of objections which for him were of a somewhat embarrassing nature. Thus she asked how it came about that, if there is indeed a God who metes out punishment, her husband should nevertheless be doing exceedingly well—which was not at all bad for a savage who but a short time ago was being fattened for consumption by her compatriots. However that may be, the truth of the proposition 'anima naturaliter christiana' was established to a quite astonishing degree and so within a remarkably brief space of time he was able to present himself before the delighted priest beside one who was a true Christian. The day on which this took place was declared by Robinson Crusoe to be the fairest day of his entire life.

The insincerity of all this, its crass tendentiousness and the mawkish sentimentality it contains are things too palpable for criticism, to say nothing of the skilful titillation of our senses by the story of the handing over of naked women, though that is, of course, related with the strictest regard for decency. These qualities surely put this work on the level of the worst kind of tract. It is nevertheless significant that just as marriage and family life play so important a part in the feelings of Bunyan that he introduces this theme into a Christian allegory, so, following a similar impulse, Defoe introduces the subject into an adventure story, which he thus illuminates—doubtless to the delight of his bourgeois readers—with a happy combination of Christianity and sentiment.

6. Defoe's books on marriage

Defoe had already bent his literary talents to serve the cause of practical religion by producing in 1715 his *Family Instructor*. In 1722 he had followed this with *Religious Courtship*. These books achieved what was at that time an enormous circulation. By 1722 the first of them had gone into its seventeenth edition, and the second enjoyed an even greater popularity than the first. As late as 1830 Defoe's biographer, Wilson, stated in a passage that was certainly intended to be taken seriously, that there were few books more suitable than the *Family Instructor* for family reading, for parish libraries or for distribution amongst people of modest means, the last named group being apparently regarded as particularly susceptible to the joys of a religious life. Defoe's third work in this field appeared in 1727, but found fewer admirers; it originally bore the somewhat catchpenny title *Conjugal Lewdness: or Matrimonial Whoredom* but then it was changed to *Use and Abuse of the Marriage Bed*.

The robust lack of inhibition which the book already displays in its title contrasts in a most marked manner with the delicacy and polish that is in evidence in the other books, nor is such crudity reserved for the title alone. Indeed the expectations of frankness aroused by the latter are by no means disappointed, for the book contains most searching disquisitions on marital chastity, the prevention of conception, intercourse during pregnancy, differences of age, and the like. Trimming his sails, as he so often did, to any breeze that blew, Defoe seems here to be making concessions to certain fashions of the day which lacked that increasing refinement of expression characteristic of a later period. But, as has been pointed out, the success of his other books was all the greater. Actually these are, so to speak, the successors of the seventeenth century's numerous conduct books which enjoyed so wide a circle of readers. They disseminated the latter's teaching and presented it partly in epic, partly in dramatic form for the benefit of a world of readers that had not remained wholly untouched by the new interest in literary art forms.

7. The stories of conversion in the Family Instructor and Religious Courtship

There is here little in the way of an explicit development of these ideas. What we are really offered in the *Family Instructor* is a series of family scenes which illustrate domestic life at a point of time when pietistic forms of life were establishing themselves. We are shown these pietistic forms of life leading to crises in that process of sharing spiritual experience that was meant to take place between husbands and wives, parents and children and between masters and servants. These rather bigoted stories of conversion would be of no interest whatever but for the excellence of the author's art, his psychological certainty of touch and the exactitude of his eye for detail, for it is these qualities which enable him to call up before our minds a picture of bourgeois life in England during this period which is unequalled in its sober precision. If, following Edmund Gosse, we set Defoe's novels beside those of Zola, their naturalistic character may quite possibly become even more palpable and we may recognize them even more fully for what they are—coherent pictures of everyday life. The figures in question are indeed the Babbits of the eighteenth century, by which I mean that they represent the characteristic type of Puritan, both in his character as an individual and as a member of a family, in a much more realistic and lively manner than was possible in the protracted theorizings of the conduct books. The thing that holds the family together—by which I mean husband, wife, parents, children, masters and servants—is the sharing in religious life. Children and servants who will not submit to the rules of that life are cut off from it with a degree of intolerance which is all the more remarkable because of the absence of any suggestion in the author's presentation of the matter that such severance separates those of exalted character from the depraved. For we surely cannot help feeling that no adequate reason is provided for driving a daughter or a maidservant from the house because the one wears a patch upon her cheek, reads Boileau, Dacier and other novels and expresses a wish to walk in the park with her brother after service on Sunday, while the other—the case is described in *Religious Courtship*—having worked industriously throughout the week, seeks a little innocent pleasure in the company of her friends. There are whole passages where we cannot rid ourselves of the confusing impression that the author would have given an almost identical account if his purpose had been to show up in a glaring light the narrowmindedness of pious people and their lack of imagination. Thus in *Religious Courtship* we have a bigoted widow who upon the death of her husband, a splendid fellow in every respect, complains that her whole life has been a failure since she could never engage in domestic worship together with him. One cannot resist the feeling that a freethinker such as the late husband could not have been portrayed with such obvious affection if the author had in his heart been on the other side of the fence.

Even so this rather misses the point. In a book which is to serve as a mirror for a religious family, the author's views should not be allowed to affect the argument at all. Certainly it is most unlikely that the ideas objectively set forth in this commissioned work were actually his own. That could hardly have been the case, for he was himself a novelist and produced the very same books that the persons portrayed in these works threw into the fire. But when he produced a handbook for people like these he consistently endeavoured to represent their point of view and did so even more crassly when it conflicted with his own. This held good even in regard to the most extreme opinions such, for instance, as the belief that all excellence and virtue counted nothing if the possessor thereof did not belong to the correct religious persuasion. The success of these books proves that this speculative backing of orthodoxy was fully justified. In so far, however, as art was thus placed in the service of its enemies Defoe has been guilty of committing something like high treason.

And yet, despite everything, this enterprise has been a blessing to literature, for Defoe is the heir to that Puritan realism whose quite astonishing influence we observed in the reflections on life made by Rogers and Gouge. It is by reason of this heritage that Defoe refuses to look at the world through rose-coloured spectacles but describes it as it is, and in this he contrasts sharply with such a writer as Madame de Lafayette in her *Princesse de Clèves* (1673)—a writer who displays an admirable psychological skill and is indeed in this field somewhat in advance of her times but who nevertheless cannot deny her literary ancestry, which is the gallant-heroic novel. Defoe however, despite the inclusion of themes more appropriate to the novel, remains in *Religious Courtship* (which in this regard is his most important work) strictly within the limits of the tract. For all that, he has moved right up to the very edge of the broad highway of literature; one more step— and that step is taken by Richardson—and the connection with the world's literary activity would be fully established.

Here too then old wine is being poured into bottles that are wholly new. For the basic thought behind these 'scenes' is the necessity of choosing none but a religious person as a partner in marriage, the ancient counsel not to be 'unequally yoked'. This thought is already very much in evidence in Bullinger-Coverdale and is thereafter to be found in Becon, who adjures fathers rather to bestow their daughters on a man who fears God though he be poor and humble than on a rich man who has not the fear of God within him and lacks the qualities that such fear brings in its train. From Becon onwards the same sentiment is to be found throughout Puritan literature though with certain very sensible reservations. In this connection it is especially worth noting that a mere difference in religious belief was never—as in Geneva—regarded as an obstacle to marriage (see page 80 ff.).

8. *The development of the feminine soul in Puritanism: Cromwell's daughter and Defoe's heroine*

Nevertheless it is precisely because he holds up the mirror to life that Defoe can make us see the impression Puritan teaching has made. We noted above how Puritanism had brought with it some measure of emancipation for woman in so far as it had made her responsible for herself, even as men were responsible for matters pertaining to religion. It had indeed instructed her to meet this obligation. That was how it was possible, in a time that was not favourable to the mental development of women, for such characters as the truly remarkable Mrs Hutchinson to exist.

Even girls benefited by the trend. Indeed up to a point we might well treat Cromwell's daughter Frances as a typical example. When she was only seventeen, she began to be disturbed by reports concerning the man she loved which threatened her whole future happiness. In this crisis she showed great energy and determination and did her utmost to get at the truth, seeking the help of all her friends (Carlyle, IV, 77). Bunyan had already attempted to draw in rough outline and with little expertise the ideal picture of such a woman in Mercy. For Mercy too, though completely feminine, is sustained by her conviction that she knows the only way which can lead her to her goal and, taking her destiny into her own hands, proceeds along it with the utmost independence of spirit. Since Bunyan's day however there had been an advance both in the views that people held and in the technique of story-telling, though the advance in views amounted to little more than the abandonment of the seventeenth-century attitude which could not stomach the idea of a daughter opposing her father even when she was unquestionably in the right—which is exactly what happened in the three family stories in *Religious Courtship*.

Indeed even Addison had on at least one occasion voiced the opinion that in any quarrel between parents and children his sympathies were on the side of the parents because of the gratitude which the children should feel towards them. This is completely in accord with the ideas of the Puritan moralists whose acquaintance we have made. Defoe however has deliberately concentrated on a situation—to which the teachings of the same authors might very well be applied—the situation in which the children's duty of obedience ceases because the father's wishes are in conflict with the duty owed to God.

In the case in point the father's conduct in forcing a marriage upon the daughter is in itself questionable, but it is doubly wrong in so far as he is endeavouring to force his daughter into a marriage with a man who is indifferent in matters of religion. For the daughter, however, the conflict is a double one, since she loves this man. Thus an artistic problem has shot up like a flower out of so much rubble from the barren dialectic of the conduct books, and it is a flower that could have blossomed nowhere else. The sincerity, depth and delicacy of feeling that had been made possible by centuries of the spiritual culture generated by Puritanism—culture which, by reason of the ruthless rejection of the arts, had never before been reflected in literature—this same depth and delicacy of feeling now suddenly acquires literary flesh and blood.

The highly articulated life of the spirit, as it pulses before us in the writings of a man like Rogers, has suddenly taken on artistic form. We see before us a woman who is a Puritan to her fingertips and nevertheless is extremely feminine. There is about her nothing of the sweet helplessness that was traditionally a part of the ideal image of a young maiden. Rather do her actions follow the directive of Baxter:

> I know you must have Love to those that you match with: But that *Love* must be *Rational*, and such as you can justify in the severest tryal, by the evidences of *worth* and *fitness* in the person whom you love. To say *you Love*, but you *know not why*, is more beseeming

children or mad folks, than those that are soberly entring upon a change of life of so great importance to them.

(*Christian Directory*, page 483)

She conscientiously examines the whole situation and when she discovers that the man towards whom her heart inclines is indeed irreligious, she will have none of him and tries to suppress the affection that has been growing up in her heart. With all the Puritan fear of *passio* she is anxious that her feelings should not involve her in a snare which would at some later time spell much suffering. Here Defoe shows us the moral man—in this case woman—battling with natural man. The double attitude towards her enraged father on the one hand and her treacherous heart on the other takes its toll of her physical strength, so that she becomes weak and ill. In this courageous wrestling with herself she admittedly reminds us of the Princess of Clèves in the famous French novel. In Defoe however everything is much more true to life. He never exaggerates and his powers of observation are superb. He does not miss a single psychological detail, whether relating to the conscious or the unconscious mind. Despite the subtlety of their shades of feeling, all these people have their feet firmly planted on the ground and belong to the world of reality. Defoe never seeks to hide the fact that the recipient of the maiden's affections has an estate which brings him in two thousand pounds a year. Even more important is the circumstance that he has none of that 'highfalutin'' character which distinguishes the Duc de Nemours, the hero of the French tale. True, the inner development of this simple hero is intended to lead up to a conversion. Indeed the conversion of men seems to have had much the same attraction for the pious as the seduction of women had for the Godless. Yet in the description of this process which gradually leads to the unravelling of the knot, and, in particular, of the inner difficulties which result in his change of mind so that the outcome is achieved without loss of dignity to either party, there are a multitude of delicate psychological perceptions of a kind which at that time were wholly without precedent. Surely it is here that we should look for the beginnings of the psychological novel in England.

V

The Convergence of Aristocratic and Bourgeois Culture

(a) THE ROLE OF THE FAMILY IN ARISTOCRATIC CULTURE

1. *The cultural seclusion of the Puritan: the views of the fashionable world*

Whoever examines the general state of culture among Puritans is struck again and again by the extent to which Puritanism is hermetically sealed off from those achievements of native culture which we are accustomed to regard as England's crowning glory. How fanatical for instance—and this fanaticism continued unabated—how fanatical was the hostility towards all that was connected with the theatre! We can learn about that from the story of Shakespeare and the fate of his work. When Gouge, to whom we have so often referred, was discussing the duties of children to parents he had occasion to deal with the case of a son who, urged thereto by his father's ghost, undertakes to revenge that father, conduct which Gouge condemns as un-Christian and contrary to the express teaching of the Gospels (Treatise 5, section 51). One immediately thinks of Hamlet. The marginal note, however, shows that the author was not thinking of Shakespeare at all but of Seneca's *Agamemnon*.

This is typical of the wide knowledge such people had of the classics of antiquity and of their contempt for any product of more recent times. The Reverend Philip Henry, who flourished in the second half of the seventeenth century, was a man of some culture, but when he constructed a list of *viri celebriores*, he did not mention a single poet. In this regard, as in so many other matters, Milton forms an exception. Thus saints are a people within a people; they are a people separated from the rest and held together by the certainty of salvation.

On the other side of the fence however, among the Cavaliers that is to say, nothing is known of the moral values that have taken shape within the Puritan movement; totally blinded by partisan feelings, as in Butler's *Hudibras* (1663), these men brand its members without exception as hypocrites and liars. Indeed the mental worlds of the Puritan and of the courtly society would no more mix than oil and water. It is only very rarely that some kind of bridge is erected between these two camps of the spirit, as is the case with the three volumes of Steele's *Ladies Library* of 1714 which recommended a way of life very much along the lines of the conduct books and which, in setting forth its case, fell back on such varied authorities as Jeremy Taylor's *Holy Living* and Locke's *Treatise on Education*. Nevertheless it is just in spiritual culture that the aristocratic side lagged far behind. We should not of course blindly accept the literature of the court as evidence of actual conduct; such literature is an indication of literary taste and not a mirror of prevailing manners. For all that, certain conclusions can be drawn from the spirit which animates it, from the whole tone in which love and marriage are discussed. Thus in Dryden's *Conquest of Granada* (II, 3, 1) marriage is spoken of as a trap and as the curse of love, and the position of the wife is referred to as a degradation from that of the beloved, lines being added which run:

> Love, like a scene, at distance should appear
> But marriage views the gross-daubed landscape near.

Here the contrast between love and marriage takes a relatively agreeable form, but when in the same poet's *Aurengzebe* the emperor is made to say:

> In unchaste wives
> There's yet a kind of recompensing ease:
> Vice keeps them humble, gives them care to please;
> But against clamorous virtue, what defence?
>
> (II, 1)

then we can acknowledge the wit in the passage but we can also recognize in it the frivolity of an entire class, a class which has completely abandoned the ordinary middle-class citizen's ideas of decent conduct (compare Reinhold).

This frivolous quality lived on in this stratum of society even after the riotous and unbridled tone set by the Stuart court had disappeared. Innumerable satirical remarks in the literature of the time bear witness to the unsatisfactory relationship between husband and wife that was characteristic of the age. When Polly in *The Beggar's Opera* (John Gay, 1728) marries the highwayman, Macheath, her mother is furious and says that if she had to marry she surely did not have to bring a highwayman into the family and declares that Polly will be as much neglected and abused as if she had married a lord.

That such remarks contained rather less exaggeration than might at first appear is evident from the theoretical observations of those who at this time were teaching the principles of social life—and here we must assuredly give pride of place to Lord Chesterfield's grandfather, the witty and relatively open-minded Lord Halifax, from whose pen there appeared in 1688 a little book entitled *Advice to a Daughter* which almost attained the rank of a classic and went into edition after edition, there being no less than twenty-five editions in all.

The degree to which in this book—almost two generations after Rogers—the subordinate position of woman is taken for granted is truly remarkable. She is regarded as completely dependent on the mercy of her husband while the latter's infidelities are treated as just another of the facts of life.

> Next to the danger of committing the fault yourself, the greatest is that of seeing it in your husband. Do not seem to look or hear that way: if he is a man of sense he will reclaim himself ... modesty no less than prudence ought to restrain her ... in these cases your Discretion and Silence will be the most prevailing reproof. An affected ignorance, which is seldom a vertue, is a great one here ... such a behaviour will at last entirely convert him. There is nothing so glorious for a wife, as a victory so gain'd.

Prudence, according to this noble Lord, consists, so far as women are concerned, in seeking to improve the disadvantageous position which nature has accorded them by relying on the weaknesses of their men. The faults and passions of husbands, he says, bring them down to woman's level and make them content to live with the other sex on a less unequal footing, something which they would in no wise consent to do if they did not have the faults in question. A woman, Halifax declares, must therefore thank God for her husband's faults. It is by no means the worst thing that could happen if he turns out to be a downright weakling, for she will then cut the better figure. Contrast this with the words of

Taylor 'It is a sad calamity for a woman to be joined to a fool or a weak person'. ('*The Marriage Ring*', page 153).

In Lord Halifax we have a man whom nobody in his own day accused of frivolity. Indeed he was a man who was most anxious that a beloved daughter should learn from his experience. Yet the idea of marriage as a spiritual harmony, as a sharing of spiritual experience, is totally absent from his work, or, at best, is forced into the background by other considerations. Even the idea of womanly dignity is only weakly developed. For it is actually regarded as a virtue in women if they close both eyes to their husbands' transgressions.

Four years after the publication of *Advice to a Daughter* there appeared Cibber's famous sentimental comedy *The Careless Husband*, in which a wife continually forces herself to be blind to her husband's faults. In the end her patience is sorely tried, for she catches him almost *in flagrante*—to be precise she catches him and her maid asleep in each other's arms. But even under this trial she manages to observe Lord Halifax's advice and master her justifiable anger—she even has sufficient magnanimity to cover her husband's head with her handkerchief, his wig having fallen off.

Such tenderness melts the heart of the transgressor and there is the great tear-jerking scene which we expect from this kind of play and in the end the husband is converted to a better way of life and the wife wins back his affection.

2. *Swift's attitude to the family. Chesterfield and Dr Johnson*

The attitudes that underlie the scene I have just described are such that anyone brought up in the Puritan tradition will find them difficult to stomach. Yet it is remarkable how little understanding there is for the genuine links of kindly feeling that hold a marriage or a family together, even when the spirit of a new age makes itself felt in the preaching of a humanity that has little in it of Cibber and his tawdry sentimentality. Swift furnishes an excellent example of this. Of course everybody's outlook is bound to be affected by their personal experience of life and we might well surmise that Swift's views on such subjects as the family and family life were to some extent determined by the fact that he himself had never known a parental home and so had no pleasant childhood memories linking him to brothers, sisters or parents. When Swift was born in Dublin his father was already dead and he was handed over to a nurse who—against the will of his mother, it is said—carried him off to her own part of the country where he remained for the best part of three years. He can hardly have lived with his mother for long, for she soon went off to England while he himself at the age of six was sent off to school, following the custom of the time.

Such physical separation does not itself of necessity imply a complete estrangement of minds, and Swift often spoke of his mother with childlike warmth. Yet he was all too ready to see in the relationship between parents and children, full of true affection as that relationship may be, only an extension which we may well keep concealed from ourselves of that self-love which his ideal of humanity forbade him to entertain. This is apparent in what he says in *Gulliver's Travels* (1726) about families in the land of the Houyhnhnms:

> They will have it that *Nature* teaches them to love the whole Species, and it is *Reason* only that maketh a Distinction of Persons, where there is a superior Degree of Virtue.

With them the number of children is strictly limited. Any pair of horses that has two male children exchanges one of them for a female. If through some unfortunate circumstance a child has been lost and the mother is already old a new child is allotted them. I might add that in Lilliput, too, children are taken from their parents at the age of twenty months, since parents are rather less suitable than anybody else to be entrusted with their education; they are then handed over to public boarding institutions, where parents can only see them twice a year and then only for a single hour. Thus the family virtually ceases to exist.

It is clear that, like the aristocratic world of his day, Swift was quite incapable of appreciating the real nature of the family, and it is with an equally complete lack of sentimentality that this same Jonathan Swift whose strange heart can overflow with tenderness towards a woman—though admittedly only on paper—can also speak of love and marriage in the land of the Houyhnhnms, where marriages are contracted as the result of the decisions of parents and relatives and are regarded as ordinary pieces of business.

A married couple pass their lives showing the same friendliness and good will towards one another as they display towards any other individual with whom they associate. There is no more amorous tenderness to be found here than there is jealousy, quarrelling or discontent. In describing the Struldbruggs, the unfortunate immortals who are found in Luggnagg, Swift attaches special importance to the fact that marriages are dissolved when the younger partner attains the age of eighty, so that the misery of those who are condemned to live everlastingly in the world shall not be doubled through having to endure the burden of a wife.

We might well find such an observation as this—and in precisely this form—in a Restoration comedy and we will be well advised to treat it here as we would treat it in the context of the comedy and not to take it too literally. We would also do well to remember that the literary *genre* of the Utopia, of which Thomas More was the pioneer, has always tended to delight in humorous paradox where certain facets of life are concerned. As against this, it shows us how strong was the dominant tradition in the outlook of the ruling class. Indeed it was so strong that a man like Swift, who was in many ways the unquestionable superior of that class, should have joined the great chorus of those for whom marriage was essentially a subject for a joke. This period of the early eighteenth century almost certainly touches rock bottom in its publicly accepted scheme of values. The practical result of this was a tendency among the educated classes to avoid marriage. The moral periodicals refer to this phenomenon, which is attested by many observers, as the greatest evil of the time. The number of bachelors among literary men is also remarkable and includes some of the greatest names in this field: John Gay, Shenstone, Thomson, Hobbes, Gray, Pope and Prior. Nay, we find bachelors even among the fictional editors of *The Spectator* in the persons of Sir Roger de Coverley, Bickerstaff and Will Honeycomb, of whom the latter alone gets married— and that in his old age—to an innocent country maid. We hear an echo of this state of things when in Rousseau's *Nouvelle Héloïse* (1765) Lord Bomston seeks a kind of politico-economical justification of the trend by declaring—and there is actually no cynical intention behind the remark—that the duty to marry is only incumbent on people who are truly useful, since otherwise the country would become depopulated. For people of quality however, celibacy was permissible, because in England there was much more likely to be a shortage of ploughmen than of peers.

In the aristocratic world such a low estimation of marriage continues to predominate and this is entirely in harmony with the

ARISTOCRATIC AND BOURGEOIS CULTURE

general acceptance of the hedonist view of life and with that contempt for women which the Cavalier contrived to unite with an extreme outward courtesy towards them. A typical representative of this point of view is Lord Chesterfield who, after contriving to secure a divorce for his brother, declared that he had rendered him the best service that can be performed for the majority of married people. When he says that it is no misfortune for sons to grow up without a father and for parents to have no children, he is reflecting an opinion that was typical of the circle in which he moved.

Dr Johnson belonged to a very different world and his attitude towards the basic questions of life was much more intensely affected by religious trends. Yet his general outlook was, for all that, not so very far removed from that described above. Indeed he too takes a view of the family that is far from favourable. Families, as he explains in *Rasselas* (1759) tend to be the scene of strife. Parents and children, the longer they live, necessarily tend to grow more and more away from one another. With his customary acumen Johnson analyses the reasons for this.

> The opinions of children and parents, of the young and the old, are naturally opposite, by the contrary effects of hope and despondence, of expectation and experience, without crime or folly on either side. The colours of life in youth and age appear different, as the face of nature in spring and winter. And how can children credit the assertions of their parents, which their own eyes show them to be false?
>
> Few parents act in such a manner as much to enforce their maxims by the credit of their lives. The old man trusts wholly to slow contrivance and gradual progression: the youth expects to force his way by genius, vigour and precipitance. The old man deifies prudence: the youth commits himself to magnanimity and chance. The young man, who intends no ill, believes that none is intended, and therefore acts with openness and candour: but his father, having suffered the injuries and fraud, is impelled to suspect, and too often allured to practice it. Age looks with anger on the temerity of youth, and youth with contempt on the scrupulosity of age. Thus parents and children, for the greatest part, live on to love less and less: and, if those whom nature has thus closely united are the torments of each other, where shall we look for tenderness and consolation?
>
> (*Rasselas*, II, pages 3–4)

There is yet another way in which the generations can be a hindrance to each other, and this applies particularly when parents have married young, though it is only an early marriage—one contracted, that is to say, before inward development has hardened into fixed forms—that gives a certain reasonable prospect of success. Yet even here, once children have begun to grow up, a disastrous rivalry between the generations is inescapable, and then there is just not room for them to live in the same house. The grown-up son wants to get pleasure from something which his father does not yet wish to renounce, the daughter begins to bloom before the mother has accepted the fact of her withering, and naturally the one wants the other out of the way. If however, parents marry late, they do not live to see their children when these have grown up and gained understanding.

It is very clear that this observation is only partly concerned with something deriving directly from human nature. In certain very important respects—e.g. when dealing with the son waiting to inherit the estate for instance, or with the mother whose vanity is hurt—it assumes the existence of certain very specific social conditions. Now it is perfectly true that, despite his pessimistic view of marriage and the family, Johnson does not recommend people to remain unmarried. On the contrary, compared with bachelordom, Johnson considers the married state distinctly preferable. Unmarried persons tend to be hard and loveless, they constitute a disturbing element in society, and do nothing to enhance the latter's happiness: 'marriage has many pains, but celibacy has no pleasures'.

It would therefore appear that Johnson is already well on the way to accepting the view that was increasingly to prevail and had already begun to replace the aristocratic way of looking at the matter which for so long had set the tone in public life. It was inevitable that the influence of the bourgeoisie, whose circumstances were so very different, should have helped prepare the way for a different set of ideals.

3. *Family propaganda in the moral periodicals*
It is customary to look upon the moral periodicals, *The Tatler*, *The Spectator* and their successors, as the pioneers of such social ideals. Brie however has rightly pointed out how very much these would-be improvers of the world were prisoners of the aristo-

cratic view (page 38 ff.). He has shown how great was their sympathy for external aristocratic forms, how tame their criticism, how friendly their mockery and how lacking in any earnest intent, and how real their concern for mere entertainment.

The justice of such a view will be particularly apparent to anyone who has engaged in the study of the kind of reformist preaching with which Puritan books had been busying themselves for over a century. In the matter of marriage and the family it is significant that some time was to pass before the contributors to the moral periodicals began to be aware of the attitudes which their whole view of life made it incumbent on them to sustain. In one of the earliest numbers of *The Tatler* (7) marriage is simply a subject for jokes, and is symbolized by a man and woman walking arm in arm along a slippery road and for that very reason sinking deeper and deeper into the mire. This is precisely the view adopted by the fashionable world to which later strong exception was to be taken. Later when the periodicals were actually writing in favour of marriage what they have to say strikes us as something deliberately flavoured by a very diluted concoction of Puritan doctrine. That the family, as is eulogistically proclaimed, is the essential unit of the state, is 'part of the Church's oldest philosophy of history' (Troeltsch). That its great merit in the eyes of God lies in the fact that it multiplies the numbers of Christians, is an observation which we can encounter in innumerable other places. Again it is said that by bringing up a large number of children a man has the chance of becoming the progenitor of a noble family in which one child may become a general, another an admiral, another an alderman, while yet another may rise to high office in the Church or distinguish himself as a lawyer or a physician. Yet this is no more than a naïve appeal to vanity which clearly betrays the influence of the social world to which reference was made above. The ways that are advocated to preserve love in marriage are very much to the point and argue a sensitive and delicate mind. We are told that love must be cultivated, that most cases of failure in marriage are due to trifles, that good humour, self-control and mutual consideration are the best props for the sustaining of married life. A number of little hints are given. The wife, for instance, is advised not to dress herself in the presence of her husband. But all this is elementary to any student of Gouge, Rogers, Baxter or Jeremy Taylor, and when it comes to a really profound treatment of the problems of married life, the ideas of the moral periodicals will simply not bear comparison with the work of the above-named writers—especially with that of Rogers.

Nevertheless the real service which these moral periodicals rendered should not be undervalued. By keeping their feet on the ground and speaking as observers of the society in which they moved, they could with greater assurance get on with the work of correcting its distorted points of view. In an age when marriage had become the butt of almost every joke in a comedy, when a correspondent could write to *The Spectator*, though admittedly in jest, 'I am ashamed to admit it, but I'm married', it was surely to the very considerable credit of these periodicals that, once they had recognized the true nature of their task, which was to regain respect for marriage and the family, they should have devoted themselves to it with persistence and quiet determination.

The moral periodicals' family propaganda contrasts sharply with that of the Puritan teachers by the largeness of heart which causes it to lay such stress on purely human factors. A whole series of descriptive scenes lets us see the quiet happiness that marriage can ensure. In due course the reader is able to watch a bachelor visiting a happy and pleasant home inhabited by a husband and wife who live together in unity of mind and have real affection for one another. We see that same bachelor leaving the place with a feeling of sadness in his heart by reason of his own poverty in spiritual treasure. Next we are given loving descriptions of the pleasure afforded by children and their games. Then in due course we witness the death of a happy wife who while dying thanks her husband for all the kindness she has received at his hands. Yet again, we see a family hard hit by the death of the mother and in their grief we become aware of the great value of feeling, of which most contemporaries were still quite ignorant. Even the physical side of the marriage of two young people is looked upon with a kindly eye.

Criticisms of the family are extremely rare. We do indeed get a complaint that a guest is unduly bothered by stories about the children, that he is expected to show interest in the signs of a four-year-old's mental development, this being a source of intense delight to its parents. Yet in the final analysis even this is made to serve as an encouraging indication of the fact that the merest trifles can enhance the happiness of family life and thus such family enthusiasms serve to make good propaganda.

What strikes us in these pictures of family life is the degree to which the family is beginning to be humanized. There is no longer a *pars imperans* and a *pars subdita*, the presence of which Baxter took for granted in any kind of family set-up. Something of course of the old Puritan view continues to linger on. On one occasion the father of a family is made to say that he looks upon that family as a patriarchal kingdom of which he is both priest and king. He appears to believe that in uttering such a sentiment—one found in every conduct book or other work of edification—he has actually made an original remark. In fact, the picture represents no real theocracy at all but merely a very close human association. Over the door to the children's playroom there is no longer the sinister warning that 'familiarity breeds contempt', nor does the 'subjection' of the wife any longer constitute a principle that threatens the peace of the marriage. The children's right to follow the dictates of their heart in contracting a marriage—provided external circumstances permit—is eagerly defended and the deceitful counsel of the ages, 'marry first and love will come afterwards', can no longer command obedience.

The wife's position in regard to her husband has improved. In particular in her capacity of mother she now holds a very central place in the domestic community. It is just this enhanced respect accorded the mother that constitutes one of the most noteworthy advances of the age. It is from the mother that there now radiates a warmth of feeling which affects the whole domestic atmosphere. To lose their mother is now recognized as the heaviest blow by which the members of a family can be afflicted. James Thomson, who wrote *The Seasons* (1730) was one of the first to give poetic expression to this thought. He did so in his poem 'On the Death of my Mother' (1725). The relations between parents and children on the other hand are wholly determined by the feelings that they entertain for each other. Each is fond of the other, and each can assert himself as an individual, even down to the small boy who is allowed to display his skill on his toy-drum. If, on the other hand, constant repressive measures on the part of the father impede the natural freedom of a growing personality, feelings of displeasure are aroused.

This essentially humane attitude is something very different from the Puritan's narrow system of ideas. It is even further removed from the predominant aristocratic view which regarded everything pertaining to marriage and the family as tainted with Philistinism. This new conception rests on a different essentially bourgeois ideal of manliness. The Cavalier can only think of affection and consideration in the context of his relation to the woman whom he is engaged in wooing. This relation he regards as *romantic* (compare Reinhold). To give rein to any gentle feeling once he is married seems to him a sign of weakness (*The Spectator* 236); while to spend his time with children whose intellects are still undeveloped argues sheer deficiency of mind. There is in such circumstance no common mental ground that might help to make a success of both family and of marriage. Once Chesterfield sought to enumerate the pleasures of a gentleman. All he could name were those of the table, of social intercourse, of play and 'gallant' conversation. Whoever exchanged the town for the country was bound to be asked by his friends whether he was pursuing some 'rural nymph', the only kind of pleasure that these people could conceive of as being available in the countryside.

The fashionable lady on the other hand continued over a period of centuries to deplore her lack of any means of occupying her time, while the boredom from which she suffered was regarded by her as a mark of her station. Thus we can well understand when somebody, speaking of his wife and himself, wrote:

> I am afraid we shall both be laugh'd at, when I confess, that we have often gone out into the Field to look upon a Bird's-Nest; and have more than once taken an Evening's Walk together on purpose to see the Sun set.
>
> (*The Tatler*, 27 December 1709)

Such pleasures were too simple for the man of quality and those who indulged in them lost something of their standing. As to any really intimate relations with children, parents tended to find this definitely embarrassing. Compare, for instance, Lord Halifax's warning to adults to be as watchful when they were with children as they would be among enemies. And he justifies this by an argument which seems to imply that the relation between mother and child is essentially one in which a cunning and greedy subordinate is continually struggling with his superior. *The Guardian* portrays a scene in which a young mother anxiously begs her guest not to laugh at the tenderness she displays to her children. As against this *The Tatler* and *The Spectator* endeavour to popularize the bourgeois attitudes towards life which was to replace delight in outward show, superficial sociability and mere sensual pleasure with a deepening of spiritual life.

4. *The family as a school of virtue. Description of the child. Cato's domesticity as a model*

Literary fashion chiefly shows itself conscious of such increase in depth of feeling in its cult of sensibility. From the end of the seventeenth century onward, the tendency towards sentimentality in literature, which was already discernible at its beginning, becomes unmistakable. Now and then, to achieve its effect, it already employs the very means whose development is here under review. We can recognize the dawning of a new age when in Southerne's *Fatal Marriage* the character of poor deserted Isabella is made even more moving by the circumstance of her having a child, of whom there is frequent mention and concerning whom her returning husband, till now presumed dead, immediately and most tenderly enquires. Admittedly the art of Dekker, Heywood and certain others was at the beginning of the seventeenth century already seeking to achieve its effects by harping on similar feelings, but what was in that case an isolated movement in a certain direction and was mixed up with all manner of coarseness and crudity of theme and expression, now begins to extend in a more refined form over wide areas of literary output. This refinement is echoed in the catchword 'tender' which is very characteristic of this age. To awaken the soul 'by tender strokes of art'—this, as Pope says in his Prologue to Addison's *Cato* (1713) is the task of the dramatic Muse. The refinement of mind by which the period is characterized is clearly in evidence in the words of Bishop Tillotson (*Six Sermons*, page 127) when he urges that, as far as this is possible, children are to be kept away from 'bloody sights and spectacles' and that any tendency to cruelty in them should be firmly checked.

It is in the nature of sentimental art that it should make frequent use of the figure of the child as a literary theme. Where the object was to touch the heart, the temptation to avail oneself of that figure was bound to be strong. The contrast between the inner world of the child with its trustfulness and incomprehension of evil on the one hand and the relentless character of the outer world upon the other—this and the child's unconscious helplessness could always be relied on to produce rewarding effects. This age with its developed feeling for charm and grace is particularly alive to the peculiar grace of the child. This is why the child keeps on reappearing, always in much the same form, as a constituent element of the sentimental family idyll, first in the moral periodicals, then in Fielding and, after Fielding, in Goldsmith. It is seen as amusing at play, at its lessons, as a chatterbox; as moving, when it is a sweetly affectionate creature, the comfort of parents menaced by misfortune; and even as edifying in its role as an angel of innocence, an unconscious guide, virtue personified, the embodiment of faith, and sometimes a creature who actually puts adults to shame. It was after this fashion, moreover, that in the eighteenth century the fine arts visualized the child.

The noble sensibility that lies behind all this, it now began to be argued, should surely develop with exceptional vigour when the sexes and generations live together. Thus it was that the family came to be regarded as that sensibility's natural soil. Here, people were all too anxious to prove those faculties must surely blossom which are the noblest that man can show: consideration, delicacy of feeling, gentleness, understanding and warmth of heart; here there is both a school and a field of action for all that is predisposed to goodness, here the truth is made manifest of the great doctrine that virtue bears within itself the reward of happiness. Away then with the brutality that puts on the airs of nobility! Away with a love that only lives in the senses! Behold him there, the father of a family and let the tear be in your eye that shows your heart is touched—behold the father of a family who can recognize his children in an adjoining room by their tread. Here indeed is a heroic ideal that lacks all precedent.

So clearly interwoven are the concepts of virtue and the family in minds such as these that when Addison composed his famous *Cato*, he made of it not only a classicizing tragedy of text-book perfection, but the means of presenting us with a picture of an ideal family life. The great Roman is shown us as the father of two sons and a daughter, who are full of reverence and affection for him and only seek to mould their lives according to his example. Every wish that he utters is for them a command. That he may dispose of the hands of his sons as of his daughter, Marcia, is treated as a matter of course. Marcia's 'ancient Roman virtue', for instance, is made manifest when she is asked whether she loves Juba and she replies:

> While Cato lives, his daughter has no right
> To love or hate, but as his choice directs.
>
> (IV, 1)

Moreover the children in their dealings with each other are prepared for any sacrifice; the heroic father himself however, is represented as a sensitive *pater familias* who is strict and merciless when dealing with the enemies of Rome, but is mild and gentle where his family are concerned. The highest tribute is paid him when it is said that he is 'filled with domestic tenderness'.

This is a very noteworthy development, for though in some ways it is, as we have seen, not wholly uninfluenced by Puritanism, it is nevertheless in its essentials a quite independent growth. It has unquestionably sprung from those sections of the solid bourgeoisie which have not become Puritanical, but, having been abundantly nourished in the humane and liberal ideas of the age, have in due course expressed themselves in the form of sentimental art. That this also produced practical results could hardly have been doubted even if we did not possess the proud testimony of *The Spectator* of 1712 that its propaganda had been successful since people were less inclined to fight shy of marriage and the quality of the ridiculous which attached to that institution was beginning to disappear. For literature in those days was still of sufficient importance to impart a definite direction to life and to do so to a degree which subsequent centuries could not imagine. Everywhere—and not least in France, whose influence continued to be very strong—people were seeking to develop an increased refinement of feeling which could not but have a beneficial effect on marriage.

5. *Family encouragement from other kinds of literature*

The sentimental comedy, which depends very largely on the bourgeois public for support, had for its basic assumption that the woman was the victim of the man (Bernbaum, page 70), and so made its modest contribution to the spread of bourgeois morality —when, as in the case of Cibber's play referred to above, it did not go morally off the rails. A good illustration of the way in which in this age moral ideas were particularly prone to change is provided by the alterations introduced by Cibber into the comedy *The Provok'd Husband*, the work of his defunct predecessor Vanbrugh. Whereas the latter had rather tended to make fun of the domesticity of the heroine, Lady Grace, Cibber, if anything, held it up (1728) as an example most worthy of emulation.

Even so, the ideal of life which she describes in very great detail is still that of a more or less idle woman of society, whose utmost demands upon her husband cannot be more clearly formulated than in the hope which she expresses that by her virtue she may persuade him to become as 'sober' as herself. This being so, it is hardly surprising that a bourgeois dramatist like Lillo should indulge in occasional eulogies on marriage and on peace at the hearth. Even so, the joys of domesticity are much more rarely shown in a poetic light than one might suppose. Thus when Thomson in his *The Seasons* describes a winter evening in the country and in the town, he never thinks of showing us parents and children engaged in a common task. He does not seek to present us with anything like a family idyll. It is only in his 'Autumn' which he composed at a later date (1730), that we are given a very momentary picture of the head of the household surrounded by chattering children who affectionately press in upon him (1234 ff.). Yet even the art of a man like Hogarth who in so many of his works expresses the bourgeois ideals of his age, is one feels, hardly emotionally alive to the special values of family life. There was an obvious opportunity to express such an idea when he contrasted the lives of the industrious and the idle apprentice (1747). The climax and consummation of the former's career should surely not come, as in point of fact it does, on the morning after his marriage to the wealthy heiress when we see him as the recipient of high civic honours. It should come a generation later when he would have received the real crown of his life, and we could behold him as the happy father of a family with his children around him. Yet the artist never seems to have thought of this at all. This is all the more remarkable in so far as at about this time (1755) Greuze in France was beginning to paint his celebrated pictures of family life, including that of the 'Father reading to his children from the Bible'.

ARISTOCRATIC AND BOURGEOIS CULTURE

(*b*) THE FAMILY AS A LITERARY PROBLEM:
SAMUEL RICHARDSON

1. *Richardson's problems*
Meanwhile however the problem of the family acquired a new relevance thanks to a writer whose thought and feeling was permeated by the Puritan teaching under the influence of which he had grown to manhood. I speak of Samuel Richardson. To the modern reader this author conveys but little, for our contemporaries simply do not understand him. Yet Gellert in some enthusiastic verses ranked him higher than Homer, Goethe paid him homage and he was admired by Alfred de Musset. His problems do not seem to us to be profound, his characters appear lifeless and his manner of telling a story fails to arrest us. We dislike his breadth of style, his ponderous morality, and his habit of speculating on the efficiency of our tear-ducts. Yet if in regard to these things the age of Richardson took a different view from our own, this is due not so much to a diminished appreciation of quality on the part of the public, as to the change in the cultural situation. Like Shaw and Ibsen, Richardson is one of those didactic writers who share the fate of all educators in that their highest ambition is to render themselves superfluous. This applies particularly to those problems which he sets himself to solve, chiefly those of the relations between the generations and the sexes. Today however he has nothing to say to us in respect of either of these things. But the same was by no means true of the age in which he wrote. It may possibly appear to us, if we bear in mind the humane and liberal tone of the moral periodicals, that he is battering on doors that are already open. We tend to assume, to give but one example, that in matters of marriage the question of the respective rights of parents on the one hand and children on the other had already been decided long before. But life and literature are two different things and it is part of the greatness of this man that he allowed his mind to be moulded not by romantic literary traditions but by the actual state of affairs that he witnessed around him. Here there was as yet no clear accepted opinion of a kind which would ensure, say, the automatic capitulation of paternal authority when confronted by the wishes of the children's hearts. It is just in the biographies of the eighteenth century that we keep encountering those

dissensions that derive from secret marriages or from marriages contracted without parental consent. We have only to recall the paternal home of Fielding, Smollett and Goldsmith. Hogarth is another case in point. The blame for these unhappy developments is two-fold. On the one side is an over-obstinate adherence to ancient privileges; on the other a loosening of religious ties, and a growing habit of marrying later in life. There is also a growing urge for freedom, to say nothing of economic factors. Thus there was sufficient justification for an attempt to clarify the position by means of a paradigm in artistic form.

2. *The significance of* Clarissa

Nothing is more original than one of the points of view brought out in *Clarissa* (1748). Clarissa, the charming, clever and witty daughter of the house of Harlowe, comes into conflict with her parents because she is being bidden to marry the son of the owner of a neighbouring estate. Puritan casuistry is full of such cases as these, and the broad lines of the views that were held concerning them have already been indicated.

One of the greatest authorities on ethics that the century produced and one to whose educative influence Richardson (born 1689) was subject, was Jeremy Taylor (Taylor's comprehensive formula for such difficulties was discussed above). On one occasion however he expressed a more detailed opinion on a certain hypothetical case which bears a striking resemblance to the story of Clarissa. There are, he says in this connection, cases (*The Rule of Conscience* Book III, chapter V, rule VIII, 33–4) where the father must not force his children into marriage. They occur when the person in question is so insufferable that such a command would be tyrannous. For there are certain kinds of people who are *turpes*, 'filthy' and repulsive, those who are deformed and intolerably ugly. But when the father chooses a husband of this kind for his daughter, she still has no freedom to 'dissent', but only the right to 'petition for liberty' for beauty is not the highest quality that redounds to a man's credit; he may still be an excellent person even if his appearance is displeasing, his behaviour and understanding may be much better than his outward looks. When however the daughter has tried everything that is in her power to get used to him, and all her efforts have been in vain, she must even then only reject him when she is quite certain that she would never be able to do her duty to him as a wife. Since she can never be certain of this in advance because his perseverance may one day bring him success and overcome her predeliction for outward trifles and her foolish imaginings, man's ugliness is no sufficient reason for a daughter to act contrary to a father's commands when these are seriously intended. For all that, a good father will not force a daughter into a marriage which is repellent to her, despite the fact that he actually has the authority to do so—unless of course it would be greatly to her benefit. Since the wishes of the daughter are expressed in such a manner that one clause of a sentence withdraws what has been conceded in the other, we can tell from this qualified expression of regard for her wishes how vast was the moral authority to which parental tyranny could still appeal and on which it could base its actions. It is however, particularly clear from the importance which Taylor attaches to a man's bodily appearance, why the unattractive suitor in Richardson's novel is equipped with repulsive features of just this kind, why we are told again and again of his clumsiness, his uncouth figure, his dumpiness and his splay-footedness. The unhappy Clarissa speaks of him as a monster, but had it not been for these extraneous additions of ugliness, her resistance, the justification of which seems so self-evident to later generations, would, no doubt, have appeared to the author to have no justification at all. The fact that Richardson has exaggerated the circumstance can to some extent be explained by the views of his age.

Yet even if Richardson did not have Taylor's *turpes* in mind and was only indulging a certain Hogarthian passion for caricature —a passion which is evident on more than one occasion in Richardson's work—we cannot fail to notice an almost excessive anxiety to find excuses for what obviously seems to him an essentially questionable attitude on the part of the disobedient daughter, and by such excuses to bring about her moral rehabilitation as best he can. He does this by contrasting the gentle young girl with her family. The father is a harsh obstinate family tyrant, the mother is naturally weak. Though her intentions are kind, she is both inwardly and outwardly entirely dependent on her husband, is in perpetual fear of him and is always apprehensive lest he should charge her with intriguing with the children against him—a form of behaviour in which, as we know from the *Paston Letters*, wives frequently engaged. The elder sister is disagreeable, jealous and malicious while her brother, who enjoys a quite remarkable range of rights against his sisters, is violent and vindictive. Since therefore in this loveless atmosphere she cannot reckon on support from any quarter—the friendly servant who had smuggled her correspondence with a distant friend in and out of the house having been discovered and dismissed—all that is left for her is to flee her home and thus escape the marriage that is being forced on her, meanwhile placing herself under the protection of her old admirer Lovelace on whose honour she relies, as it turns out, mistakenly.

3. *The battle against the Cavalier ideal: Steele as pacemaker*
Here we begin to come up against the second problem which held Richardson's attention throughout his literary career—I speak of the battle against the Cavalier ideal which prevailed at that time. This battle too, in a certain sense, was an ancient Puritan heritage. From the first beginnings of the Puritan movement we are made very much aware of the irreconcilable conflict of the reformist views on the one hand and the hedonistic and life-affirming attitude of the Cavaliers on the other. The Puritan had a low opinion of the good manners to which the Cavalier attached so much importance. As we have seen, Puritan writers go to some pains to show that good manners do not in any way contradict 'principles'. When it comes to luxury and idleness however, which contrast so sharply with his own way of life, the Puritan pursues these vices with unflagging hatred, and shrinks back in horror from what Baxter regards as the nobility's marks of honour: sensuality and pride.

Such, no doubt, were the views amidst which Richardson grew up, for his family came from the lesser bourgeoisie. What we know of his youth shows us the typical characteristics of the Puritan child; the fact that Richardson was not a Dissenter but an Anglican is here quite irrelevant. The precocious moralizings of Richardson as a little boy have their exact counterpart in little Lucy Hutchinson who on Sundays would instruct her mother's maids and would direct their idle chatter to more worthy objects. Even his first essays in the literary art, which consisted in the composition of letters—*Pamela* was born out of just such attempts—show him to be moving along the same road. Yet he underwent a change, a change that was characteristic of the higher bourgeoisie, which ever since it had come into being, had been making concessions to the nobility, to the more questionable side of whose characters it showed itself singularly accommodating. We see this very clearly in the contributions of Addison and Steele to the moral periodicals. These writers were always going through the motions of securing for the bourgeoisie the position in society which was their due (see *The Guardian*, 12 March 1713), and then somehow failing to bring it off because they were still too subject to aristocratic influence and could not escape the impact of aristocratic views.

It is very much the same with Defoe, who, despite his sharp criticism of the aristocracy, continued to show undiminished respect for it as a social class. Above all the old Puritan objection to idleness was now rarely heard. Becon had insisted that even the rich were in duty bound to engage in some work, for nobody should be idle (folio 550b), but all such voices had now fallen silent. It is true that such a man as Steele, who more than any other had concerned himself with the creation of an ideal of bourgeois personality, makes occasional fun, as in *The Conscious Lovers* (1723) of the nobility's lack of occupation:

> We never had one of our Family before, who descended from Persons that did any thing.
>
> (Act V, scene 1)

Steele thus endeavoured to divorce the ideal of the gentleman from the concept of class. It is much the same when he maintains that 'courtier, trader and scholar' all have an equal claim to the title of gentleman since

> The appelation of gentleman is never to be affixed to a man's circumstances, but to his behaviour in them . . . There are no qualities for which we ought to pretend the esteem of others, but such as render us serviceable to them; for free men have no superiors but benefactors.
>
> (*The Tatler*, 207, 1710)

Even Taylor had once ruled: 'better than another, that is, of more use to others' (*Holy Living*, chapter IV).

This was almost a matter of course in an age which, along with a tremendous increase in trade and industry, the type of sober, public-spirited middle-class citizen spread ever more widely and took on an ever-increasing importance to the State. Such sentiments indeed seem particularly natural in the case of men whose views, like those of Steele, amongst others, were shaped by religious influences. Had not Steele in *The Christian Hero* (1701) followed in the wake of Puritan teaching in contrasting just the democratic virtues of meekness or humility over against the more outmoded ideals? His Christian hero was 'quick to see his own faults and other men's virtues and at the height of pardoning every man sooner than himself . . . to treat him kindly, sincerely, and respectfully' (chapter III).

Yet it is instructive to note that in Steele, as in others, we can observe the phenomenon to which a recent historian draws attention, namely that the new estimation accorded the middle-class, an automatic consequence of the new respect for business and trade, only applied to public and civic life. The social ideal is still personified by the gentry and the nobility. Steele, too, is familiar with the 'fine gentleman' who appears to him to be the very flower of society but also to be its ornament. He draws us a picture of such a fine gentleman in *The Guardian* of 20 April 1713. It shows us a man who, possessing all the necessary means of education, deepens his learning at court, in the field and in foreign countries, who has widened his horizon and acquired the graces of society, including the ability to dress with taste, while displaying in all his words and actions that quality of charm which Lord Chesterfield considered more important than any other. Along with all this however the fine gentleman possesses religious principles to which he cleaves, firm and undaunted, he is free from all base passions, and is full of gentleness, sympathy and benevolence. Considerable emphasis is thus still placed on qualities which only those can acquire who have grown up in circumstances of affluence. We find the same in Richardson. He too starts out from the same essentially bourgeois conception that in judging people what matters is their usefulness, the degree of their achievements. His heroine, Clarissa, has chosen the motto 'Rather useful than glaring' and the author also slips in a number of other observations which have a distinctly democratic ring. There is, for instance, the remark about the use of simple words which have a more important function to perform than pompous combinations—an image of the classes. Again the author comes out with a forthright statement that the lower and uneducated orders are the more useful elements in the State, since they represent the working part of the population. Nevertheless no further inferences are made from these reflections, because the author's respect for the aristocracy is too deep-rooted. All that later social struggles understood by the term 'class-consciousness' is still in the very distant future. Actually the crossing of the bourgeois conscience with aristocratic forms of life appears to Richardson most likely to realize the highest ideal of human personality.

Yet there is one aspect of the aristocratic character which he makes the object of his most vehement attack and this is the Cavalier's attitude towards women. That every member of the fashionable world is something of a woman-chaser and likes to boast of the scalps taken in such conquests, ignoring the low estimation of women as human beings that this implies; that the overcoming of feminine innocence is a proof of manliness and proclaims a man to be a dashing fellow, Richardson rejects with contempt. These ideas constitute a cancerous growth whose presence we should in no wise accept with a tolerant smile, which was actually what the moral periodicals were continuing to do. These, despite many fine words about respect for womanhood, still seek to arouse sympathy for such a character as Will Honeycomb, who is 'that sort of man, who usually is called a well-bred fine gentleman . . . where women are not concerned, he is an honest worthy man'. Now no doubt the contributors to the moral periodicals made the rejoinder that besides the moral, there was also a humorous side of things, but they would have a hard time to convince the author of *Clarissa*, for he was a man who never allowed moral questions to be made the objects of a joke. That is why, in order to work out the problem of the relations between the sexes as brutally and unequivocally as he can, he confronts the type of man who moves among the very peaks of society with the most spiritually developed type of womanhood, why he confronts the Puritan woman with the Cavalier (compare Reinhold).

4. *Clarissa Harlowe and the Puritan family*

Now this heroine who once made all educated Europe weep comes directly out of the Puritan family. We have already encountered two of her ancestors: Mercy in *The Pilgrim's Progress* and the young girl in the first story of Defoe's *Religious Courtship*, both very feminine and sensitive creatures who are easily moved to tears but who are nevertheless worlds apart from those idealized figures of non-Puritan literature which the age produced. These figures might well be accounted natural and balanced personalities but they are the slaves of their feelings and remain creatures of luxury who in their sweet helplessness can only find fulfilment in a man. Those other women however have that 'noble steadfastness' which their habit of rational thought imparts—which means that they have complete control over their emotions.

Take for instance the passage in which Clarissa explains to a friend the reasons which induced her to transfer to her father a legacy which she has received from her grandfather (I, 19). In doing so she submits the various motives of her action to detailed analysis. Her renunciation of independence for instance, was due to something other than sheer magnanimity. It was due to a prudent, somewhat unexalted calculation—unexalted in the sense that it chiefly had regard to the impression her action would have on the minds of others. It was in that spirit that she had really weighed up the moral difficulties that such independence on the part of a young girl would clearly bring in its train. At the same time she examines her conscience in order to ascertain to what extent even the good intentions which the money would help her realize might possibly open the door to vanity and secret ambition. This is an absolutely perfect example of that Puritan practice of self-examination, and also of that mingling of morality with cool utilitarian considerations which we encounter elsewhere in this work.

The attitude displayed by this woman towards love is very characteristic. Clarissa Harlowe, when the elegant Lovelace, the social lion, begins to visit her with his attentions, seeks to find out which of his attributes it is that he hopes will win her regard.

This reminds us again of Mercy and of Defoe's heroine who will not give their hearts away until they are quite certain what kind of person their suitor is. True, Richardson's heroine stands much closer to the real world than Defoe's, but then Defoe's book was designed exclusively for ecclesiastical circles. With Richardson however, it is morality rather than religious sentiment that is the prime concern. Is Lovelace a 'man of principle'? That is the question which must receive an affirmative answer before she can free her heart which she has for the moment bound tightly to practical good sense.

But Clarissa also proves herself a faithful pupil of Puritan teaching where the family is concerned. Even as Defoe's heroine rises to well-nigh superhuman heights in scrupulously observing the obligations of filial piety despite the fact that her father's conduct towards her is excessively strict and even unjust, Clarissa will not permit Lovelace to utter a single derogatory word about her cruel father. Indeed her whole conduct, just like that of Defoe's characters is governed by the principle which, as we have seen, was the iron core of Puritan morality; that where two people have duties towards one another, the circumstance that one party fails to fulfil that duty in no wise releases the other from performing the duty incumbent on it. The mere carrying out of this duty in such circumstances argues a certain greatness of character. But this becomes even more striking when, as with Clarissa, the waves begin to break over her head. For Lovelace is anything but a man of principle. When all his seducer's arts prove vain, he takes her by force, but the psychological effects of this are so terrible that Lovelace himself is overcome and he offers to restore her honour by marriage.

5. Richardson the moralist

Large numbers of people showed their lack of taste by urging Richardson to give his story a happy ending. His refusal to do so not only enhanced his good name as an artist but, above all, confirmed the genuineness of his moral feeling. Despite the aberration in his first novel *Pamela*, he undoubtedly possessed a strong moral conviction and he refused to allow any literary convention to weaken it. To show us the old sinner Lovelace as a kindly father or grandfather after the manner of Soames Forsyte in *The Forsyte Saga*, would ultimately have proved impossible. Despite all his sentimentality and his respect for the aristocracy, Richardson possessed too much of the harsh greatness and incorruptibility of the Puritan moralist for such a compromise. His Clarissa Harlowe never for a moment entertains the thought of such a solution. Her life is ruined and she drifts slowly towards death, but to the end an almost superhuman firmness of resolve and peace of soul never deserts her, thus proving that the moral victory is really her own. These moving death scenes, though they are much too long drawn out to suit the taste of a later age, betray the Puritan. The reactions of the sick and suffering to their environment is a subject which is treated in very great detail in Jeremy Taylor's *Holy Dying*. Taylor is concerned, before everything else, to show how the good and the faithful should depart this life. The manner of one's conduct in the moment of death is, after all, something with which religious people have always been very much preoccupied. Indeed in his *The Life and Death of Mr Badman* (1680) Bunyan shows us the poor ill-treated wife of wicked Badman addressing kindly and soulful advice, before closing her eyes, to each member of her family. If we glance at the conduct books, we shall find that they contain definite instructions, worked out paragraph by paragraph, enjoining the dying Puritan to exhort his dependents in this fashion, dependents who at such a time would already be deeply moved and thus more accessible to this kind of advice.

6. *The Janus-head of Richardson's art. The receding of the religious element. Family problems old and new*

Yet, though Richardson had inherited the Puritan view of life in its entirety, his art was Janus-headed in a manner that was very typical of his age. It has already been made plain from whence Clarissa's essential character derives, and the nature of that character shows us beyond all shadow of doubt where we should look for the moral forces which at a distance determine its behaviour.

Yet when we examine the purely artistic quality of this picture of life, we become aware of a very different and very striking phenomenon. Even in his own day people greatly admired Richardson's astonishing realism—and rightly so. The fact that he introduced the reader in a quite unprecedented fashion to the intimate details of domestic life constituted one of the principal charms of his writing. The evidence for this is considerable. The Marquise du Deffand, for instance, the clever and witty friend of Walpole, stressed this fact on more than one occasion. Thus in a letter dated 4 July 1769 she writes:

> J'aime tous les détails domestiques; j'aime les lettres de Racine parce qu'elles en sont pleines. Dans les lettres de Mme de Sévigné c'est un des articles qui me plaît le plus; enfin je les préfère dans les romans à tous les grands événements et aux belles descriptions; c'est ce qui me fait préférer les romans de Richardson à ceux de La Calprenède, et à tous nos romanciers.

Yet there are limits to that faithfulness to minute details of domestic life which distinguishes the work of Richardson and was so gratefully appreciated by his readers, for the events Clarissa describes in her letters would in reality have taken in many respects a very different form. It is an astonishing fact that the most powerful force by which these people were moved has—thanks to a kind of retouching process—been almost completely made to disappear from the picture. For Clarissa's father would surely have tried to persuade his recalcitrant daughter by means of religious arguments. She would have been prayed for at family prayers. She would have had the Bible quoted at her and all moral means available to the family theocracy would have been used to break her obstinacy. As for herself—it would have been regarded as a matter of course in that particular world of ideas that she should have prayed God to help and guide her so that the conflicts in which she had been caught up might be resolved. Yet it is precisely at the birth of the bourgeois novel that we encounter a phenomenon which was to mark this *genre* throughout the whole of its life, namely the complete ignoring of the religious factor.

From this counterfeit world all religious features were erased and the same might well be said of everything connected with sex. This fact is much more striking in *Clarissa* which was published in 1748, than in Richardson's first novel *Pamela* which had appeared eight years before. Moreover this characteristic continued to remain more or less unchanged throughout the years that followed. Who, for instance, would recognize what was in this particular the real state of affairs in the mirror held up to life by Dickens and Thackeray? Who would find in that mirror any reflection of that suffocating cloud of pietistic smoke, which at that time was billowing across England, a cloud fed by millions of domestic altars, on which every Sunday there was a sacrifice of all innocent pleasure? Not even the naturalism of a later period made any significant change in this regard—save for certain noteworthy exceptions such as Samuel Butler.

Why was it that in art a kind of *noli me tangere* attitude was thus ascribed to religion as manifested in daily life? It is a little surprising to find in the introduction to the first edition of *Pamela* a relatively bald statement of the reason for this. Religious passages had to be condensed so that they should not simply be skipped by people of a different persuasion who more than any others had need of them. In *Clarissa* this regard for the so-called 'world' underwent a considerable increase. It is a regard characteristic of that Janus-headedness which we have already noted in Richardson's art. Naturally it manifests itself not only in *Clarissa*, but in such works as *Pamela* and *Sir Charles Grandison* (1754) which have found less favour in the eyes of posterity.

This however does not diminish its socio-ethical importance. We should therefore be slightly off the mark if, following Edmund Gosse, we treated the second part of *Pamela*, the story of her marriage, as hardly worth inclusion among Richardson's works. To take this view of the matter is really to see things from the same misleading angle as was done in regard to the continuation of *The Pilgrim's Progress*. What has happened here is that there has been concentration on the artistic intention to the exclusion of everything else. But nobody would have been more inclined to shake his head over this than Samuel Richardson himself since he was primarily concerned with advising his readers as to the right way of solving the problems of life. He could therefore no more pass over marriage than could Milton, Bunyan or Defoe.

What strikes us about this ideal wife is the high degree of 'subjection' which both sides appear to assume as right and proper in her case and which must in no wise be attributed to the fact that Pamela had once been Mr B's servant. We have the case of a wife who in a solemn letter written just before her confinement, a letter she intends as a parting greeting in the event of her dying in childbirth, signs herself 'Your dutiful and affectionate wife and faithful servant'.

This accords with Richardson's view of marriage, as is made plain from his correspondence with Lady Bradshaigh. Richardson has a very high opinion of women's intelligence as such. For instance he lets Pamela write an essay in which she states her views on Locke's theory of education and vigorously opposes the superstition of his day that education was harmful to women—in this respect he was much in advance of Fielding. In this he is fundamentally a follower of Puritan teaching, which, in matters of religious knowledge and education, put woman on the same level as man. Yet he also accepted the inherited ideas of his age, and could never wholly free himself from certain ancient views regarding the relation of a wife to her husband. A considerable part of the correspondence with Lady Bradshaigh consists of an argument provoked by Richardson's remark that a marriage would be all the better if parties were not only united by love but if, in addition, the husband was able to excite a certain amount of fear in his wife. His correspondent never ceased to insist that fear can have no place in a love that is perfect.

But Richardson's ideas do not by any means lead him to deny a wife the right to views of her own. This comes out very clearly in Pamela's first quarrel with her husband, the grounds of which take us right back into the world of the conduct books. For Pamela will have no wet-nurse but wants to suckle her child herself. Her husband however does not want her to fulfil this part of her maternal duties which he finds somewhat bothersome to himself. All the arguments of the conduct books are repeated, but in the end the wife falls in, though not without a certain faint bitterness, with the wishes of her husband, who, it may be added, has obtained the support of the clergy.

On the next occasion the conflict has a rather different ending. During the last part of his wife's pregnancy the noble-hearted Mr B has started a love affair. Lord Halifax's advice to his daughter in this event was to shut both eyes, a doctrine which such a play as Cibber's *The Careless Husband* had made more plausible by transposing into dramatic form. But Richardson's conception of the dignity of womanhood was diametrically opposed to the view of women that was customary in the aristocratic world. Pamela knew how to maintain that dignity. Despite all her inward excitement, she keeps herself completely under control and not a single word that might give offence to her husband is allowed to pass her lips. But, anticipating some of Ibsen's women in the severity of her moral demands, she determinedly confronts him with the choice either of ending his love affair or agreeing to a divorce.

Such a scene as this might very well have occurred in Defoe's *Family Instructor*. Yet with Richardson we are, for all that, in a wholly different world. We can see that from the very nature of the problems which Richardson selects for treatment; they are problems in dealing with which he looks the real world straight in the face. We have for instance—to name but a few—the question of how a woman, in this case Pamela, should behave towards a child of her husband's that had been born to him prior to his marriage, or again what attitude a son should take, in this case Grandison, towards his dead father's mistress. To what point may a Protestant, again Grandison, make advances if he wishes to marry a Catholic girl? The old conduct books have nothing to offer in cases such as these. Richardson, in answering the questions that they pose, applies to them a principle that could never do itself justice within the context of rigid religious dogmatism, he applies to them the principle of humanity. The basic character of this humanity is not changed even when it often gets watered down into mere sentimentality.

Richardson also has a strangely modern air when he shows that he has an eye for the difficulties that arise quite naturally when the generations live together. He is the very first to understand the extremely delicate problem posed by the relations between mother and daughter. In his Anna Howe whose joint housekeeping with her mother leads to continual petty frictions, despite the love that unites the two, he bears witness to a certain typical alternation between attraction and repulsion in the relation between parents and children which literature could only much later move into the forefront of its artistic concern. Fielding is still quite a stranger to such tasks.

VI

The Family as a Literary Public

1. *Women's education and literature*

When Samuel Richardson was working on his first novel (1739) he read each new addition to his work to his wife and to a young woman friend of hers every evening and let them encourage him to continue. Certainly Dryden and Milton and Shakespeare did not work in quite this way. The stimulation of creative work by outstanding women is something with which the history of art is unquestionably familiar, but we are speaking here of something different, for we are observing the birth of a new kind of art that is coming to life in and to some extent *for* the atmosphere of the domestic community. One could indeed say that it was born out of the spirit of bourgeois family life. What enabled it to come into being was actually a change that had taken place in that very atmosphere, a change brought about by a variety of causes.

The steady rise in the eighteenth century of the average level of education among women was one of the most important causes. Around 1700 women's education was rather poor. Among the higher non-Puritan bourgeoisie and among the aristocracy it was held that woman could only claim a very small share of the learning of the day. This is very apparent from certain passages in Pepys' *Diary* (1659–69) which relate in one case how the diarist had to spend an entire Sunday afternoon explaining to his wife the different natures of addition, subtraction, multiplication and division, and in another tells us how during a carriage drive, her insufferable tales from her reading of *The Great Cyrus** were a most sore trial to Pepys' nerves. A generation later nothing seemed to have changed. We find Swift complaining that out of a hundred women not so much as one could put her thoughts onto paper and Dr Johnson recollects that in his youth a woman was considered to be educated if she knew no more than how to spell. Richardson's friend, Lady Bradshaigh, saw fit to declare that she

* Mlle de Scudéry, *Artamène ou le Grand Cyrus*, 1649–53.

had no objection to women being taught to read and write (letter to Richardson of 28 December 1750), while Mrs Delany commented adversely on the fact—and was probably quite justified in doing so—that Richardson, who was so consistently true to life, had in his *Sir Charles Grandison* let women use such words as 'intellect' and 'ethics' (*Correspondence* I, clxiii–iv).

The emergence of one species of literature can only be attributed to this well-nigh incredible neglect of female education. It is the literature which was specifically designed for female consumption, to wit the 'gallant heroic' novel which glorified a wholly non-existent type of manhood, one that combined a positively staggering masculinity with an equally staggering tenderness and so represented a quite ludicrous exaggeration of those combined qualities which women in all ages have found particularly attractive in men.

During the first decades of the eighteenth century a slow change became perceptible which was not wholly unconnected with improvements in the education of men. We can see, for instance, from the diary of Elizabeth Raper (1758) how around the middle of the century the basic question of the education of women had become a topic of conversation—even in the country. In town circles however a much earlier attempt had already been made to treat this subject in an open-minded way. Such female education was predominantly literary. The moral periodicals had recommended that women should concern themselves with literary study as a means of correcting the terrible idleness that marked their lives.

There are many examples of pioneers of education. A Miss Talbot, for instance, who was born in 1721, is representative of a definite type. This lady's mother had known no language other than English and her letters were full of spelling mistakes. The daughter however understood French and Italian and also a little Latin and later learned German. In the circle of the so-called blue-stockings, that is to say of Mrs Montague, Mrs Carter, Mrs Delany, Mrs Thrale, Hannah More and others, women's cultural ambitions may be said very largely to have attained their goal. The contemptuous nickname which their contemporaries applied to them—it had originally been used of both sexes—is really misleading in that it seems to assume that literary interests can only be fostered if social forms are neglected. But the real characteristic of this new type of woman, who most certainly did not limit herself to the blue-stockings proper, was that she brought together certain attitudes which up till then had existed in separation from each other.

It is in women of this kind that we first encounter that complete synthesis which Steele had already visualized as an ideal and which later became characteristic of the 'higher bourgeoisie'. This synthesis united the social forms of the aristocratic world both with the elements of culture and with that moral attitude towards life which had developed among the bourgeoisie. That women in this particular were in advance of men is explained by the circumstance that men who professed to think along these lines were expected to surrender their privileges. This last applied particularly to the relations between the sexes.

2. *The lady and literature*

Now of course such a combination of qualities as that alluded to above is further determined by the factor of sex. For this highly developed delicacy of feeling has something pronouncedly feminine about it or, better said, something lady-like or old-maidish. The lady's attitude to life is a rather special one, in so far as it has not been given an edge by any participation in the struggle for existence. Sense of humour on the other hand tends among women to be somewhat weakly developed. The result is a distinctive basic tone. Violent objection is taken to coarseness and indecency, though these still play a prominent part in public life, a fact which can be substantiated by a multitude of examples. Thus the custom prevailed in the theatre of ending even the performance of a tragedy with an epilogue full of coarse *double ententes* which caused the male members of the audience to delight in the embarrassment of their female companions. Richardson lets Pamela express her indignation at this practice, and there can be no doubt that in this he was making her the mouthpiece of the ladies' world.

These feminine objections were however not always as rigorous as the limits which later generations imposed upon the artist. There is a certain story about one of the best-known members of the blue-stocking circle, the excellent Mrs Carter. It is not any less indicative of the influence of the feminine public because it happens to be concerned with a Punch and Judy show.

She went once to a puppet-show at Deal, with some respectable friends, and Punch was uncommonly dull and serious, who was usually more jocose than delicate. 'Why, Punch,' says the Showman, 'what makes you so stupid?' 'I can't talk my own talk,' answered Punch, 'the famous Mrs Carter is here.'

(Memoirs, page 35)

This complaint from Punch may well be said to reflect the fate which was later to overtake so much of English art.

The coarse virile realism that sets down what from its own experience it knows to be true can often count on little sympathy from a feminine audience. Down to earth artists such as Hogarth who takes the viewer along with him into the brothel or into a criminal dive, and shows us a decadent nobleman seeking out a quack to cure him of venereal disease, and Fielding, whose sensitive brush paints the inside of a debtors' prison or a dubious grog shop, are all too likely to fall under the feminine ban.

As against this however women have more aptitude for psychological empathy and are more adept than men in the analysis of feeling. The artist is often very much alive to this quality in women and where he can display an appreciation of it, is likely to earn their applause.

3. *Richardson and the ladies*
The prevailing atmosphere in this ladies' world now begins to exercise its influence on Richardson, the greatest novelist of the day, and brings him wholly under its spell. Originally Richardson was a petty tradesman and the philistine quality of the views by which his home atmosphere caused him to be dominated is shown by certain passages in his letter writer, that very early publication from out of whose general plan *Pamela* took shape. I refer to those passages in which he inveighs against women's riding clothes and the instruction of women in music—views which would scarcely have accorded with those of the world in which he was later to move. There was also the story of the abortive seduction of Pamela with its very detailed descriptions of the enterprising Mr B's efforts to slip disguised into the virtuous heroine's bed, a story that would have accorded ill with the more refined taste of his later admirers. After this however he begins to associate with ladies of the kind described above, ladies from the higher strata of society,

whom he continually observes and by whose whole way of thinking he tends to be influenced. These are made to serve as his psychological models.

This is clearly shown by his six volumes of correspondence. They afford an excellent insight into the minds of these strangely advanced types of women, who were in many respects the intellectual leaders of their day. Certain remarks in this connection of Lady Bradshaigh's are particularly significant; she insists that the laws governing the relations between men and women had been made by men and that these were simply serving their own interests. She also claims that in marriage there should only be love and would not hear any mention of fear. How far such emancipated ideas had already progressed among women is shown by Richardson's own creation in *Clarissa* of Miss Howe, for here for the first time in literature we are shown a woman who views the world and all the circumstances by which she is surrounded with prudent judgment and yet wholly from the woman's standpoint.

But this is not the only result of Richardson's association with women. The really remarkable thing is that in his whole way of feeling Richardson completely reflects the feminine world. Indeed, his image of the ideal male, as displayed in his *Sir Charles Grandison*, shows features that are definitely feminine. His character is governed by 'delicacy', by refinement of feeling, which for Richardson had become a kind of key virtue, the root from which all other excellences spring. Though in some ways Steele anticipates it, this is fundamentally a feminine way of regarding virtue. Richardson found it among the women who surrounded him.

There is a letter which very clearly substantiates this dated 23 December 1751 addressed by his friend, the aforesaid Miss Talbot, to Mrs Carter who was very much her intellectual superior. The writer expresses her delight over *Sir Charles Grandison*, a delight which she knows her correspondent to share. Her pleasure is all the keener, because this character is in large measure their joint creation, since they were both very much concerned in bringing it to life. They are indeed in their admiration 'two Pigmalionesses'. If now the whole coming generation were to form themselves after this pattern, she jestingly continues, it would be too late for both of them.

This observation is very instructive. True, the world has not shaped itself after the Richardsonian or Talbot-Carterian model;

nevertheless literature has followed firmly in Richardson's footsteps. The line from Richardson via Rousseau to Goethe's *Werther* is only the most obvious among many.

We can therefore say that it is from this point onwards that the triumphant procession of the feminists begins its progress through the literature of Europe, the way having of course been prepared for it by the moral periodicals with their large circle of woman readers. Naturally the first significant victories were won on native soil.

4. Fielding and the ladies

Of this last we are made especially aware in the art of Fielding. The wit displayed in Fielding's *Joseph Andrews* (1742) in making fun of Richardson's *Pamela* sometimes leads us nowadays to believe that it seriously impaired the effects that the latter had on his public. Nothing could be more mistaken. This is particularly apparent from the fate of Fielding's last novel. *Amelia* (1752) whose reception was a great disappointment to its author. He too told the story of a marriage and in doing so had displayed the full maturity of his art. For our own day this novel has many attractions. The scenes in a debtors' prison and those depicting shabby domesticity have a colourful realism which has something Hogarthian about it. The character of the hero, Booth, is not very profound; nevertheless with its mixture of good and bad it is a life-like study drawn from a real world. As to the heroine, Amelia, critics such as Thackeray have voiced the most enthusiastic opinions about her. Yet, despite all this, in Fielding's own lifetime *Amelia* proved a complete failure. The critical periodicals, which admittedly did not attain a very high level, for the most part made fun of it and the public would not buy it. It was a long time before a second edition became necessary.

What is the reason for this? Fielding felt impelled to have the matter out with those who thus rejected him. He did so in the *Covent Garden Journal* (1752) of which he was editor, letting the whole argument take the form of a legal trial in which Amelia herself appeared. It is highly instructive to read of the circumstance to which the author attributes his defeat, for proceedings in this trial begin with the calling of Lady Dilly Dally to bear witness against Amelia. It is clear that Fielding knew where a great part of his enemies was to be found. Among the accusations now brought against *Amelia* a certain very trite charge was often made, a charge intended to discredit any artist who looked for his subject matter in certain circles of life—namely, that some of his scenes and characters were 'low'.

We can observe how society and literature have joined forces and how important a part Fielding himself allots to women in that society. It is also not unworthy of note in this connection that certain deprecatory and even contemptuous remarks were made about this excellent person and gifted writer which seem to indicate that he did not move in those London circles that really set the tone. One thinks of Zola, who had long to pay a heavy social penalty because of his insistence on remaining true to life. How right Fielding was in regarding the ladies as his principal enemies—and indeed some who certainly could not be called 'Dilly-Dally'—is plain from certain letters of that time. We ourselves can now recognize such figures as Sophia in *Tom Jones* (1749) as artistic achievements of the highest order. But a great proportion of Fielding's women readers, being moved by ethical considerations which Richardson appears to have satisfied, took a very different view. Thus Miss Talbot writes to Mrs Carter (22 April 1752) that Mr Fielding's heroines are always 'silly, loving runaway girls'. Or again we find Mrs Delany complaining to Mrs Dewes that some element which would have made the scenes of misfortune in *Amelia* truly moving was somehow lacking (18 January 1752). Although there was some truth in this—and after what has already been said I need not further stress the point—yet as literary criticism the statement is invalid. For the ground of offence in this instance was simply that certain things were brought into the story which were considered unsuitable for ladies' ears.

It is evident that at this particular point of time a greatly increased regard was beginning to be shown towards women and their wishes. To despise them as a public was something which no author could afford. True that such a man as Sterne continued to hold his own against them: *Tristram Shandy* is essentially a book for men. But it is instructive to observe the powerful resistance which in many cases he still encountered in public taste, a taste which may well be regarded as having been born from the essence of femininity. This was in 1759. It was a very significant gesture on the author's part when he dedicated the continuation of the book 'The Story of Poor Le Fever' to a woman, Lady Spencer.

Incidentally the great humourist himself had a higher opinion of this book—in my view, a mistaken one—than of any other of his works.

5. *Fordyce's sermons*

A few years later we can trace the gradual change that has taken place in the sermons of a well-known preacher, Dr Fordyce. These sermons, which went into edition after edition, exercised, as we learn from the biographers of the day, a not inconsiderable influence, and that influence was made all the stronger by reason of the fact that they were assisting in the changes in circumstance that were already taking place.

Now Fordyce in his *Sermons to young women* of 1766 and also in that series of sermons that came ten years later strongly recommended close and regular association between the two sexes, since women seem to have the ability to make men more civilized. He noticed a great difference in this particular between England and France, woman's influence being definitely the dominant one in the latter country, a fact as much in evidence at the court of the king as in the poor man's hut. This does not always appear to the advantage of French youth of the male sex but once they attain a more mature age, Frenchmen, thanks to their continuous association with women, are much more courteous and kind than Englishmen and also more cultured and entertaining. For when there is a fairly close association between the sexes the influence of women on men is much stronger than that exercised in the opposite direction. Of course, for this to be so, women must naturally be cultured themselves. Indeed Fordyce's sermons are veritable hymns of praise, glorifying the culture and education of women, for on these the virtue of women, their dignity and their good fortune depend. All this is set forth with an eloquence that often attains poetic levels, but it is worth noting that literary interests are viewed as lying at the very heart of any culture a woman may possess.

It is here that the seed sown by Richardson begins to produce its harvest. The creator of *Clarissa* had declared women to be natural authors. The nobility in their way of thinking, the gentle quality of their feelings and the liveliness of their imagination gave them an advantage in this respect over men, who in expressing themselves frequently tended to be unnatural, dry and bombastic. Fordyce voices similar views. To compensate for their lack of depth and strength, nature has given women a greater refinement of mind and a stronger urge toward morality. Their psychological skills are superior to those of men. For this reason they are very close in spirit to the literature of that day which depends so much on 'sentiment and character'.

Such reasoning, which demonstrates the closeness of the tie between women and the more cultured clergy, and shows us the clergy urging women to recognize in imaginative literature their most formidable weapon in the cultural struggle, makes plain that a revolutionary change has taken place. Literature has become the subject of sociable conversation to a quite unprecedented degree and this is the vantage from which woman, as the guardian of accepted social habit, exercises her influence. The more advanced representative of the clergy grasps the importance of this fact and his advocacy is one of the forces which causes women's preoccupation with literature to grow and which also tends to enhance woman's importance as the propagator of good taste. Moreover Fordyce is something of a typical figure. We keep encountering clergymen among Richardson's personal associates.

It is also at about this time that imaginative literature begins to play quite a new part in the education of youth. The young girl becomes a serious factor in the formation of literary taste. This is tellingly exemplified by Goldsmith's publication in 1767—with special mention of Fordyce—of an anthology entitled *Poems for Young Ladies* in the Introduction to which he stresses the fact, as though it were of more significance than anything else, that the volume only contains 'such pieces as innocence may read without a blush'. The author adds—and his observation says much for the part played by literature in social intercourse, that poetry is of value through:

> The pleasure which it gives, and indeed the necessity of knowing enough of it to mix in modern conversation...

It is no accident that this form of words should be very similar to that used in the introduction to the notorious Dr Bowdler's *Family Shakespeare* which was published half a century later in 1807, words which the aforesaid Dr Bowdler employs to inform us that everything has been eliminated that 'was likely to raise a blush on the cheek of modesty'. There is here clearly an identity of basic attitude. It is true that Goldsmith includes much of which Dr

Bowdler could hardly have approved. There are for instance the concluding lines of the poem 'On a Girdle' by Edmund Waller (1606–87):

> Give me but what this ribband bound,
> Take all the rest the sun goes round.

These would not have been received with favour in a later age. It is however here that the development assumed a definite shape for the first time. Bowdler lived from 1754 to 1825 and was personally associated with the blue-stocking circle. He thus grew up under the influence of a set of ideas which just at this time were becoming articulate. The truth is that when Fordyce observed that the influence of women in France was much greater than in England, he was saying something that would soon no longer apply to English literary circles, for though in the French *salon* one saw many more men than women, even though a lady might conduct it, corresponding institutions in England were freely visited by both sexes.

The women who set the tone here were, above all else, thoroughly respectable. To marry for love was treated by them almost as though it were something immoral. A number of prominent ladies of this period—Mrs Delany, Mrs Montague and Mrs Thrale, for instance—were married to men old enough to be their fathers and when one of them became a widow and showed signs when remarrying of wishing to follow the dictates of her heart, there was a positive outcry; it was as though the unfortunate woman were proposing to commit incest. This shows us how, despite all the changes that an age can bring, certain basic ideas from the religious outlook of the past can continue obstinately to persist. Indeed at one point in his letter-writer, the work which began his literary career and which has been so strangely overlooked, Richardson (*Letters written to and for Particular Friends*, etc.) lets a father address the following words to a daughter whom he is seeking to persuade to give her hand to a considerably older man:

> it is every bit as much Credit to a *young Lady* to marry a worthy Man, *older than herself*, as it is *Discredit* for an *older Woman* to marry a young Man.
>
> (page 131)

A generation later when the influence of the clergy had grown still greater, such views had hardly changed at all. Even the increasing enthusiasm of the age for nature and the natural had in many respects left them untouched. Actually by what they call 'the natural', the women of this world really mean no more than the bourgeois. They look upon themselves, above all else, as the guardians of a very narrow type of morality. When Fanny Burney made the acquaintance of Madame de Genlis and Madame de Staël and happened to hear something that did not do overmuch credit to their reputations, she immediately broke off all relations with them. Hannah More, one of the spokeswomen of the circle, declared that propriety was as essential for the woman as Cicero had said action was for the orator (*Strictures*, pages 4-5).

6. *The humanizing of the family: relation between parents and children*

Nevertheless, compared with previous centuries, progress in the humanizing of the family was immense. Whereas formerly, thanks to the iron compulsion governing the Puritan domestic community the influence of the mother could never really make itself felt in the way it should have done, a welcome change now becomes perceptible. There is a loosening of strict Old Testament forms, while a more thorough education has made it possible for women to have a larger share in setting the family course. The mother can also carry weight with her children as a spiritual and intellectual guide. A good example of this is the daughter of the famous classical scholar, Bentley, the lady who became the mother of the dramatist Richard Cumberland. Cumberland tells in his memoirs (1807) how his mother took note of his intellectual interests and, like Goethe's mother, stimulated his earliest flights of imagination and helped form his taste. One could cite large numbers of similar cases. I will only mention that of Gibbon, whose development as a human being was pre-eminently due, not indeed to his mother, but to an aunt, who managed to attune herself completely to him and formed a friendship with him which was in every way like that between adults. She shared all his thoughts and found happiness and a rich reward in observing the first blossomings of his spirit.

This is typical of the generation that was born between 1725 and 1740. The relation between children and fathers now also begins in many cases to change and the principle that for centuries had been respected that 'familiarity breeds contempt' begins to lose its validity. Even the wise Bacon had believed that he was singing the praises of friendship when he declared:

> A man cannot speak to his son but as a father; to his wife but as a husband; to his enemy but upon terms; whereas a friend may speak as the case requires, and not as it sorteth with the person.
>
> *(On Friendship)*

A century and a half later however people became less unbending. They began to follow Steele's counsel (*The Tender Husband*, 1705). He said that children can only be won over by an appeal to their inclinations. Things now move so fast that they actually catch up with Richardson himself, who in *Clarissa* had so effectively championed the rights of children against their parents but had now to defend himself against the charge, brought by his lady friends, that he was too stiff and formal with his daughters. His answer was the somewhat negative one that, whereas condescension befits the parental character, it is befitting for the child to show that he is not offended by it (*Correspondence* I, cli ff.). He countered the reproach of stiffness and undue formality by saying—this being but one of his arguments—that he had often joked with them and freely spoken his mind in front of them. He hoped, he said, that his children had put a good part of the distance behind them which he had endeavoured to help them overcome. Incidentally, they addressed him as 'honoured Sir'.

Of course there have always been understanding fathers—Milton's father was one of them—but they were the exception. Now however there is a radical change in the whole relation between fathers and children. When Erasmus Darwin complains about his father, who died in 1754, and says that 'he kept them', the children, 'at an awful kind of distance', the very fact of such a complaint is indicative of the changes and the fresh needs that the new age had brought along with it. Similar complaints are to be found in other memoirs. Thus the Reverend John Newton remarks bitterly on the spiritual distance which his father maintained between them (*Letters*, page 14).

But this great gulf between the generations which, as we saw, Dr Johnson still regarded as part of the order of nature, now began to close. In the course of correspondence (*Memoir of the Life of*

John Bowdler, Esq. 1824) the father writes to his twenty-one-year-old son on 18 March 1767, that he hopes that he will always be that son's best friend:

> I remember your Sister once made an observation to me which I have often thought of, and which I believe to be a very just one, and that is, that every body thinks others reserved; ... Perhaps there are very few who are quite free from reserve to any one body, yet this I think I am to you, and I wish you to be as much so as you can to me.
>
> (pages 53–4)

Somewhat later we have the mother of the twelve-year-old Maria Edgeworth telling her daughter that she hopes to be with her in every regard as her equal, irrespective of age (letter, 10 October 1779).

It is undeniable that the circumstances thus described are typical. Naturally in families whose point of view was very much that of the Church, and also among the aristocracy, things remained largely unchanged, but in the case of the great majority of the bourgeoisie, even in those among whom there had been some loosening of the religious bonds, we can still encounter something of the old stiffness. Interesting evidence for this is furnished by the 'scene' between father and daughter which Richardson set down for his friend, Lady Bradshaigh, as a kind of foretaste of possible things to come (*Correspondence* VI, 29 f.). The father is in despair because his daughter has lost her heart to a man who is unworthy of her. If the advice of Gouge, Baxter or Jeremy Taylor had been followed, the father would simply have asserted his authority. In Defoe's *Family Instructor* religion would have been used as a means of bringing the daughter to her senses. Yet there is now nothing of any of this. The frightened father seeks to influence the daughter by love alone, and before all else he seeks the cause of the trouble in himself:

> I am of a harsh, a severe temper; so say my censurers; perhaps, because I penetrate their disguises; and think I have reason to have a mean opinion of all mankind. Your mother, however, (indeed she is all goodness, all excellence!) has not been unhappy with me. My children's reverence seems to have exceeded their love for me. I have been, perhaps, too little solicitous to shew the companionship to them, in my outward behaviour, that it was always in my heart and in

my judgement to shew them. You, my dear, have started up, as I may say, into woman, unawares to me. I looked upon you too long as a child, because I loved my child. You have found yourself out to be marriageable, before I had considered you as such. If anything disagreeable, stiff, distant, be imagined by you, in my temper or behaviour; if you find, in your own heart, more awe of me than love for me; and if to get out of my power, be one of your motives; I will endeavour wholly to change this my outward behaviour. I will, if possible, overcome your fear, and engage your love. I will make you my companion, my friend, and my third self. Your mother, your good, your indulgent mother, shall be only my best self.

(pages 34–6)

And he lets her look forward to enjoying complete freedom in the house, she is to pay and receive visits as she pleases and is to be independent financially and none is to hinder her. Not even in Dickens could a father speak to his daughter with greater tenderness, greater love or with more complete forgetfulness of self. It is easy to see how vast a change is coming about. It is a change whose effects no one can foretell.

7. Reading aloud in the family
Wherever a harmonious relationship exists between people, they tend to search for some activity in which they all can engage. That is why agreement in matters spiritual or intellectual finds expression in a sharing of the pleasures of reading. Reading aloud in the family circle is of course, a very ancient practice—at least where certain forms thereof are concerned. Of course, neither the adventures of *Beowulf* nor *The Canterbury Tales* reached their public in quite this way. It was for the most part some form of religio-ethical literature that was sometimes enabled thus to communicate its message. The books chosen for this purpose were works like Dan Michel's fourteenth-century *Ayenbite of Inwyt*, which in a very involved manner expounded the Ten Commandments, the twelve articles of faith and similar matters. There was also *Dives et Pauper* which was inspired by a very similar spirit. Then there was *The Legend of the Saints*. We can see another very ancient custom surviving in Shakespeare's *Titus Andronicus*, that of making children read aloud to their elders. No doubt the reason for this custom is to be found in the circumstance that the adults

THE FAMILY AS A LITERARY PUBLIC

had lost the ability to read. After the Reformation *The Legend of the Saints* was replaced by Foxe's *Book of Martyrs* which describes the sufferings and struggles of the martyrs for the new doctrine.

In the Puritan family however reading had a significance which went far beyond any mere literary interest such as had stimulated it in the past. The woman who, when not busy about the household, 'always had a good', i.e. religious, 'book in her hand' is a very typical figure, and it will be remembered that the dowry of John Bunyan's wife consisted of nothing save two works of edification.

Even today anyone who collects this kind of seventeenth- and eighteenth-century religio-ethical and didactic literature will be struck by the frequency with which an entry in faded ink on the first page or inside the cover discloses the name of a woman as the owner of the book. Woman however is by nature communicative and she welcomes the opportunity that reading aloud provides of making others familiar with whatever is engrossing her own thoughts. But idle listening is not enough to satisfy the pietist. It is best that such listening should be accompanied by active work. So in the sixteenth century we could frequently have witnessed a scene in which a bevy of maids was engaged in the embroidery of wall hangings and other objects while their mistress sat in their midst—or possibly as in Lady Hoby's house, the chaplain did so—and read aloud from a book of sermons. A vivid picture of such a scene—though in this case there was no actual mention of work—is conjured up by some words of Baxter's:

> *When you read to your family or others, let it be seasonably and gravely, when silence and attendance encourage you to expect success; and not when children are crying or talking, or servants busling to disturb you.*
> (*Christian Directory*, page 580)

Of course the works he actually recommends for the purpose in question consist for the most part of tracts and religious books on such subjects as the practice of piety and life in God, etc. He certainly does not recommend the 'books of the Devil' like 'idle Tales, and Play-books, and Romances or Love-books, and false bewitching stories . . .' (page 580).

In the introduction to his famous work, for instance, we are expressly told that it should be read aloud by fathers to the family circle.

And indeed I began it rudely, with an Intention of that Plainness and Brevity which Families require . . . And I thought it not unuseful to the more Judicious Masters of Families; who may choose and read such parcels to their Families, as at any time the case requireth.

In order to arouse their interest an early attempt was often made to bring the children into these affairs. Actually the reading aloud by children from the Bible, alternating verse for verse, was a practice with which people had been familiar for a very long time indeed. No doubt it was because of this custom that Defoe's *Family Instructor* and *Religious Courtship* attained such a gratifying number of editions. When in the eighteenth century the breath of time began at last to melt the ice of orthodoxy, and such men as Steele and Addison began to produce a worldly literature which pious opinion considered harmless, the concept of family reading began to take on a new quality.

Sermons of course still provided the backbone of this kind of reading. We have unfortunately no knowledge of the nature of the contents of the short-lived *Family Magazine* which was published in 1740 by John Osborn, for not a single copy of this publication has survived. But some nine years previously ideas were in the air concerning a special kind of art specifically designed for the family. Indeed so marked was this trend that Fielding could make fun of the excessively instructive quality of theatrical entertainment of the day with the words:

> This Opera was writ, sir, with a design to instruct the world in economy. It is a sort of family Opera. The husband's vade-mecum; and it is very necessary for all married men to have it in their houses.
> (Preface to *The Grub Street Opera*)

Besides this, the art of Richardson provided ample material for family reading. The great majority of times when his name is mentioned in letters shows that his works were read aloud. It is this practice of reading aloud that explains the rhetorical character of many works. A good instance of this is provided by words in the introduction to Johnson's *Rasselas:*

> Ye who listen with credulity to the whispers of fancy and pursue with eagerness the phantom of hope; who expect that age will perform the promises of youth, and that the deficiencies of the present day will be

THE FAMILY AS A LITERARY PUBLIC

supplied by the morrow; attend to the history of Rasselas, prince of Abyssinia.

It is scarcely possible to think of these words otherwise than as being read aloud. In Richardson's own descriptions there is frequent mention of reading aloud. Clarissa's friend, for instance, entertains her mother by such reading on winter evenings while—again in winter—Clarissa herself, though only on weekdays, gathers the young girls of the neighbourhood around her to listen to her—just as Lady Hoby gathered her maids—and these too bring their work along with them. For attendance at a reading session together with some kind of handiwork was deliberately being made to take the place of cards, with which for generations ladies of the upper classes contrived to kill time. When there was no reading aloud, there was often reading in company and Richardson was given a charming account of this by his friend Aaron Hill (1685-1750) who described his young feminine companions as surrounding him like damp flowers in April.

Meanwhile the practice, which I have already described, of getting children to read aloud continues to live on. The reading of a story therefore by little Dick, the son of Parson Abraham Adams in *Joseph Andrews*, is a picture from a perfectly real world. It is much the same when we read Mrs Trimmer's account (page 15) of her husband's habit in the 1770s: on coming home of an evening he would gather a little group of listeners around him and then get one of his children to read from Milton or Pope, from Hume's *History of England* (1754-61), from one of Shakespeare's historical plays, from Blackstone's *Commentaries on the Laws of England* (1765-9), from the moral periodicals, from the works of Johnson or Burke or from sermons or Holy Scripture. No doubt most of what was read was well above the heads of the young listeners.

So far we remain within the tradition of religious domestic reading. But even this changes in the course of time. An earlier world had been unable to understand the childish inclinations, nor could it get inside a child's mind. In a letter to a nine-year-old child, Chesterfield makes satirical remarks about the Catholic Church, gives *Tom Jones* to yet another child and presents a fourteen-year-old with the story of an unhappy passion, namely that contained in Madame de Lafayette's *Princesse de Clèves*. Now, however, a real children's literature begins to appear on the market, such for instance as that produced by Goldsmith's publisher, John Newbury.

In these circumstances it was natural enough that reading aloud should in the course of time come to be recognized as something of an art in its own right. Indeed in the case of Clarissa it is definitely reckoned to her credit that she displayed considerable virtuosity in this field. Dr Fordyce himself works into his sermons (1766) a long dissertation in which he seeks to determine what course of instruction will be most likely to provide the aspirant with the necessary skills, recommending him to begin with short pieces of prose then to pass on to passages requiring more intense feeling and ultimately to those that are definitely rhetorical, from when it is but a step to the passionate and the sublime. Even though the writings first to be selected in this connection had of necessity to be the classics—for when the audience consists of both adults and adolescents it is natural that the classical writers should be considered before any others—it is nevertheless instructive to observe how, as the result of all this, the family becomes more receptive and more eager to appreciate what is being set before it and continually becomes more worthy of serious consideration as a literary public. Since moreover, there is nothing to restrict literary appetites to the family circle, the most varied efforts are made to meet demands from such other groups as boarding schools. Among other things anthologies were produced which, like William Enfield's *The Speaker* (1774), a work that went into many editions, seem to have had their material deliberately chosen in pursuance of the Dr Fordyce's instructions, for they usually start with a few aphorisms or proverbs, following these with short narrative pieces and ending with some sentimental poems.

8. *Importance for literature: discovery of the family as a theme*
The effect of these developments on art itself was of various kinds. The first discovery of family art was the family itself, as depicted by Richardson and then by his rival, Fielding. Fielding's professional career started with a few satirical comedies and then passed on to the novel of married life, a work full of gentle feeling and sincerity, reflecting something of the spiritual transformation that marks the course of the eighteenth century which substituted the bourgeois attitude to life for that of the aristocrat. How Fielding himself discovered the charms of this bourgeois life is evident

from a number of passages in his works. I draw particular attention to one in which he speaks of the magical intimacy of home life, a thing which would hardly have captivated any member of the aristocratic world. He thus describes Amelia (1752) preparing supper in the kitchen:

> And, if I may speak a bold truth, I question whether it be possible to view this fine creature in a more amiable light than while she was dressing her husband's supper, with her little children playing round her.
>
> (XI, chapter VIII)

Who, reading these words, would not immediately think of the scene where Werther finds Lotte so infinitely charming as she serves supper to her little brothers and sisters? The same words however also awaken a memory of a certain descriptive passage in *Paradise Lost* in which Eve is admired as she goes about her domestic duties, a passage that is surely already inspired by a thoroughly bourgeois spirit. However, even as a portrayer of marriage, a subject to which in the opinion of his day he never did justice, Fielding never became the special prophet of this bourgeois spirit. Yet how important this subject was becoming is evident from the very views of those who disliked what it stood for. For Goethe was surely right, when he recognized in Sterne's *Tristram Shandy* a tendency to hold up to scorn the whole bourgeois family atmosphere and treat it as a manifestation of Philistinism. And indeed the advanced nature of Sterne's ideas could hardly be considered to favour the family's cause. Sterne was never touched in his person by the kind of religious influences among which Richardson grew to manhood, and what distinguished him from his forebears of the aristocratic world who made fun of marriage as a 'ludicrous misfortune' were simply the new and original means he employed to make us see life more directly and more immediately than was ever done before. Delicacy of mind, consideration, mutual respect and tactful understanding of the other's point of view—these qualities might quite properly be ascribed to the brothers in their relations with one another. In marriage however there is for Sterne but one essential matter—namely that which Tristram's father, when he winds up the big clock once a month, brings into indissoluble relationship with the passage of time—and even in these significant moments the husband uses a deprecatory tone that sometimes gives way to downright irritability while the wife's thoughts are busy with household matters.

It is indeed most indicative of Sterne's whole attitude that the butt of his brilliant wit is always woman—with her lack of any scientific interests, her obstinacy, her curiosity which impels her to listen at key holes, a creature who is in every way inferior to the men of the house. The confrontation of the innocent Uncle Toby, so touchingly portrayed, with the scheming widow Wadman who, though trying to catch him, is doubtful about certain physical consequences of his war-wounds—all this is inspired by much the same set of ideas. Shandy's position as head of the house also provides a number of essentially comic opportunities. Yet the very manner in which these subjects are treated—even when they are seen under an essentially humorous light—is symptomatic of the steadily growing interest in family life. Nothing shows this more clearly than the change in the work of Smollett who in his last book, *Humphrey Clinker* (1771), draws for us in the domestic life of Squire Dennison a most charming family idyll, thus abandoning his old realism in favour of a more kindly and sympathetic portrayal of life, an attitude that recalls the art of Goldsmith.

In Goldsmith's *The Vicar of Wakefield* (1766) the glorification of family life had already risen to heights that clearly marked a new stage of development. Efforts have been made (Sells) to discern in all manner of French models the ultimate sources of Goldsmith's inspiration. But the argument is unsound. Goldsmith did not need to be influenced by Rousseau, he had only to follow the road indicated by the moral periodicals. Edward Moore in *The World* (1753, 16) had already painted a similar idyll in miniature, and this may well have moved Goldsmith to try his hand on a larger canvas. It is indeed difficult to say which of the two efforts is more completely divorced from reality, that of Moore who shows us the inhabitants of the vicarage in a remote Yorkshire village leading a positively paradisial life on a stipend of fifty pounds a year and, along with their children, once more becoming children themselves, or that of Goldsmith who, having become an out and out townsman, imagines that agricultural work consists essentially of haymaking.

But with Goldsmith the emphasis is now on the warm and friendly atmosphere. A type of human association has come into being which extends its influence over almost all departments of life. The family sits in the arbour and drinks tea surrounded by hawthorn and honeysuckle, has meals from a table set up in a field, takes little walks, feeds the blackbirds and the robins or arranges innocent games with visiting neighbours, games in which the mothers take part, while the fathers look on. Musical entertainments are organized, as are dances and a guitar recital, poems are read and there are literary discussions. The children are friendly and full of love towards each other and when brother Moses goes to market his sisters show concern for his clothes, his hat and his hair and plait a black ribbon into his pigtail. At length a picture is painted of the whole family, showing the vicar's wife as Venus, the two little ones as cupids, Olivia as an Amazon on a hill of flowers, Sophia as a shepherdess and the squire as Alexander the Great at Olivia's feet. The general sharing of interests even permits a discussion of the daughters' respective prospects of marriage which are examined in the family circle much as though its members were considering the price that might be fetched by a horse. And yet it is precisely in this complete sharing of heart and mind that we observe the total abandonment of views that had once prevailed unchallenged. Mr Primrose, the Vicar, speaks of the members of his family as of a small republic, and indeed he himself is free from any dictatorial attitude whether in regard to his wife, whose not inconsiderable failings are in his estimation amply offset by her excellence as a housewife, or towards the children, whose freedom no one seeks to disturb.

The whole conception of the family has undergone a change. Where are Baxter's *pars imperans* and *pars subdita*? Where is the father's part as the organ of vindictive justice? When his disobedient daughter is overtaken by misfortune, no harsh word is heard. The father's conduct expresses nothing but love; misfortune only causes them all to draw closer together. So long as that misfortune comes from without in the form of loss of fortune and the like, the vicar loses none of that 'cheerfulness' which we hear extolled as one of the greatest virtues that the passage of centuries has produced.

Finally, the moral intention of this work is to exalt moderation. The real enemies of man are shown to be the unbridled passions. Childhood, a childlike disposition, the simple pleasures of life are the fairest things it has to offer. How close this view of life already comes to that of Wordsworth! The background to all this—and how everyone longs for it when they are away from home—is provided by the rustic roof of thatch, the warmth of the fireplace, the breakfast room and the arbour in Milton's *Paradise Lost* which in Germany became the actual symbol of family life, which will only disappear from the social scene along with the family itself.

VII

Conclusion

The idyllic transfiguration of family life in Goldsmith's poem in prose shows the immense change in literary taste which the eighteenth century brought in its train. In the early part of that century the trend had been towards rationalism, a rationalism that inclined towards satire as the art-form most adequate to its mood. In the second half of this same century this was replaced by warmth, feeling and a passion for nature. This great change is closely connected with the imposition upon culture of a bourgeois stamp. The bourgeoisie's most outstanding achievement is the transformation of the family into a real community. It takes time for this new entity to come into being, for the condition of its existence is a harmony both spiritual and intellectual between its members. There must be the opportunity for a community of ideas, temperament and material goods. This means that there must not only be time, place and occasion for the cultivation of mutual interests but also a certain relationship of mind on the part of the children towards each other and between the children and their parents. Above all, if family life is really to exist at all, there must first be a true marriage based on a complete sharing between wife and husband in all spiritual and—so far as this is possible—in all intellectual matters. As we saw earlier, it was some time before these conditions could be realized. Yet we cannot help asking to what extent they ever were really present in England at all, and whether, in a word, the family of Mr Primrose ever really contrived to win a victory over the Harlowes.

It is all too evident from the picture that woman of genius, Jane Austen, painted of her compatriots that this was not the case for some time.

Jane Austen (1775–1817), contrary to her predecessor Richardson, who was idolized on the Continent, remained almost unnoticed in Germany. Not least among the reasons for this is that her wonderfully exact observation of the real world showed it to be a world of the family, an institution for which—particularly in the day of the German Romantics—there was in Germany very little interest. It is all too true that Jane Austen mirrors with superb realism, profound psychological insight and masterly artistry, the crises, spiritual struggles and character development of people coming from the world of the higher bourgeoisie, the provincial gentry. Yet how insular they are! One notes with astonishment how negligible are the changes that have taken place within the space of two generations. How similar to the old conceptions—as Annelies Döring has pointed out—are the views on love and marriage, on 'propriety' and 'principles', how completely everything is dominated by the ideal of 'sobriety' which, along with the 'necessity for self-denial and humility' referred to in *Mansfield Park* (1814), in this context underlies all delineation of character.

How closely related to Mercy in *The Pilgrim's Progress*, or to the youngest daughter in the first part of Defoe's *Religious Courtship* and especially to Richardson's Clarissa are such heroines as the cool Elinor of *Sense and Sensibility* (1811) with her conscientious dissections both of herself and other people. The very title *Sense and Sensibility*, with its odd contrast, is a phrase that is eloquent of the tendencies at work within the author herself. It obviously needed the revolutionary change that ushered in what we call the 'early Victorian' for human beings to be viewed in a wholly different way.

The urge towards a new literary *genre*, which laid the main stress on the description of feeling and sentiment attained its summit in the sequence of Charles Dickens' works. His art is nourished by humour and by a humanity which has impressed into its service an unexampled poetic imagination and an unprecedented wealth of observation. Now feeling comes into its own but it cannot dispense with descriptions of the family. The great novelist himself is at his best in its atmosphere. 'No man,' says Forster, his biographer and friend, 'was so inclined naturally to derive his happiness from home concerns.' It is not to be marvelled at that he had a most lively admiration for Oliver Goldsmith. Just as for the latter, the warmth of the home can for Dickens heal the effects of the worst blows of fortune. He paints family happiness or family disaster in soulful colours. Yet, original writer that he is, one really feels that there is nothing specifically English about his writing, above all nothing that could remind one of Jane Austen and the conduct

CONCLUSION

books of a bygone age. Rather do we unmistakably recognize the power of the age. Indeed the feminine ideal in Dickens differs only in nugatory fashion from that prevailing in Germany, France and America at the time, in the stories of Mörike, Raabe, Stendhal, Fennimore Cooper and others.

When—again half a century later—naturalism sought to portray 'a coherent piece of reality', we encounter in the novels of its representatives, Galsworthy, Arnold Bennett and Wells, a quite different sort of family—and this time it is really an English one—which they behold with the loveless eye of the critical sociologist. Does it betray traces of a Puritan way of life in the culture of the age ? It most certainly does—and it is precisely against these that the mind of these authors is set. We see as we examine them that what we once referred to as 'the humanizing of the family' has quite surprisingly contrived to get stuck half-way. It is true that in this context we shall have to distinguish between a wide range of human relationships, some more advanced than others. Nevertheless—and this is the important point—the conception is still very much alive of a *pars imperans* and *pars subdita* which implies an inescapable spiritual separation between parents and children, a separation which once obtained everywhere in earlier stages of cultural evolution, but was especially cultivated and preserved by Puritanism—even in circumstances where the religious grounds for it had ceased to exist. Indeed this realism in art makes us aware of an unfeeling quality in the relation between one generation and another, which often is nothing short of frightening to the Continental beholder. The lack of confidence in one another, the independent manner in which members of a family come to decisions by which their whole lives may be affected, the tone used by children in speaking of their parents—all these things and many others like them argue a coldness of heart between members of a family which make it impossible for anything that could be described as happiness coming from shared experience to come into being at all. The battle of the generations, as described in such a work as Samuel Butler's *The Way of all Flesh* (1903), seems positively to be part of the order of nature, everything else being no more than a mask. To the reformer Shaw (1856–1950) the contemplation of the family is the occasion of his unkindest paradoxes (compare Erna Cohn). Shaw's personal credo declares the economic and ideal grounds of family life to be invalid. There can be no thought of a natural affection between parents and children. 'The family ideal is a humbug and a nuisance,' he says. Even the love between brothers and sisters is not innate. The family is merely a product of capitalism and must perish along with it. A thousand years from now it will be accounted bad taste even to know one's parents. One would tend to view arguments of this kind as so many ludicrous quirks if they did not accord so closely with certain observations of Galsworthy's and even more with remarks by Bennett and Wells, authors whom nobody would accuse of deliberate excursions into the kind of bad taste with which Shaw all too often anticipates the grotesque absurdities of an age that was still to come.

In the meantime changed circumstances are compelling millions of human beings to shape their lives in such a fashion that the family ideal must appear Utopian, but many consider even this Utopia to be no longer attractive. The bourgeoisie in the old sense of the term has been unable to keep up with developments and many of its ties are loosening. Even art, which was once nourished out of the depths of human feeling, seems now to prefer a taste in which emotional values play little part. It must be left to our indestructible faith in human nature to save us from the fear that we may be moving towards an impoverishment of feeling, and with it ultimately to an impoverishment of the Muses.

Bibliography

ADDISON, Joseph, *Cato*, 1713
—— *The Tatler*, 1709-11
—— *The Spectator*, 1711-14
—— *The Guardian*, 1713
AGRIPPA von Nettesheim, *De nobilitate et praecellentia foeminei sexus*, 1532
AITKEN, George Atherton ed., *Romances and Narratives*, London, 1895
AUSTEN, Jane, *Sense and Sensibility*, 1811
—— *Mansfield Park*, 1814
BACON, Francis, *Essays*, 1625, ed. Rych Foster Jones, New York, 1937
BATTY, Bartholomew, *The Christian Man's Closet*, trans. William Lowth, 1581
BAXTER, Richard, *Christian Directory*, 1673
—— *Reliquiae Baxterianae*, 1696
BAYLY, Lewis, *The Practise of Pietie*, 1613
BECON, Thomas, *Catechism*, 1560
BERNBAUM, Ernest, *The Drama of Sensibility. A Sketch of the History of English Sentimental Comedy and Domestic Tragedy 1780-96*, Harvard Studies in English, III, 1958
BOWDLER, Thomas, *The Family Shakespeare*, 1807
—— *Memoir of the Life of John Bowdler, Esq.*, London, 1824
BOWND, Nicholas, *The Doctrine of Sabath plainely layde forth*, 1595
BRIE, Friedrich, *Englische Rokoko-Epik 1710-1730*, Munich, 1927
BUNYAN, John, *Christian Behaviour*, 1663
—— *The Pilgrim's Progress*, 1678
—— *The Life and Death of Mr Badman*, 1680
—— *The Holy War*, 1682
BURNEY, Fanny, *Diary and Letters of Mme D'Arblay (1778-1840)*, ed. Charlotte Frances Barrett, 7 vol. London, 1842-6
BUTLER, Samuel (1612-80), *Hudibras*, 1663-78
BUTLER, Samuel (1835-1902), *The Way of All Flesh*, London, 1903
CALVIN, John, *Christianae religionis institutio*, 1536
CAMPBELL, Douglas, *The Puritan in Holland, England, and America*, 2 vol., London/New York, 1892
CARLYLE, Thomas ed., *Letters and Speeches of Cromwell*, 1845
CARTER, Elizabeth, see: Pennington
CHAMBERS, Raymund Wilson, *The Place of Sir Thomas More in English Literature and History*, London, 1937

CHOISY, J. Eugène, *La théocratie à Genève au temps de Calvin*, Geneva, 1897
CHESTERFIELD, Lord, see: Dobrée
CIBBER, Colley, *The Careless Husband*, 1692
—— *The Provoked Husband*, 1728 cf. also Vanbrugh
CLARK, Samuel, *Self Examination explained and recommended*, 1761
CLEUER, Robert and DOD, J., *A godlye forme of household Gouernment*, 1630
COHN, Erna, *G. B. Shaw und die Familie* (Diss.), Leipzig, 1927
COLLIER, Jane, *An Essay on the Art of ingeniously Tormenting* etc., 1753
COULTON, George Gordon, 'The High Ancestry of Puritanism', *Contemporary Review* 88 (1905), pages 221–30
COVERDALE, Miles, *Christian State of Matrimonye*, 1541
—— *Letters of Saints*, 1564
CRANMER, Thomas, *The Marriage Vow*, 1547–9
—— *Preface to the Common Prayer Book*, 1549
CROMWELL, Oliver, see: Carlyle
CUMBERLAND, Richard, *Memoirs of Richard Cumberland*, London, 1806/7
DARWIN, Erasmus, see: Krause
DAVEY, Henry, *A History of English Music*, 2nd ed., London, 1929
DEFOE, Daniel, *The Family Instructor*, 1715
—— *Robinson Crusoe*, 1719
—— *The Religious Courtship*, 1722
—— *The Great Law of Subordination* etc., 1724
—— *Everybody's Business is Nobody's Business*, 1725
—— *Political History of the Devil*, 1726
—— *Use and Abuse of the Marriage Bed*, 1727
—— see: Aitken
—— see: Wilson
Dives et Pauper, RIche and pore etc. by Henry Parker, Carmelite of Doncaster, London, the v. day of Iuyl, 1493
DOBRÉE, Bonamy, ed., *The letters of Philip Dormer Stanhope, 4th Earl of Chesterfield*, 6 vols., London, 1932
DÖRING, Annelies, *Das puritanische Erbe in den Romanen von Jane Austen* (Diss.), Leipzig, 1944
DOWNAME, John, *A Guide to Godlynesse*, 1622
DRESSLER, Bruno, *Die Entwicklung der englischen Erziehung im 17. Jahrhundert* (Diss.), Leipzig, 1927
DRYDEN, John, *The Conquest of Granada by the Spaniards*, 1672
—— *Aurengzebe*, 1676
DYKE, Daniel, *Two Treatises*, 1618
EBNER-ESCHENBACH, Marie von, *Aphorismen*, Wiesbaden, 1948, Insel Bücherei 543
EDGEWORTH, F. A., *A Memoir of Maria Edgeworth with a selection from her letters by the late Mrs. Edgeworth*, ed. by her children, 3 vol., London, 1867
EDGEWORTH, Maria, see: Edgeworth, F. A.

BIBLIOGRAPHY

EICKEN, Heinrich von, *Geschichte und System der mittelalterlichen Weltanschauung*, Stuttgart, 1887
ELYOT, Sir Thomas, *The boke named the Governour*, 1531
ENFIELD, William, *The Speaker*, 1774
FIELDING, Henry, *Joseph Andrews*, 1742
—— *History of Tom Jones, a Foundling*, 1749
—— *Amelia*, 1752
—— *Covent Garden Journal*, 1752
FORDYCE, James, *Sermons to young women*, 2 vol., 1766
FORSTER, John, *The Life of Charles Dickens*, 3 vol., London, 1872-4
FOX, John, *Actes and Monuments*, 1563
—— *Book of Martyrs*, see: *Actes and Monuments*
FRIPP, Edgar Innes, *Shakespeare's Stratford*, London, 1928
FROUDE, James Anthony, *John Bunyan*, London, 1880 ['English Men of Letters', ed. John Morley]
GAIRDNER, James, *Lollardy and the Reformation in England*, 4 vol., London, 1908-13
—— *Paston Letters*, 1422-1509 with notes and an introduction by James Gairdner, 6 vol., Exeter, 1904
GALSWORTHY, John, *The Forsyte Saga*, 1906-21
GASQUET, Francis Aidan, *The Eve of the Reformation*, London, 1900
—— *Parish Life in Medieval England*, Northampton, 1906
GAY, John, *The Beggar's Opera*, 1728
GILBERT, A. H., 'Milton on the Position of Woman', *Modern Language Review* 15 (1920), pages 7-27
GODFREY, Elizabeth, *Home Life under the Stuarts 1603-49*, London, 1925
GOLDSMITH, Oliver, *The Vicar of Wakefield*, 1766
—— *Poems for Young Ladies*, 1767
GOODSELL, Willystine, *A History of the Family as a Social and Educational Institution*, New York, 1915
GOSSE, Edmund, *A History of Eighteenth Century Literature (1660-1780)*, London, 1902
GOUGE, William, *Of Domesticall Duties, Eight Treatises*, 1622; 2nd ed., 1626
—— *The Whole Armour of God*, 1619; 2nd ed., 1627
GRIFFITH, Matthew, *Bethel: or, a forme for families* etc., 1633
Hali Maidenhad, An Alliterative Homily of the 13th Century, ed. Oswald Cockayne, London, 1866 [E.E.T.S. 18]
HALIFAX, Lord, see: Savile, George
HALLER, William, *The Rise of Puritanism*, New York, 1938
HAMILTON, John, *Catechism of the Kirk of Scotland*, 1552
HARTMANN, Eduard von, *Ausgewählte Werke*, Berlin, 1885-96
HAUTKAPPE, Franz, *Über die altdeutschen Beichten*, Münster, 1917
HAYWOOD, Eliza, *The Tea-Table*, 1725
HENRY, Philip, *An Account of the Life and Death of Mr Philip Henry*, 1712
HILL, Aaron, *Progress of Wit*, 1730

HITTMAIR, Rudolf, 'Der Begriff der Arbeit bei Langland' *Luick Festschrift*, Marburg, 1925, pp. 204-18
HOWARD, George Eliot, *A History of Matrimonial Institutions*, 3 vol., Chicago, 1904
HUTCHINSON, Lucy, *Memoirs of the Life of Colonel Hutchinson* etc., London, 1806
JOHNSON, Samuel, *A Dictionary of the English Language*, 1755
JOHNSON, Samuel, *Rasselas*, 1759
—— *Dinarbas*, 1760
—— *The Rambler*, 1750-52
JONAS OF ORLEANS, *Libri tres de institutione laicali*, 1723 ed.
KIRBY, Sarah, *Some Account of the Life and Writings of Mrs Trimmer*, London, 1814
KLUCKHOHN, Paul, *Die Auffassung von der Liebe in der Literatur des 18. Jahrhunderts und in der deutschen Romantik*, 2nd ed., Halle, 1931
KRAUSE, Ernst, *Erasmus Darwin*, trans. by W. S. Dallas, London, 1879
KYD, Thomas, *The Spanish Tragedy*, 1587
LAFAYETTE, Mme de, *La princesse de Clèves*, 1673
LANGLAND, William, *The Vision of William concerning Piers the Plowman* etc. 1362-99, ed. Walter W. Skeat, 2 vol., 2nd ed., London, 1924
LATIMER, Hugh, *Hys ·7· sermons vpon the Lordes prayer*, Ed. Augustine Berner [27 Sermons preached by . . . Maister Hugh Latimer] London, 1562
LECHLER, Gotthard Victor, *Geschichte des englischen Deismus*, Stuttgart, 1841
—— *Johann von Wiclif und die Vorgeschichte der Reformation*, 2 vol., Leipzig, 1873
LESSING, Gotthold Ephraim, *Sämmtliche Schriften*, ed. Karl Lachmann, 12 vol., Leipzig, 1857
LOCKE, John, *Some Thoughts concerning Education*, 1693
LOWTH, William, see: Batty
LUPSET, Thomas, *An Exhortation to yonge Men*, 1530, 2nd ed., 1534
LYDGATE, John, *Pilgrimage of Man*, an English metrical version written in 1426 of Deguilleville's *Pèlerinage de la Vie Humaine*
MANNYNG OF BRUNNE, Robert, *Handlyng Synne*, 1303, ed. Frederick J. Furnivall, London, 1901 [E.E.T.S. 119/123]
MARTIN, Alfred Henri, *Exposé de l'ancienne législation genevoise sur le mariage*, Geneva, 1891
MEADS, Dorothy ed., *Diary of Lady Margaret Hoby 1599-1605*, London, 1930
METEREN, Emanuel van, *Pictures of the English in Queen Elizabeth's Reign*, trans. from the Dutch, 1865
MICHEL, Dan, *Ayenbite of Inwyt, or, Remorse of Conscience*, 1340, ed. Richard Morris, London, 1866 [E.E.T.S. 23]
MILTON, John, *Of Education*, 1644
—— *Paradise Lost*, 1667
—— *Samson Agonistes*, 1671
MOORE, Edward ed., *The World*, 4 vol., London, 1753-6

BIBLIOGRAPHY

MORE, Hannah, *Strictures on the Modern System of Female Education* etc., 4th ed., Dublin, 1799
—— *The Life of Hannah More with Selections from her Correspondence* [*The Library of Christian Biography*, superintended by R. Bickersteth, 7] London, 1856
NEWTON, John, *Letters, Sermons, and a Review of Ecclesiastical History*, 3 vol., Edinburgh, 1780
ORDERICUS VITALIS, *Historia Ecclesiastica*, 1120–41, ed. Auguste le Prevost, 5 vol., Paris, 1838–55
Paston Letters, see: Gairdner
PECOCK, Reginald, *The Repressor of Overmuch Blaming of the Clergy*, 1495, ed. Churchill Babington, London, 1860 [Rolls Series, 19]
PENNINGTON, Montagu, *Memoirs of the Life of Mrs. Elizabeth Carter* etc., 2 vol., 2nd ed., London, 1808
—— ed., *A Series of Letters between Mrs Elizabeth Carter and Miss Catherine Talbot from the year 1741 to 1770* etc., 2 vol., London, 1808
PEPYS, Samuel, *Diary 1659-69*
PERKINS, William, *Oeconomia Christiana*, 1590
Poema Morale, ed. Richard Morris, London, 1873 [E.E.T.S. 53] cf. also E.E.T.S. 29 and 34
POWELL, Chilton Latham, *English Domestic Relations 1487-1653* etc., New York, 1917
RAPER, Elizabeth, *The Receipt Book of Elizabeth Raper* etc., ed. Bartle Grant, London, 1924
REINHOLD, Heinz, *Puritanismus und Aristikratie*, Berlin, 1938
Relation of England, *A Relation, or rather a true account of the Island of England*, trans. from Italian by Charlotte Auguste Sneyd. Camden Society 37, London, 1847
RICHARDSON, Samuel, *Pamela*, 1740–1
—— *Letters Written to and for Particular Friends on the most Important Occasions*, 1741
—— *Clarissa Harlowe*, 1748
—— *Sir Charles Grandison*, 1754
—— *The Correspondence of Samuel Richardson* etc., ed. Anna Laetitia Barbauld. 6 vol., London, 1806
—— *Selected Letters of Samuel Richardson*, ed. with an introduction by John Carroll, Oxford, 1964
ROGERS, Daniel, *Matrimoniall Honour*, 1642
ROUSSEAU, Jean Jacques, *Julie ou la nouvelle Héloïse*, 1765
RYF, Andreas, *Une chronique suisse inédite du XVI*e *siècle*, ed. E. Meininger, Basle, 1892
—— Baseler Beiträge zur vaterländischen Geschichte IX
SASEK, Lawrence A., *The Literary Temper of the English Puritans*, Louisiana State University Press, 1961
SAVILE, George (Marquis of Halifax), *A Lady's New Year's Gift, or Advice to a Daughter*, 1688
SCHÜCKING, Levin Ludwig, 'Zu den Anfängen des Familienlebens in England 1200–1600' *Die Neueren Sprachen* 32 (1924), pages 1–18

SCHÜCKING, Levin Ludwig, 'Literatur und Familie zu Anfang des 18. Jahrhunderts in England', *Hoops Festschrift* Heidelberg, 1925, pages 184–94
—— 'Die Grundlagen des Richardsonschen Romans' *Germanisch-Romanische Monatsschrift XII*, 1924, pages 21–42 and 88–110
—— 'Die Familie als Geschmacksträger in England im 18. Jahrhundert' *Deutsche Vierteljahrsschrift* IV, 1926, pages 439–59
—— *Essays über Shakespeare, Pepys u.a.*, Wiesbaden, 1948
SCHÜTZE, Johannes, *Dickens Frauenideal und das Biedermeier* (Diss.), Erlangen, 1948
SCUDERY, Mlle de, *Artamène, ou le Grand Cyrus*, 1649–53
SECKER, William, *A Wedding Ring fit for the Finger*, 1658
SELLS, A. Lytton, *Les sources françaises d'Oliver Goldsmith*, Paris, 1924
SHAW, George Bernhard, *Back to Methusela. A Metabiological Pentateuch*, London, 1921
SINGER, Helmut, *Das Verhältnis von Herrschaft und Dienstbote im Puritanismus* (Diss.), Leipzig, 1940
SMOLLETT, Tobias G., *The Expedition of Humphrey Clinker*, 1771
SNAWSEL, Robert, *A Looking Glasse for maried folkes* etc., 1610
SOUTHERNE, Thomas, *Fatal Marriage*, 1694
STEELE, Richard, *The Christian Hero*, 1701
—— *The Tender Husband*, 1705
—— *The Ladies' Library*, 1714
—— *The Conscious Lovers*, 1723
—— *The Tatler*, 1709–11
—— *The Spectator*, 1711–14
—— *The Guardian*, 1713
STERNE, Laurence, *The Life and Opinions of Tristram Shandy*, 1759–67
—— *Sermons of Mr. Yorick*, 2 vol., 1760
STUBBES, Philip, *A Perfect pathway to Felicitie*, 1592
SWIFT, Jonathan, *A Tale of a Tub*, 1704
—— *Gulliver's Travels*, 1726
—— *Directions to Servants in General*, 8 vol., 1745
TAYLOR, Jeremy, *The Rule and Exercises of Holy Living* etc., 1650
—— *Ductor Dubitantium or the Rule of Conscience* etc., 2nd ed., London, 1671
—— 'The Marriage Ring', *Illustrations of the Liturgy and Ritual of The United Church of England and Ireland* etc., ed. James Brogden, III London, 1842, pages 117–60, republished as *The Mysteriousness of Marriage*, Abergavenny, 1928
TEELINCK, Willem, *Huysboeck*, 1639
THOMSON, James, *The Complete Poetical Works of James Thomson*, ed. J. Logie Robertson, 2nd ed., London/New York/Toronto, 1951
TILLOTSON, John, *The Wisdom of being Religious: A sermon preached at St Paul's*, 1664
—— *Six Sermons . . . of Stedfastness in Religion* etc., 1694
TRENCHFIELD, Caleb, *A Cap of Gray Hairs, for a Green Head* etc., 1671
TREVELYAN, George Macaulay, *English Social History*, London, 1944

BIBLIOGRAPHY

TRIMMER, Mrs, see: Kirby
TROELTSCH, Ernst, *The Social Teaching of the Christian Churches*, trans. by Olive Wyon, London/New York, 1931
TYNDALE, William, *The Obedience of a Christen man* 1528, ed. R. Lovett, 1888
VANBRUGH, Sir John, *The Provoked Husband, or, a Journey to London* etc., 1728
VIVES, Juan Luis, *The Instruction of a Christian Woman*, trans. by R. Hyrde, London, 1540
WALLER, Edmund, *Poems, written by Mr Ed. Waller of Beckonsfield* etc., 1645
WALPOLE, Horace, *The Yale Edition of Horace Walpole's Correspondence*, ed. W. S. Lewis, London/New Haven, 1937
WARTON, Joseph, *Biographical Memoirs . . . of Joseph Warton*, ed. J. Wool, London, 1806
WATTON, John, *Speculum Christianorum*, 1490
WEBER, Max, *Gesammelte Aufsätze zur Religionssoziologie*, 3 vol., Tübingen, 1920-1
WHITE, Thomas, *A little book for little children*, 12th ed., London, 1702
WHITFORDE, Richard, *A werke for householders, or for them yt haue the Gydyonge or Gouernaunce of any Company* etc., 1533
The Practice of Christian Graces or The Whole Duty of Man, London, 1659
WILSON, Walter, *Memoirs of the life and times of Daniel De Foe* etc., 3 vols., London, 1830
YOUNG, Edward, *The Complaint: or, Night-Thoughts on Life, Death and Immortality*, 1755
ZEUNER, Martin, *Das Problem der Generationen im englischen Naturalismus* (Diss.), Leipzig, 1930
ZIEGLER, Theobald, *Die geistigen und sozialen Strömungen des 19. Jahrhunderts* [Schlenther, Paul, *Das 19. Jahrhundert in Deutschlands Entwicklung* etc., 1] Berlin, 1899

Index

Addison, Joseph, 87, 127, 141–2, 149, 174
Advice to a Daughter (Lord Halifax), 131, 132
Agamemnon (Seneca), 129
Aitken, G. A., 101
Amelia (Fielding), 164–5, 177
Aquinas, Thomas, 43
Artamène ou le Grand Cyrus (Scudéry), 159
Aurengzebe (Dryden), 130
Austen, Jane, 181–3
Ayenbite of Inwyt (Michel), 21, 172

Babington, C., 19
Back to Methuselah (Shaw), 15
Bacon, Francis, 170
Barrett-Browning, Elizabeth, 41
Batty, B., 75
Baxter, Margaret, 8, 53
Baxter, Richard, 18, 19, 111, 112, 137, 139, 148, 179; influence of, xiii; on sobriety, 8; on marriage, 21, 24–7, 36, 40, 45, 53; on women, 42–3, 45, 53; on the family, 56; on education, 70, 74; on children; 74, 76, 171; on idleness, 79; on mothers, 87; on childless marriages, 91–2; on leisure of children, 92–3; on servants, 99; on love, 127–8; on reading to the family, 173
Bayly, Lewis, 93, 98
Becon, Thomas, 97; on sobriety, 7; influence of, 19; on children's instruction, 63, 69, 92; on keeping the Sabbath, 64; on children, 73–6, 91, 92; and industry, 78; and marriage, 80, 83; on servants and masters, 98–100; on ideal of Puritan maiden, 119; and marriage of daughters, 126; and the aristocracy, 149
Bede, 71
Beggar's Opera, The (Gay), 131
Bennett Arnold, 183, 184
Bentley, 169
Beowulf, 172
Bernbaum, E., 143
Bethel: or, a forme for families (Griffith), 19
Blackstone, W., 175
Boileau, N., 7, 124
Book of Martyrs (Foxe), 173
Bowdler, Thomas, 167–8
Bownd, Nicholas, 64
Bradshaigh, Lady, 156, 159–60, 163

Brie, F., 136–7
Bullinger, Heinrich, 19, 25, 126; influence of, 18; on women, 45; on children, 63; on servants, 99
Bunyan, John, xv, 173; on Old Testament, 21; on the family, 56; on children, 76–7; on servants and masters, 98, 100–2; on marriage, 108; as husband and father, 114–5, 116–7; compared to Milton, 114; on woman, 116–20, 126; and family life, 118, 122, 156; and conduct at death, 154
Burke, Edmund, 175
Burney, Fanny, 169
Butler, Samuel, (1612–80), 130
Butler, Samuel (1835–1902), 155, 183

Calvin, John, 65, 104; influence of, xii, xiv, 4–5, 37, 66; on marriage, 43; on the family, 59–60, 97
Campbell, Douglas, 65
Canterbury Tales, The (Chaucer), 172
Careless Husband, The (Cibber), 132, 157
Carlyle, Thomas, 126
Carter, Elizabeth, 160–3, 165
Catechism (Becon), 7, 63, 69, 74
Chesterfield, Lord, 92, 131, 132, 135, 140, 150, 175
Chambers, R. W., 6
Cato, 141–3
Choisy, J. E., 60
Christen State of Matrimonye (Bullinger), 19, 63
Christian Behaviour (Bunyan), 56 100
Christian Directory (Baxter), 19, 42, 56, 70, 74, 76, 92, 93, 128, 173
Christian Hero, The (Steele), 150
Christian Man's Closet, The (Batty), 75
Cibber, Colley, 87, 132, 143–4, 157
Cicero, 20, 169
Clarissa (Richardson), 146–8, 150–3, 155–6, 163, 166, 170, 176, 182
Clark, Samuel, 10
Cleuer, R., 83
Cobham, Eleanor, 32
Cohn, Erna, 183
Collier, Jane, 102
Colossians, 97
Commentaries on the Laws of England (Blackstone), 175
Conjugal Lewdness: or Matrimonial Whoredom (Defoe), 123
Conquest of Granada (Dryden), 130
Conscious Lovers, The (Steele), 149

192

INDEX

Contemporary Review, 23
Cooper, John Fennimore, 183
Coriolanus (Shakespeare), 29, 86
Coulton, G. G., 23, 116
Covent Garden Journal, 164
Coverdale, Miles, 19, 45, 63, 98, 126
Cranmer, Thomas, 20, 22, 64
Cromwell, Bridget, 51
Cromwell, Elizabeth, 95
Cromwell, Frances, 126
Cromwell, Mary, 90
Cromwell, Oliver, 8, 50-2, 67, 84, 93-5, 126
Cromwell, Richard, 84
Cumberland, Richard, 169

Dacier, A., 7, 124
Dante, 108
Darwin, Erasmus, 90-1, 170
Davey, Henry, 93
De institutione laicali (Jonas of Orleans), 75
De nobilitate et praecellentia foeminei sexus (von Nettesheim), 31
Deffand, Marquise du, 154
Defoe, Daniel, xiii, xv, 7, 18, 41, 59, 102, 107, 174, 182; on religion, 12; on marriage, 26, 31, 39, 85; on religious instruction, 68, 69; and relationship of father-daughter, 89, 127; and children in the family, 89-90; and lack of cultural interests, 94; on servants, 97, 100, 102; on angels, 107; and relationship husband-wife, 110; on women, 111; on Milton, 114; on the Puritan maiden, 119; and marriage, 80, 120, 122-4, 156, 171; and mental development of women, 126-8, 151-2, 157; and the aristocracy, 149; and family life, 156
Dekker, Thomas, 141
Delany, Mrs, 160, 165, 168
Dewes, Mrs, 165
Diary of Samuel Pepys, 94, 159
Dibelius, W., 54
Dickens, Charles, 155, 172, 182-3
Dinarbas (Johnson), 71, 87
Directions to Servants in General (Swift), 102
Dives et Pauper, 7, 20, 22, 31, 61, 82, 108, 172
Dod, J., 83, 113
Döring, Annelies, 182
Downame, John, 10, 33, 50, 64, 73, 74, 77, 94; on children, 92; on servants, 98, 100
Dressler, B., 72, 79
Dryden, John, 130, 159
'Duties of Husbands' (Gouge), 120
Dyke, Daniel, 13, 57, 96

Ebner-Eschenbach, Marie von, 15
Ecclesiasticus, 74
Edgeworth, Maria, 171
Ehebuch, see Christen State of Matrimonye
Eicken, H. von, 108
Elizabeth I, xi, 22, 65, 66, 79
Elyot, Thomas, 68
Enfield, William, 176
English Domestic Relations (Powell), xiii
English Social History (Trevelyan), xi
Ephesians, 75
Erasmus, 18, 25, 33, 45
Essay on the Art of ingenuously Tormenting, An (Collier), 102
Eve of the Reformation (Gasquet), 61
Everybody's Business is Nobody's Business (Defoe), 102
Everyman, 115-17
Exhortation to yonge Men, An (Lupset), 3, 80

Family Instructor (Defoe), 7, 41, 59, 69, 89, 94, 110, 123-4, 157, 171, 174
Family Magazine, 174
Family Shakespeare (Bowdler), 167
Fatal Marriage (Southerne), 141
Faust (Goethe), 108
Fielding, Henry, 142, 146, 156, 158, 162, 164-5, 174, 176-7
Fordyce, J., 116-17, 168, 176
Forster, J., 182
Forsyte Saga, The (Galsworthy), 153
Foxe, J., 173
Frederick of Würtenberg, 29
Fripp, E. I., 80, 106
Froude, J. A., 115
Fuller, T., 87

Gairdner, J., 81, 82
Galsworthy, John, 183, 184
Gasquet, F. A., 61, 65
Gay, John, 131, 134
Gellert, C. F., 16, 145
Genesis B, 111
Genlis, Madame de, 169
Gibbon, Edward, 169
Gilbert, A. H., 105, 108
Gloucester, Humphrey, Duke of, 32
Godfrey, E. L., 50
Goethe, J. W. von, 108, 145, 164, 169, 177
Goldsmith, Oliver, 142, 146, 167-8, 176, 178-9, 181-182
Goodsell, W., 20
Gosse, Edmund, 124, 156
Gouge, William, 19, 77, 113, 137; influence of, xiii; on self-examination, 9; on the Stoics, 13; on Old Testament, 21; on marriage, 26, 33-9, 45, 46, 49, 53, 108; on women, 29, 30, 33-9, 43, 45; on children,

193

Gouge, William—(continued)
  73, 75–6, 89, 92, 129, 171; and sinecures, 80; and position of mother, subordinate to father, 88; and criticisms of mothers, 88; on servants and masters, 98–100; and physical love, 104; and duty of sharing, 106; and hospitality, 107; on duties of husband, 120; influence of Defoe on, 125.
Governor, The (Elyot), 68
Gray, Thomas, 134
Great Cyrus, The, see *Artamène ou le Grand Cyrus*
Great Law of Subordination consider'd or, the Insolence and unsufferable behaviour of servants in England duly enquir'd into (Defoe), 101
Greuze, Jean Baptiste, 144
Griffith, Matthew, 19, 76
Grub Street Opera (Fielding), 174
Guardian, The, 140, 149, 150
Guide to Godlynesse, A (Downame), 10, 33, 74
Gulliver's Travels (Swift), 133

Hali Maidenhad, 24
Halifax, Lord, 131, 132, 140, 157
Haller, William, xi, 113
Hamilton, John, 62
Hampole, Rolle von, 78
Hartmann, Eduard von, 12
Hautkappe, Franz, 41
Haywood, Eliza, 13
Hebrews, 107
Henry IV (Shakespeare), 3
Henry V (Shakespeare), 4
Henry, Mrs, 50, 52
Henry, Philip, 52, 103, 129
Heywood, Thomas, 141
Hill, Aaron, 175
History of England (Hume), 175
Hittmair, R., 78
Hobbes, Thomas, 134
Hoby, Lady, 59, 173, 175
Hogarth, William, 144, 146, 147, 162, 164
Holbein, H., 3
Holy Living and Dying (Taylor), 19, 39, 91, 130, 149, 153
Homer, 20, 145
Howard, G. E., 81
Hudibras (Butler), 130
Hume, David, 175
Humphrey Clinker (Smollett), 178
Hunne, Richard, 65–7
Hutchinson, John, 36, 52, 84, 93
Hutchinson, Lucy, 8, 36, 50–1, 69, 84, 93, 126, 148
Huysboeck (Teelinck), 47

Ibsen, Henrik, 145, 157

Jacqueline of Holland, 32
Johnson, Samuel, 11, 87, 113, 132, 135–6, 159, 170, 174–5
Jonas of Orleans, 75, 107
Joseph Andrews (Fielding), 164, 175
Julius Caesar (Shakespeare), 7, 86

Kluckhohn, P., 18, 48,
Kyd, Thomas, 96

La Calprenède, 154
Ladies Library (Steele), 130
Lafayette, Madame de, 125, 175
Langland, William, 21, 22, 65, 78
Latimer, Hugh, 78, 97
Lechler, V., 65
Legend of the Saints, The, 172, 173
Lessing, G. E., 90
Letters Written to and for Particular Friends (Richardson), 90, 168
Life and Death of Mr Badman, The (Bunyan), 154
Lillo, George, 144
Literary Temper of the English Puritans, The (Sasek), xi
Little Book for Little Children, A (White), 69
Locke, John, 70, 87, 96, 130
Looking Glasse for maried folkes, A (Snawsel), 42
Lowth, William, 67
Luke, 97
Lupset, Thomas, 3, 80
Luther, Martin, 22, 23, 37, 48, 59–61, 82, 97
Maidstone, 8
Mannyng, Robert, 75, 84
Mansfield Park (Austen), 182
'Marriage Ring, The', (Taylor), 36, 132
Martin, A. H., 81
Mary I, xii
Matrimoniall Honour (Rogers), 19
Memoir of the Life of John Bowdler, Esq., 170
Merry Wives of Windsor, The (Shakespeare), 29
Meteren, Emanuel van, 29, 30, 55
Michel, Dan, 21, 172
Milton, John, xv, 92, 129, 156, 159, 180; and sobriety, 8; and personal dignity, 15; and sexual morality, 38, 67; education of, 70; and simplicity, 77; and lack of knowledge of mother 87; and music, 93; and Puritanism expressed in *Paradise Lost*, 103, 113; and hospitality, 107; and significance of marriage, 108, 113, 116; and nature of women, 109–10; and weakness of women, 111–12; and despotic power of husbands, 113; women, contradictory attitude to-

INDEX

Milton, John—(continued)
  wards, 113–14; compared to Bunyan, 114; and relationship with father, 170; reading aloud of, 175
Montague, Mrs, 160, 168
Moore, Edward, 178
More, Hannah, 160, 169
More, Thomas, 6, 41, 61, 62, 73, 134
Mörike, 183
Much Ado About Nothing (Shakespeare), 30
Musset, Alfred de, 145
Mysteriousness of Marriage, The (Taylor), 48

Nettesheim, Agrippa von, 31
Newbury, John, 176
Newton, John, 170
Nouvelle Héloïse (Rousseau), 134
Night Thoughts (Young), 64

Obedience of a Christen man, The (Tyndale), 22, 33, 73, 98
Oeconomia Christiana (Perkins), 19, 38
Of Domesticall Duties, Eight Treatises (Gouge), 19, 26, 29, 33, 104
'On a Girdle' (Waller), 168
On Friendship (Bacon), 170
Ordericus Vitalis, 71
Osborn, John, 174

Pamela (Richardson), 73, 90, 148, 155–7, 161, 162, 164
Paradise Lost (Milton), xv, 8, 13–14, 16, 38, 77, 103–13, 177, 180
Parish Life in Medieval England (Gasquet), 65
Paston Letters, 147
Pecock, Reginald, 19, 31, 65–6
Pepys, Samuel, 94, 159
Perfect Pathway to Felicitie, A (Stubbes), 59
Perkins, William, xiii, 19, 35, 38, 40, 45, 75, 80
Piers Ploughman, see *Vision of Piers Ploughman*
Pilgrim's Progress, The (Bunyan), 21, 115–20, 151–2, 156, 182
Plato, 105
Plutarch, 13, 18, 49
Poema Morale, 116
Poems for Young Ladies (ed. Goldsmith), 167
Political History of the Devil (Defoe), 107
Pope, Alexander, 134, 141, 175
Powell, Chilton L., xiii
Practise of Pietie (Bayly), 93, 98
Princesse de Clèves (Lafayette), 125, 175
Prior, Matthew, 134
Provok'd Husband, The (Cibber), 144

Raabe, Wilhelm, 183
Racine, Jean, 154
Raper, Elizabeth, 160
Raphael, 93
Rasselas (Johnson), 11, 87, 135, 174
Reinhold, H., 130, 140, 151
Relation to the Island of England, A, 72
Religious Courtship, The (Defoe), 12, 26, 85, 89, 102, 123–5, 127, 151, 174, 182
Reliquiae Baxterianae (Baxter), 87
Represser of Overmuch Blaming of the Clergy, The (Pecock), 19, 31
Richardson, Samuel, xv, 125, 167, 170, 182; Anglican Home of, xiv, and self-knowledge, 13, 16; on pride, 16; on marriage, 34, 45; and children, 73; and law, 80; and relationship between children in families, 90; on single men, 92; on daughters, 92, 170, 171; and ideal of Puritan maiden, 119; opinions about, 145; influence of Taylor on, 146, 177; background of, 148; and the working class, 150–1; and the aristocracy, 150–1; and women in love, 152; as a moralist, 153–4; and domestic life, 154–5, 176; view of marriage, 156–7, 168, 171; and dignity of womanhood, 157; humanity of, 158; and problem of different generations, 158; and the ladies' world, 161–3; and literary ability of women, 166; reading aloud of, 174–5; and the family, 176; popularity of, 181
Rise of Puritanism, The (Haller), xi
Robinson Crusoe (Defoe), xiii, 120–2
Rogers, Daniel, 19, 67, 104–5, 112, 127, 131, 137–8; influence of, xiii; on marriage, 25–8, 34–6, 38, 46–51, 53, 92; on women, 30, 43–4, 46–7; on the family, 57; on children, 74, 75, 81, 92; mother's importance subordinate to father, 88; and physical love, 104; influence of Defoe on, 125
Romans, 107
Romeo and Juliet (Shakespeare), 83
Roper, 6
Rousseau, J. J., 134, 164, 178
Rule of Conscience (Taylor), 84, 146
Ruskin, John, 69
Ryf, Andreas, 59–60

St Augustine, 22, 57, 61
St Chrysostom, 45, 99
St Paul, 32, 34
Samson Agonistes (Milton), 8, 112, 113
Sasek, Laurence A., xi
Scudéry, Mlle de, 159
Seasons, The (Thomson), 139, 144

Secker, William, 23
Self-Examination explained and recommended (Clark), 10
Sells, A. L., 178
Seneca, 13, 63, 98, 129
Sense and Sensibility (Austen), 182
Sermons to young women (Fordyce), 166
Sévigné, Madame de, 154
Shakespeare, William, 159, 172; views of the English character, 3, 5, 7, 15; portrayal of English women by, 28–30, 47; and love, 37, 48; and children, 73, 90; and position of mothers, 73, 86; and music, 94; and marriage, 106; and the ideal woman, 111; Puritan attitude towards, 129; reading aloud of, 175
Shaw, G. B., 15, 145, 183–4
Shenstone, W., 134
Singer, H., 96
Six Sermons (Tillotson), 68, 100, 101, 141
Sir Charles Grandison (Richardson), 156–7, 160, 163
Smollett, Tobias, 146, 178
Snawsel, Robert, 42, 49, 59
Song of Songs, 104
Southerne, Thomas, 141
Spanish Tragedy, The (Kyd), 96
Speaker, The (Enfield), 176
Spectator, The, 134, 136, 138, 140–3
Speculum Christianorum (Watton), 78
Spencer, Lady, 165
Spenser, Edmund, 113
Staël, Madame de, 169
Steele, Richard, 87, 130, 149–50, 161, 163, 170, 174
Stendhal, H., 183
Sterne, Laurence, 165, 177–8
Strachey, Lytton, 63
Strictures (More), 169
Strindberg, A., 111
Stubbes, Philip, 59, 73, 77
Summae, 18
Swift, Jonathan, 93, 102, 132–4, 159

Talbot, Catherine, 160, 163, 165
Talbot, Ch., 45
Tale of a Tub, A (Swift), 93
Tatler, The, 136–7, 140–1, 149
Taylor, Jeremy, 19, 130, 137; influence of, xiii, xiv; on marriage, 24–5, 36, 38, 47, 83–4, 130, 132, 171; on children, 91; on masters and servants, 98; influence on Richardson of, 146; and importance of physical appearance, 147; on gentlemen, 149; and conduct in death, 153–4
Tea-Table, The (Haywood), 13

Teelinck, Willem, 57–8, 60, 63, 64
Tempest, The (Shakespeare), 86
Tender Husband, The (Steele), 170
Terence, 74
Thackeray, William, 155, 164
Thomson, James, 134, 139, 144
Thrale, Mrs, 160, 168
Tillotson, John, 19, 70, 76, 101; influence of, xiv; on wet nursing, 68; and diligence, 79; views on mothers, 88; advantages of religion, 100; on children, 141
Titus Andronicus (Shakespeare), 172
Tom Jones (Fielding), 165, 175
Treatise on Education (Locke), 130
Trevelyan, G. M., xi
Trimmer, Mrs., 175
Tristram Shandy (Sterne), 165, 177
Troeltsch Ernst, 18, 66, 137
Tyndale, William, 22, 33, 60, 73, 80, 82, 98, 99

Use and Abuse of the Marriage Bed (Defoe), 123
Utopia (More), 41, 134

Vanbrugh, John, 144
Vicar of Wakefield, The (Goldsmith), 107, 178
Victoria I, 63
Vision of Piers Ploughman (Langland), 21, 65
Vives, Juan Luis, 42–3

Waller, Edmund, 168
Walpole, Horace, 154
Warton, Joseph, 87
Watton, John, 78
Way of All Flesh, The (Butler), 183
Weber, Max, 14
Wedding Ring Fit for the Finger, A (Secker), 23
Wells, H. G., 183, 184
Werke for householders, A (Whitforde), 61
Werther (Goethe), 164, 177
Wesley, John, 25
White, Thomas, 69
Whitforde, Richard, 61, 73
Whole Armour of God, The (Gouge), 9
Whole Duty of Man, The, 23, 68, 82
Wilson, W., 123
Wordsworth, William, 180
World, The (Moore), 178
Wycliff, John, 31, 32, 40, 65

Young, Edward, 64

Ziegler, Theobald, 43, 76
Zola, Emile, 124, 165

For Product Safety Concerns and Information please contact our EU
representative GPSR@taylorandfrancis.com
Taylor & Francis Verlag GmbH, Kaufingerstraße 24, 80331 München, Germany

www.ingramcontent.com/pod-product-compliance
Lightning Source LLC
Chambersburg PA
CBHW070608300426
44113CB00010B/1452